DATE DUE

FEB 0 8 1997	
OCT 1 5 1999	
APR 1 2 2000	
Richmond Pub. Lib. Due Sept 22/01	
BRODART	Cat. No. 23-221

Within
the
Wall
of
Denial

Conquering Addictive Behaviors

Within
the
Wall
of
Denial

Conquering Addictive Behaviors

ROBERT J. KEARNEY, Ph.D.

W.W. Norton & Company • New York • London

A NORTON PROFESSIONAL BOOK

Library of Congress Cataloging-in-Publication Data

Kearney, Robert J.
    Within the wall of denial : conquering addictive behaviors /
Robert J. Kearney.
        p.   cm.
    "A Norton professional book."
    Includes bibliographical references and index.
    ISBN 0-393-70210-3
        1. Compulsive behavior—Treatment.   2. Denial (Psychology)
    I. Title.
RC533.K43   1995
616.86—dc20   95-22942   CIP

W. W. Norton & Company, Inc., 500 Fifth Avenue, New York, NY 10110
W. W. Norton & Company, Ltd., 10 Coptic Street, London WC1A 1PU

1 2 3 4 5 6 7 8 9 0

Contents

Acknowledgments

This book has been in process for over twenty years. It would not have been possible without the assistance of many people. Most of all I wish to express my gratitude to Dr. Vin Rosenthal for his wisdom and encouragement. His experience as a therapist, writer, and editor has been, and continues to be, invaluable. Thanks to his unique humanist/existentialist world view, the book and the author have been humanized. His voice was gratefully heard and, I hope, faithfully reproduced on nearly every page. The other friends and colleagues who have directly shaped its form include Dori Fuji, M.S.W, who insisted that an earlier draft make sense, Mifta MacNeal, whose craft insured that its final form was English, and Maxine Topper, who assisted with the proofreading.

I am also deeply indebted to Dr. Ken Moses, who has allowed me to share in his work and graciously permitted me to use his concepts about the dynamics of grieving. Thanks also to Dr. Harris Berenbaum, who introduced me to working with denial; to Dr. Samuel Cardone and Jim Brady, who first taught me the ways of alcoholism; and to Dene Stamas, who taught master classes. Special thanks to Dr. Judith Piat, who made a major contribution to the celebration of this book, and to Susan Munro of Norton whose patience and skill made a manuscript into a book at last. Thank you all.

Introduction

Why a book about denial? For one thing, because, like the mountain that inspired Everest conqueror Sir Edmund Hillary, "It's there." For another reason, like Claudia Black's elephant in the living room, everyone is affected by it and no one talks about it.

Denial is an unconquered mountain in the middle of American life. Consider the following: Approximately one person out of three in America either has the disease of chemical dependency or is affected by it. However, many of the most impaired victims would deny that they *are* suffering or assert that it is not *that* bad. Even those who admit there is a problem may not seem to *do* anything about it. Minimizing a problem and not acting to correct it is part of denial. Denial is a mountain of "NO" under which a volcano of pain is seething.

Chemical dependency has been called a disease of denial. Denial facilitates the development of the disease, it blocks the early diagnosis and treatment of the disease, and it contributes to its relapse. Denial can easily be seen in the attempts by the abuser to hide from criticism or escape from the pain of withdrawal, or from the threat of being fired for his or her absenteeism. But denial also alienates abusers from their family and friends and therefore estranges them from help. With help being held at arm's length, the harm being done by the disease is prolonged and exacerbated. So the disease grows, spreading destruction and despair. All the while, the disease develops, and the abusers claim that nothing is really wrong.

Denial is everywhere. It is in the failure to acknowledge problems and take effective steps to change behavior. It can be seen in each of the signs currently used to diagnose the disease of chemical dependency: (a) maladaptive pattern of use; (b) impairments of social and occupational functioning; (c) preoccupation with drug-related activities surrounding the supply, use, and recovery from use; (d) concealment and the neglect of medical consequences or use; (e) interpersonal problems consequent to use; (f) shifting of priorities in the substance user's life so that the main focus of every day is one of the issues listed in (a) through (e).

Denial becomes both cause and effect in the disease process and creates barriers to seeking help. It does not stop there. It spills over into the treatment process where it can slow recovery and contribute to relapse. Counselors are trained to understand, recognize, and intervene effectively on denial. Yet denial is not just a problem between patients and counselors. All those who care and want to help feel the impact of denial. So it is important for family and friends to understand denial as well. That is why a book about denial. It is for all of us who are involved in substance abuse.

Is that all? No. that is not all there is to denial. Even with the vast number of people caught up in the problem of substance abuse, the problem of denial is not limited to chemical dependency. It can be seen in many other situations. After all, the analogy to alcoholism is the basis of such adaptations of the 12-step program as Overeaters Anonymous, Gamblers Anonymous, and Sex-aholics Anonymous. So we can expect to see denial having its pernicious effect in other addictive disorders. Seven major groups of addictive and compulsive behaviors have now been identified. Alcohol and substance abuse form the first group of disorders. Eating disorders (including overeating, undereating, and binge/purge cycling) form another. Gambling and other high risk activities (whose compulsive pursuers are sometimes called "action junkies") form a third group. Compulsive sexual behavior and sexual addiction form the fourth; spending disorders (including out-of-control "debting"), the fifth. "Workaholism" forms the sixth and "rageaholism" (episodic or chronic use of interpersonal violence or the threat of it) forms the last group.

Of course these behavior disorders do not exist in a vacuum. The people who have them are surrounded by family and friends who need protection from painful truths. Their denial is often called "enabling" and their relationship with a person who is addicted is called "co-dependency." Their recovery also follows a 12-step model in such groups as Al-Anon and Co-Dependents Anonymous (CODA).

Denial is not limited to addicts and co-dependents. It is just as powerful (if somewhat less obvious) in problems that we take to be "medical" diseases, such as diabetes and heart disease. Denial becomes a factor in these diseases when patients do not change their dietary habits or "forget" to take their medicine or to exercise. When these patients do not alter their life styles, the impact of denial can be just as devastating to them and their families as it is in addictive disorders.

Denial becomes a major problem in purely "psychological" disorders (such as depression, anxiety, or stress reactions) when the patient will not seek or accept help. It is very much a problem in "nonmedical" problems, such as child abuse and spouse battering, and may become a problem in other family disruptions, such as divorce or death. A family in crisis that insists on being left alone is a family in denial.

Denial can interact with *any* disease process (or disease-like process) from chronic heart disease to child abuse; and when it does, it contributes to the disability and delays the recovery. When it interacts with any human problem from marital stress to grief, it distorts communication and may even prevent healing.

The presence of denial can be detected in human affairs, from petty vanities to life-rending tragedies. It plays a role in all human misery. We are forever being struck by denial and finding that we are stuck with it. It is a constant companion of suffering, and suffering can enter our lives at any time. Wherever we are, it is. Perhaps because it is so uniquely human, it is so pervasive, or vice versa. All of "us" use it some of the time, and some of "them" use it all of the time. This book is for "them" . . . and "us."

Within
the
Wall
of
Denial
Conquering Addictive Behaviors

1

What Is Denial?

Denial is a form of self-protection. It is a *psychological* process people use to protect themselves from *psychological* threat. It is a wall, a barrier, a shelter from fright. When people are suddenly confronted by shocking news they often respond by saying, "I don't believe it!" "It's not true!" We can almost see them trying to shut out the news, close a door on it as if they could avoid this blow. Even while we watch them reacting to the news that is destroying *their* sense of security, *we* still believe that our own is assured. Which of us is truly safe from bad news? Whose feeling of safety and sense of well-being is not fragile? What normal life cannot be destroyed at any time by a knock on the door? Who is there? The wolf! When the wolf is at the door, we close and lock it. There are a lot of things to fear these days. Not all the wolves are in the woods or fairy tales.

We recognize the need for people to defend themselves from sudden threats, and use the word "shock" to describe their response to unexpected news. When bad news is heard for the first time we expect people to be stunned and to say, "Oh NO." As we listen to their reactions, however, we translate their "I don't believe it!" into "I don't *want to* believe it." We hear their "It's not true!" as meaning "*I hope* it's not true."

If the people getting the news are friends or loved ones, we wait for this shock to wear off. But when the news is no longer new, or to our way of thinking it should have been accepted long ago, we lose our patience and say (loved ones or not), "The time has come to face the facts." When in *our*

1

judgment it has become time to accept the truth and respond to it, we insist *they* must stop defending against the threat the truth represents. In time, our loved ones' shocked refusal or stunned inactivity will seem dangerous to us and we will start making demands on them. We may even say, "*You* keep on denying the truth." Maybe they are, but inside us is another truth that should not be lost: *We* may be threatened by their inaction and *we* feel angry or frightened.

Ironically, the person who remains in denial in the face of a growing threat becomes increasingly at risk of the very danger from which he or she is seeking shelter. For example, one may have a disease like cancer or addiction and delay getting treatment. That is why it is so frustrating for *us* to see what *they* don't, can't, or just plain won't see.

Why don't people face the truth, even when it hurts or frightens them? Isn't it always better to face the wolf? Maybe it is—when we can be assured that the wolf won't win, or is only a blowhard, like the villain in the *Three Little Pigs*. It was the pig with the strongest house, after all, who took on the wolf, and even then he had the help of his two brothers! Together they were able to shut the door against the wolf. We may not be so lucky. Life rarely sends us real wolves (or, for that matter, happy-ever-after endings). It does send us hard work and small joys. And it does send us bad news. It never comes at the right time. Someone gets sick, hard times come, a dream (most of all one of our own cherished dreams) is lost. Against these metaphorical wolves we try to shut a psychological door. We deny, again and again, even mortal danger.

IS DENIAL NORMAL?

Denial is as normal as flinching. It is as simple as that. When we are hurt or frightened, we want protection. We want assurance that everything will be okay. We want to know that the threat will end without our psychological world being turned upside down. Faced with a blow to our self-esteem, world view, or sense of how things "should be," we want assurance that our psychological house will not be blown down. We want the protection of believing things are not *that* bad and so will be better soon. Most of the time things are not that bad; being late does not get us fired, a sniffle does not mean we have to spend our day off in bed. Most of the time there is no big emergency. It *can* wait until tomorrow.

In the story of *The Three Little Pigs*, the first two pigs certainly were lazy enough, but they did get around to building themselves houses. Their houses were poor, but the fact that they built any shelter at all teaches us something about denial and danger. The houses got built precisely because the wolf was not hanging around threatening the pigs every moment. They had enough freedom from current danger to think about the future. The third one even had enough freedom while the wolf was dealing with the first two to build a fortress. The brothers had some degree of safety. They did not have to devote all their energy simply to hiding. They could go out and gather sticks and straw to cover themselves. With some kind of reassurance or protection, we too can build for the future, we too can be brave, and do what needs to be done. Without it, we must seek shelter, any shelter, until the storm blows over. In the face of physical danger, physical shelter is sought in order to survive. Denial provides psychological shelter from psychological storms. Denial is a psychological survival strategy.

Denial and Survival

Survival strategies provide partial shelter when total protection is not available. In an emergency one survives by finding ways to minimize the impact of a threatening force. A turtle dives down, tucks in its head, and waits for the danger to pass. Like turtles, people using denial try to evade the full brunt of a threat. They try to protect themselves, and wait until the coast is clear, the danger is past, and the reason to be afraid is gone. Of course people in denial are frightened; that is why they are using denial. Their world has stopped being safe. They feel alone, scared, and unprotected. What could be more natural than to seek protection? The issue is not the threat or safety *outside*. The issue is the sense of that safety *inside*. People use denial because they have lost their internal sense of safety; maybe it is lost for just a moment, but for that moment it is gone.

Yes, there are good ways of protecting and bad ways. Aren't we all taught as little children that we must protect ourselves? Isn't that why we teach the story of the three little pigs in the first place—to teach children to take precautions, to be sure they are protected?

Most people learn their lessons well, so most of the time people do a good job of protecting themselves from harm. They take precautions to avoid dangers. They lock up valuables, look both ways before crossing streets, and sometimes even take an umbrella when it looks like rain. They protect themselves by treating threats to their well-being as though they were real, imminent, and present, not imagined, remote, and unlikely.

But sometimes people don't take good care of themselves. They are careless, forgetful, and sometimes even reckless. Such behavior is a manifestation of denial. Careless people seem to treat a threat as though it is not real, or they are in some magical way protected from harm. People say, "It can't happen to me," "I just want to forget that," or "I don't believe it." It seems as though they are putting their heads in the sand, or as if they are pulling into a psychological shell, trying not to be affected by something that is happening to them. They behave as though a danger is not real, as if nothing has to change. *We* say *they* are in denial. It is easy for *us* to say that when *we* are safe. However, not everyone has a big brother with a brick house guaranteeing that safety.

Denial and Adaptation

If denial is a process for *not* changing, then the opposite of denial must involve change. Indeed, the opposite of denial is adaptation. Adaptation is changing to meet a new circumstance, force, or threat. Unlike survival, which is designed to help us endure without change, the essence of adaptation is change. Change requires facing or meeting the threat, believing that it is real, and coping with it. Since denial is a survival strategy, the essence of denial is resistance to change.

At times resistance to change is called for. Resistance is a necessary component of such laudable acts as heroism, fidelity, and self-sacrifice. Yet we might also ask ourselves, "Is a hero being *brave*, or being *reckless*? Is the long-suffering spouse being *loyal*, or *denying* the seriousness of her family's distress?" To answer those questions we must look at the consequence of being "brave" or "loyal." If the resistance increases blindness to the threat, it is probably denial masquerading as virtue. If the bravery or loyalty includes awareness of risk and effective protection, we may be seeing real virtue. One person's steadfastness is another's denial.

Loyalty, courage, and determination all involve resistance to change. Life calls for small virtues almost daily. People have countless plans for their lives — tasks that need doing, commitments that need to be met. Then something goes wrong, something changes. We have to decide whether any particular change is necessary or desirable. By shielding ourselves from some of life's blows, we save the energy, even the will, to keep on doing what we feel is necessary.

The spouse of an alcoholic is sometimes called a "booze widow." Like a real widow, she is often awarded bouquets of flattering adjectives, such as "brave" and "loyal." "Look at all she has to cope with!" Her real virtues may be lost in the scramble for survival. Aren't we equally likely to cluck disapprovingly at a young bride who "goes home to mother" instead of "working it out"? Sometimes facing one problem has the effect of distracting from another. One of the hallmarks of chemically dependent families is that they are in constant crisis. They put out one brush fire after another, while not facing the core issue, the source of the flames.

Much of life is lived balancing between the two ends of a teeter totter called change. Move too far toward one end of the board and adaptation becomes instability and chaos. Move too far toward the other end and constancy becomes denial, rigidity, and maladaptation.

Denial and Time

Behind the wall of denial the force to change is resisted, or at least slowed. Denial prevents change by keeping people from being aware of the full impact of some painful, life-changing truth. Denial is a normal response to confrontation with such a truth. Shakespeare's Macbeth, upon being told of his wife's death on the eve of the defense of his kingdom, responds:

> *She should have died hereafter;*
> *There would have been time for such a word.*
> *Tomorrow and tomorrow and tomorrow*
> *creeps in this petty pace from day to day*
> *to the last syllable of recorded time.* (Act V.v)

Thus begins one of literature's most eloquent appeals for more time. Denial buys time. What difference would it have made if Lady Macbeth died the next day, or the day after? She would still be dead. What did Macbeth need the time for? He claims that he was not prepared to mourn her properly. He was not ready to cope with the task. Why not? He was under attack — literally. He was not ready to deal with her death then. Who would be? You don't bury the dead during the battle. You fight for your own life. Are any of us so free from life's battles that we can take on another? Are any of us ready for the next crisis, threat, or danger? Yet these unwanted callers come knocking, and when they come we need time to solve the problems they create, time to identify the resources the crises require, and time to locate the support we need.

Of all the things denial buys time for, the most important is support, face-to-face contact with people who are important to us. In times of great trial we seek the support of loved ones. With their comfort and support it will be possible to face the emotional threat. Their presence makes it possible to let the full weight of what has happened become real. They make it possible for us to respond. How? By crying with us, cheering with us, and cheering for us. They do not actually have to do the crying and cheering. They do not even have to be physically present for us to be helped. What is important is that we have to *feel* their presence and support. We have to sense they are *offering a promise as big as the threat* we are facing. Then we can face the threat because we are assured of the support of those who care. We are not alone in our terror- or grief-filled hearts. It is in our hearts that we feel the aches, and it is there that we must feel the connection if we are to face the danger outside. It was not to the safety of a house that the first two little pigs ran; they sought the safety of each other.

The contrast between a family gathered at a coronary care unit and a family gathered at a chemical dependency unit may illustrate this point. Both families are dealing with a crisis that may become the turning point in their lives. Indeed, the Chinese character for crisis has two parts: one signifies danger; the other, opportunity. One family is gathered in support and the other is gathered in confrontation. One is cheering for recovery; the other, demanding that the truth be said out loud at last. But which is which? We may imagine that it was the family in the coronary care unit that was being supportive, but not necessarily. There may come a point in the heart patient's treatment when the family might start confronting the patient's lethal life style. At that point we might see the barriers of denial going up in the cardiac patient's family. Perhaps some family members will argue about who is to blame for the stress in the family's life style. Others may withdraw into stony silence: "I'll talk to him later, after this hospital thing is over and things are back to normal." Across the hall where the chemically dependent family is talking, there may come a point when the persons who had been walled off from one another try to find a common ground of support. They must connect with one another if the treatment is to be maximally successful.

Denial may be seen in both of these patients and their families. Both families have run into resistance against a full, open discussion of "the problem" somewhere in the course of each of the diseases. Both families have encountered resistance to change. If the solutions to the problem seem ineffective ("Maybe I should cut down some on sweets"), or the offer of support seems ingenuous or unrealistic ("You know, I haven't been spending enough time with the boy. Maybe we could go fishing this summer"), identified patients and families alike will retreat into denial. The danger outweighs the opportunity. They shut off their feelings, become rigid in their behavior, resist intrusion on their privacy, and reject the offers of help. They will retreat from each other behind their walls.

Since the demand to change and face problems comes from the people around the identified patient, it is often his or her own support system that he or she is retreating from. Another of the many ironies about denial is that people provide the only real safety, and the only real threat. Just as one can feel alone in a crowd, one can feel *not* connected in a crisis. Even with family and loved ones around saying soothing, comforting things, one can still feel the need to hide behind the wall.

Trauma and loss can happen at any time. We know this, but we "just don't think about it." We cannot be prepared for all forms of disaster, so we all need some denial. We all use denial some of the time to keep us focused. We really don't think about all that could go wrong. Thinking about the endless range of things that could go wrong, such as an oncoming car suddenly crossing the mid-line of the highway, or harm befalling loved ones, would cause us endless worry and paralyze us with fears and vigilance. We would be too afraid of life to live it. We must put these possibilities out of, or at least at the back of, our minds in order to do simple tasks such as driving to work, shopping for the family dinner. It is important to see the place of denial in everyday life so that we don't think of it as a strange aberration that only happens to others, or only to people who are weak or bad. There is a little bit of it there all the time. And when a crisis does arrive, in the face of an awful truth, we may well avoid, escape, hide, postpone. We may minimize, rationalize, excuse. We may deny. We may stall for time. And rightly so; we will need the time to identify believable resources. Sometimes that resource is an expert such as a physician or lawyer or a special "place" where they help people with this sort of problem. Sometimes it is a survivor, someone who has "been there," who "understands." Often it is a resource in ourselves, a way to find the time or money, or the sense of mastery of a skill that is new.

Of course the time we buy may be purchased at great expense. Many people who have turned to credit cards and loan sharks to bail them out have discovered that. The debt itself becomes a new stress. The time purchased with denial can have many costs, some of them quite high. The highest costs are increased danger and alienation. The price is paid by the person in denial *and* those around him or her. The current view of the chemically dependent family emphasizes that covering up "the secret" causes problems in every member of the family. The way the time is bought is a problem in itself.

DENIAL, DEFENSE, AND CONFLICT

"Denial" can be used as a general term for the whole range of protective processes people use to shelter themselves from the impact of powerful, frightening, or lifechanging truths. It always involves a conflict between knowing and not knowing. For the sake of description we can divide conflicts into two categories, *interpersonal* and *intrapersonal*. Interpersonal denial, *between* individuals, will be used when the message is coming from the outside. Intrapersonal denial, denial *within* the individual, will be used when the conflict is generated by internal messages, such as the voice of a nagging conscience, a "stuffed feeling," or a deeply buried pain. Denial, in its largest sense, is a way of protecting awareness from unacceptable threat, and a way of buying time to cope with that threat. These protective processes cover a wide range of human behavior and reactions. The range extends from the intrapersonal processes, which psychologists call defenses (such as repression), to interpersonal processes, such as manipulation of others and outright lying. Denial is generated by conflict the way heat is generated by friction. Things get hot because they are rubbed and people go into denial because they are being pushed. Just as they can be pushed from the outside by messengers of an unwanted truth, they can be pushed from their own insides by internal conflicts, torments, or regrets.

Conflict and Intrapersonal Denial

Psychologists say that defenses keep unacceptable ideas, emotions, and impulses from flooding one's awareness. They classify denial as a kind of defense and give it a specific meaning, which we will discuss later. For now, the intrapersonal aspects of denial are roughly equivalent to what psychologists call *intrapsychic* defenses.

Perhaps the simplest and most graphic version of a defense in operation is seen in the response to physical pain. In the face of unbearable pain, people may lose consciousness—"pass out from pain"—a simple, graphic, and admittedly extreme example of shielding oneself. Such extreme measures are not usually necessary. For lesser stresses we can use simpler tricks, such as changing television channels when the news is disheartening, playing golf to relax and forget work problems, or jogging to relieve stress. The examples of losing consciousness and running are deliberately chosen to emphasize the breadth of alternatives open to an individual. Somewhere in the middle of the intrapsychic range falls rationalization, and the phenomenon we call "not being honest with yourself."

Often the truth we avoid is in the form of an expectation or demand we make of ourselves. It takes the form of a *should* (e.g., "I should lose 5 pounds"), or a *have to* ("I have to save more money"), or a *must* ("I must give up smoking") that is nagging us. When we do not do what we *should*, *must*, *have to*, we feel the same painful sense of failure that we do when we do not meet expectations of others. To get relief from this pain we shut off the nag. We resist change, even change we choose ourselves. Anyone who has ever dieted can verify this. The diet starts tomorrow. Our resistance generates an inner conflict and denial emerges in response to that conflict to insulate us from the heat of it and to harden us to the pain of it.

Conflict and Argument

Denial is often an interpersonal struggle as well as an intrapersonal struggle. Denial shields by protecting awareness from the intrusion of self-generated thoughts, such as internal nags and old uncomfortable feelings, as well as by protecting awareness from external intrusions, such as the demands of others to "face facts." As an interpersonal struggle, denial can take the form of an argument between someone who is "trying to help" (the "helper") and some-one who has a problem (the "helpee") and who is resisting change. It is an argument that is all too familiar. In these arguments it is easy to hear the resistance to change take the form of rejection of help, or even rejection of the helper. When the one with the problem does not change as the helper wishes, the helper says the other is resisting help, or denying some danger. The helpee uses such phrases as, "It is hard," "I'm afraid," "I'll deal with it tomorrow," "It's unfair," "It's not my fault." Then the helper argues with that resistance, "Don't you want my help?" "Don't you see how serious this thing is?" The helper argues for action, coping, adapting to the threat. But the helper's words are becoming just that—an argument. Then surprisingly the one with the problem claims that it is the helper who is not seeing things clearly. The helper does not understand how difficult, painful, stressful the matter is. So how can he or she help? The person with the problem feels misunderstood. At this point in the dialogue, the helpee does not feel the support the helper intended and the helpee needs. They are beginning to move apart and become antagonistic toward each other. Soon they will be separated by a gulf neither can cross. Sometimes denial is a wall, sometimes it is a canyon.

When the helper is not urging the helpee to take some action, but is complaining about some action he or she has taken, an atmosphere of moral judgment emerges. The aura of condemnation leads even more inevitably to the same impasse. The helper asks the helpee (who is already retreating from pain) to see more pain, to see what he or she has done as harmful, wrong, or dangerous. The helper urges the helpee (who has in fact already demonstrated his or her need to shut down and buy time) to accept personal responsibility for some act or to accept the consequences of not acting. Again, the task is to accept some painful truth, to see oneself or one's actions in a very negative way. The one with the problem says, "I couldn't help myself," and is told that he is "impulsive." He says, "It's hard. You do it for me," and he is told that he is "manipulative." He says, "It's not my fault," and hears that he is "rationalizing." This dialogue can only end with the helper being pushed away and the person at risk being confirmed in the need to retreat behind the wall and widen the gulf separating him or her from the other.

Denial and Intrapersonal Arguments

We all talk to ourselves from time to time. As outsiders, of course, we do not *hear* intrapersonal arguments (although we may overhear one side of it when someone is "talking to himself"), but we do *see* the consequences of this internal falling out. We may, for example, know that a friend is having trouble with his or her spouse and notice that he or she is having difficulty concentrating and becoming increasingly irritable at work. We see the change in his or her behavior and we can infer the internal argument causing it.

In an external argument, the conflict ends in anger and rejection. The helper is told to shut up, go away, mind his or her own business. What happens when the conflict is internal? Who is there to banish? What would "shut up" mean here? If we could overhear such a discussion, we would hear it also end with denial, just like an interpersonal argument. We could hear how someone banished a part of himself. Denial is used to shut off internal conflict by altering one's awareness of one's own thoughts, feelings, and behavior. It is like rejecting the part of one's self that is playing the role of the helper.

An internal shut up, shut down, and shut off can be inferred from the mismatch between a person's thoughts, feelings, and behavior. The people we are trying to help seem out of touch with what is going on around them and out of touch with themselves ("He's been laid off for six months and he just sits around the house, not even trying to find work"). We may challenge them about the mismatch between what they do and what they say ("I thought you said you hated school and were going to quit!"), or between what they do and what they feel ("You say you are not mad, but you are frowning and shaking your finger at me"). We may even complain about the special mismatch of a broken promise ("You said the check was in the mail"). People may even report the mismatch themselves. They may describe the dislocation between what they feel and the circumstances surrounding them ("When Charley died, I didn't feel anything. It was like living in a dream"). We may complain, but the incongruity continues.

2

The Layers of Denial

In Chapter 1, denial was described as a psychological defense that allows a person to buy time until the resources and safety necessary for the incorporation of a painful truth can be marshaled. Denial protects awareness from that painful truth until it can be incorporated. It was described as necessary, natural, and altogether human. It can also run amok and ruin lives. In that sense, denial is a little like the human immune system. The white blood cells can help us fight off invading pathogens. In some circumstances they can also multiply rapidly, even dangerously. When that happens there is no doubt that the body has a disease. The same can be said for denial. Our psychological defenses can turn against us and when they do, the disease is usually addiction. This chapter is about the way denial operates both naturally and as a disease process.

Addicts who are practicing their addiction (such as chemically dependent persons who are actively using alcohol or drugs) can make it quite clear that they just do not want to give up using. They may agree to cut down or even stop for a while, but they will not give up their *right to use*. No matter how much trouble others have with their behavior, addicts claim that they do not *want* to change, or plead that they *cannot* change. And they are willing to argue about it. The arguments and rationalizations seem endless, and they always end in the same place: The behavior does not change. Their resistance to change is often creative and sometimes violent, but it is quite predictable.

It is predictable because it is organized to create the most effective defense the user can muster.

The organization of that defense consists of several layers of denial, which protect the individual by forming a veritable wall of "NO." The layers of this system are named, respectively, the *denial of facts*, the *denial of implications*, the *denial of change*, and the *denial of feelings*. The configuration of these layers (see Figure 2.1) looks like a set of nested boxes with an inner space surrounded by four shells. The inner space holds the deep feelings and values that people have and rarely talk about except with their most intimate loved ones (and even then, only when circumstances call forth their strongest emotions). This core contains people's sense of who they are, and what matters most to them. For that reason, the space is depicted as being occupied by a little child. Sadly,

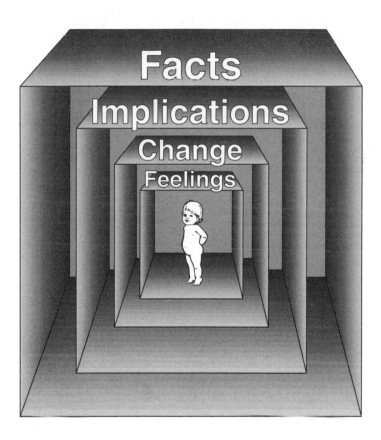

this inner core is often a negative self-image generating low self-esteem. It may be a very rigid but false self-image, rather than a true sense of self. The origin of this self concept will be discussed in Chapter 4. Surrounding this core are four distinguishable layers of denial which protect that core from threat. Although each layer will be discussed separately in a linear fashion as though there is no overlap or moving back and forth between them, arguments or confrontations with someone in denial are never like that; they bounce around like a bag of spilled marbles.

The layers of denial, and examples of responses utilizing each of these protective strategies is presented in Table 2.1.

DENIAL OF FACTS

The denial of facts is the outermost layer of the protection. It is the most frequently used form of denial and consists of *conscious* diversion of attention away from something that is unpleasant. It is simple, easy to do, and happens

Table 2.1
Layers of Denial: Typical Protective Responses

Layer of Denial	Examples
Denial of facts	"I have not been drinking." "You have no right to accuse me." "That's not true."
Denial of implications	"Okay, I had a few, but I wasn't drunk." "Sure I like to drink, but that doesn't mean I'm an alcoholic." "Your brother drinks more than I do."
Denial of change	"So, I'm an alcoholic—so what?" "I'll try to stop." "It's not my fault."
Denial of feelings	"It doesn't bother me." "I am not angry—fighting makes me tense—I have a headache." "That's an interesting idea." "I don't remember anything about that time in my life—everything was fine."

a thousand times a day. It is as simple as changing the television channel when a movie becomes too horrific, or turning the newspaper page when the headlines announce that one's favorite team has lost—again. It can become a character trait or slogan, as it did with Scarlett O'Hara in *Gone with the Wind*, who made the famous statement, "I'll think about that tomorrow."

"Out of sight and out of mind" is a key phrase in the denial of facts. When there are no facts to cause a reaction, there is no stress—for the moment—and so more time is bought. This outer layer, which is made up of both selectively perceiving and selectively admitting, is therefore called the "denial of facts" because it seeks to block out objective data.

Denial of facts is likely to be elicited first in confrontations. It is a "No" said to someone, a stone wall. The person using it has a conscious purpose of maintaining control, stopping the criticism, or protecting his or her right to do it his or her way. Denial of facts is typified by the simple negation, "That's not true." It is termed denial of facts because facts or data supporting some unwanted truth are being negated. In response to the question, "Were you high last night?" one gets a simple, perhaps even reflexive, "No." The "No" is meant to end the discussion right then and there. This kind of denial may also come with great vehemence, or even be a conscious act of bullying. It says, "No, I don't want to talk about it," and implies, "I'll make your life miserable if you try to make me." Sometimes the same effect is achieved by employing the distraction, ruse, or other manipulation, con job, blarney, or charm that users are famous for employing.

The denial of facts layer includes the conscious lying referred to earlier. In fact, the need to resort to lies by persons who otherwise see themselves as honest is a great source of pain in the development of addiction. Whether the person is pained or blasé, the entire system below this layer can be maintained if he or she is successful in covering up the evidence. Desperate times call for desperate measures. Lying is a desperate measure. It is exactly the kind of "means" one has to justify by citing a vital "end." If one can get a traffic officer to accept "No, I have not been drinking," "I only had one or two beers," or some other assertion, one may easily be able to escape the painful consequences of one's chemical abuse that a DUI would bring. It is not just the ticket per se, nor the trouble (court, suspended license, etc.) it represents, that can be avoided by successful use of denial of facts; it is the awful awareness of the mess one's life has become, which is also avoided by lying.

Included in this layer of denial is the frequent demand by users that others around them pay no attention to what happened last night, last week, last year. "Forget about the past. Pay attention to the promise I am making to you today!"

In front of others, the function of this layer is simply to avoid or escape negative consequences. "Tell him anything, honey. If the boss finds out, I'll be fired!" The internal function of this outer layer of denial is simply to block out all of the data or observations that establish the presence of the problem in one's own eyes. One might call this the ostrich approach. Abusers seem to be behaving as if the problem will go away if no one is looking at it. Thus, while they are *consciously* fooling (or trying to fool) others, they are *unconsciously* fooling themselves. They are playing a very dangerous shell game with the truth. It is they, not the others, who are hoping the problem will disappear when the evidence is hidden. Meanwhile, lies eat away at the abuser's self-esteem. That too is part of the price of addiction.

DENIAL OF IMPLICATIONS

One needs additional layers to maintain protection in case something penetrates this outer defense; that is, when a fact becomes established. That fact could be used to prove that an even larger problem exists. Another DUI could be used to prove that chemical dependency exists. The next inner level of denial, denial of implications, is used when some threatening fact does get established in awareness. Perhaps a woman has her third DUI arrest. Her driver's license may be lost, but even worse, now *they* are really going to prove she has a drinking problem. At that point, the woman may seek refuge by calling on the next layer of denial. Yes she was arrested, and yes she failed the field sobriety test, but it was because she was tired and the drinks "hit her hard." It certainly *does not mean* that she has a problem with alcohol.

When irrefutable facts have been made public that could link the individual to great threat, the link can be rejected even when the facts cannot be covered up again. The idea that the facts "mean anything" is resisted. In a legal analogy, denial of facts is equivalent to a motion to suppress evidence. "Your Honor, the search warrant was invalid; therefore, the stolen TV sets cannot be used as evidence that my client is a thief."

Continuing the analogy, denial of implications is like an objection that someone is calling for a conclusion on the part of the witness. "Your Honor, Mrs. Jones is not qualified to conclude that Mr. Jones is an alcoholic. That requires the judgment of a medical expert; and since none is present in the court, I move for immediate dismissal of all charges."

The essential argument in denial of implications is, "Okay, that may be true, but it doesn't mean what I don't want it to mean." Using this level of denial, persons can mount an endless stream of arguments about why something is not so, does not have any meaning, doesn't *really* count. They may seem to delight in this battle of wits—especially if they think they are winning. "Your brother drinks more than I do" or "Ernest Hemingway drank more than I." Again, the argument can turn angry and attacking—"Who made *you* a psychiatrist all of a sudden?"

Minimization

Minimization is one of the most common forms of denial. The essence of the minimization argument is, "It's not *that* bad." This argument may be based on minimizing the *kind* of chemical use ("I only smoke pot."); it may focus on the *amount* of use ("Three, four drinks, a couple of highballs, what's that?") or on *how* often ("only on weekends"). Another target of the argument may be the *extent of damage* from the use ("What's the harm? Work hard, play hard! Hey, I'm the one with the hangover, right?").

Minimizing can also take the form of picking some extreme as a point of comparison. The family and friends of an alcohol abuser are often frustrated to hear him or her say, "The guy down the block drinks more than I do and he's not an alcoholic." It is particularly frustrating if it is true. The person minimizing says the data are correct, but not *big* enough, or will *change* in time, so they do not warrant the conclusion *implied* by the data. Minimization is essentially any technique that can be used in arguing the position that addiction cannot be concluded from the evidence presented.

Diagnosis and the Denial of Implications

The foremost implication to be dealt with in the field of addiction is the diagnosis itself. Addicts have a hard time accepting the idea that they have a chronic, progressive disease with a horrible name, and which has a tendency toward relapse. Often they will suggest another diagnosis as preferable. If the counselor asks, "How would it be different if you had alcoholism rather than problem drinking?" and the patient replies, "Oh that would be much worse. I've heard those poor bastards at AA meetings; they're really sick," the counselor can hear the denial of implications clearly. The patient is threatened by the implication of being a "sickie."

Often there is some implication or meaning attached to a diagnosis that is two or three associations down the line ("If *that thing* is true, it means *this thing* over here is true; and *THAT* would mean . . . Oh boy!"). For many patients, this dreaded implication is simply that they will have to stop using (see next layer of denial below). For others, it is the implication of weakness and moral culpability attached to the general public's concept of an addict. A man with a "drinking problem" can claim to be "under stress"; he can make a claim for sympathy. An *alcoholic* might be scorned, ridiculed, or, worse yet, pitied. Ironically, these negative implications are the implications that the disease concept of chemical dependency is designed to address. By fighting the diagnosis, the patient is fighting for protection from the assertion that he or she is "bad" or "weak."

People who cannot stave off such labels are in trouble. Bad people are punished and lose their freedoms. Weak people are often restricted as well, sometimes "for their own good." Statements such as "I can do what I want," "It's a free country," "If I want to get high, I will," etc., seem to be straightforward claims to the right to choose chemical use (or some other addictive behavior) or to be free of criticism for using. Given the dynamics of addiction, such behavior is not really a free choice. The implication that one is "hooked . . . really hooked" comes along with the diagnosis of addiction. Consider the woman with the three DUIs mentioned earlier. She has just had an accident at work and has already missed five days of work this month because of her drinking. Suppose she is admitted to a hospital on Saturday night because she took some sleeping pills after drinking and overdosed. The admitting physician may find these facts persuasive evidence leading to the conclusion that she has the disease of chemical dependency. On Sunday morning she agrees "to think about the diagnosis," but by that afternoon she has checked out AMA (against medical advice). She rejects the referral for rehabilitation. She will "try on her own." Is this denial of implications? Possibly. Is the emphasis on the *thinking* or the *leaving*? Was this the first time she heard the diagnosis, or the second . . . or third . . . or fourth? It turns out that she had tried many times to stop by herself. She believes she has kept her failures a secret. If she fails again (as she secretly believes she will) her disguise will be uncovered. Every one will know that she is "hooked, weak, and bad." She would feel defenseless against the implications of shame. It is not that she does not want to stop, but that she *fears* failing. By using denial, the image of failure and the self-concept of worthlessness, which this woman associates with her alcoholism, are pushed behind the wall.

Once a diagnosis has been made, that event, like the other symptoms of the illness become part of the body of facts which the denial system is designed to hide from self and others.

DENIAL OF CHANGE

For another patient admitted for detoxification (also for the third time) the issue clearly is stopping itself. The diagnosis holds no special peril. "An alcoholic huh? Well I've been called worse than that. Okay Doc, thanks a lot. I'll be on my way." For him the denial of implications was breached long ago. He is operating on the next layer down. Patients operating at this level do not let the diagnosis of alcohol dependence bind them to *do* anything about their inability to control their drinking. Consequently, they can accept the logic of the diagnosis and still be protected. If they try and fail, they can always say that it is not really their fault. "I tried to stay sober but something happened." Their denial seems to reject the idea that they are the ones who have to do something. They seem to deny that there is any real requirement on them to change as a consequence of the diagnosis. In fact, they are actually resisting having to make any *real* changes. They are in the next level of denial, denial of change.

Denial of change is the denial of the need for change in one's life, and the personal responsibility for making those changes. Under the cover of denial of change, old maladaptive behavior is maintained, and new or adaptive behavior is avoided. Procrastination is the simplest form of denial of change. "I don't have to do it now. It can wait. There'll be no penalty for being late."

The person in denial of change resists the idea that his or her action or inaction is impactful or consequential in ways for which he or she can be held responsible. If the consequences are unavoidable, the person in denial will claim that the situation is not his or her fault, he or she didn't do it on purpose. The consequences of both inaction and action are distorted in denial of change. "Why should I apologize? What's the big deal? I was just a little high, nobody got hurt. Forget it."

Although chemically dependent persons may admit they did something that has caused problems, they will often try to excuse the behavior by saying that it happened while they were intoxicated. The implication is that such behavior is to be overlooked. They are not to be held as *responsible* as they would be *if they were sober*. In effect they are claiming that the problem was not really their fault. Over time it becomes apparent that they have difficulty accepting responsibility for most of their actions. The excuses accumulate, while the number of things to be blamed for mounts. They do not see themselves as the cause of anything. There is no act for which they are culpable nor any causal role for which they are responsible. The sheer volume of excuses is a tip-off that some form of denial is involved. What is being kept from awareness? Well, if they were responsible for what was wrong, they would be responsible for fixing or changing it; the resistance to that responsibility is the essence of denial of change.

Most people see responsibility as an all-or-nothing proposition. If one is responsible for the consequences of one's behavior, then one is responsible for all of one's behavior and for making whatever changes are necessary to make one's life work and one's relationships mutually gratifying. From this point of view, one should be responsible in all areas. By extension, when people are resisting, their resistance is often equally pervasive.

One of the most important areas that denial of change affects is the assumption of responsibility for recovery. Counselors working with chemically dependent persons often find that recovery is delayed or sabotaged when they encounter an elaborate system of excuses found at the level of denial of change. If a person in this level is forced to make changes (for example, court-ordered attendance at an outpatient rehabilitation program), he or she will go to great lengths to make others responsible for the success of those changes. For example, a man may only keep appointments when his wife drives him there; he may leave the insurance forms at home, etc. Many patients who have already agreed to the facts that establish the diagnosis of chemical dependency and agree that they are addicted, still don't seem to get involved in their own recovery. They miss meetings, lose contact with sponsors, and always have some explanation; some "Yes . . . but . . . " The patient resists making meaningful changes and presents the counselor with endless excuses for why he or she didn't go to an AA meeting or can't stop drinking this week, or was late for therapy appointments. "I can explain everything" is the beginning of a set of disclaimers for the consequences of the person's behavior.

Excuses and the Denial of Change

Denial of change is manifest in excuse making. Great emphasis is placed on the issue of intention rather than execution or impact, how he or she wanted things to turn out rather than how they really did. The person in denial of change demands to be judged on the promised behavior rather than the delivered behavior. Statements such as "I wanted to stay sober . . . I couldn't," "I did not mean to . . . ," "Give me another chance, I promise . . . ," and even the more manipulative "You owe me that" may accompany the excuse.

Listening to excuses can get confusing when they also seem to be probable explanations. "The car wouldn't start." But excuses and explanations are different. An explanation is a statement of cause. An excuse is a plea to be relieved of responsibility, promise, or consequence. The same dead battery cited above plays a role in both of the following examples. In one it leads to a missed appointment at the dentist; in the other it prevents cashing in a winning lottery ticket. The dentist gets a phone call, hears, "I'm sorry, the car wouldn't start," and then hears the phone click. There is not even time to reschedule the appointment. One bad start and the whole thing is off. The lottery officer hears, "Wait! Wait! I'll take a bus, walk, crawl . . . but *I'll be there*."

Denial of change is seen when patients attempt to persuade themselves and others that their behavior was not the result of choice; there were no alternatives and, therefore, there was no choice. Persons operating at this level of denial frequently explain their behavior as though it were automated, compelled. "Hey, what could I do? It was Charlie's retirement party. I had to drink a toast." When there are no choices there are no responsibilities and no valid criticisms. Without choice there is no responsibility. The pressure to change is cushioned. The behavior can continue to function as a protection and an outlet of tension.

People in denial of change are among the most difficult patients to help. They want help to relieve pain, but not to create change. They do not want changes that work. It can be confusing because they do not reject the help directly, in fact they often plead for it. When an offer comes, they always seem to find a flaw in it. It is a nice idea, but . . . and there is always a *but*. Eric Berne (1964) called this kind of dialogue *Why Don't You, Yes But*. He pointed out that it always ends the same way. The helper gets angry and the person with the problem looks hurt. "What's the matter with you? Can't you see how hard I'm trying?"

Denial of Change in Couples

The chemically dependent person is often in a complex relationship with persons who are trying to help. The only "help" they seem willing to accept is the help that doesn't work. Offering help that is accepted but does not work can easily turn into what is called *enabling*. Enabling differs from helping because it does not bring about change and only maintains the status quo. The terminology may be harsh, but it provides an opportunity to see the enabling relationship (sometimes called the dependent/co-dependent dynamic) as being influenced by the denial systems of both parties. When the co-dependent excuses the behavior of the patient, they both behave as if no blame shall be placed . . . this time. Excusing the behavior is dangerous because it feeds into both the user's and the enabler's denial.

Anyone who has "baby-proofed" a house knows that infants must be protected from the consequences of their behavior. Children are not responsible; adults are. To treat an adult as though he or she was not fully responsible is to treat him or her like a child and to become parental oneself in the bargain. While ostensibly remaining adult peers (and denying contrary facts), the user/enabler (or dependent/co-dependent) couple move into a kind of parent/child relationship. This is not a true role shift because neither has completely given up all of the tasks, privileges, or responsibilities of their adult places in the family. Their new roles are a burlesque of true parenting and actual or natural childhood. It is a dress-up game of house. One spouse is in the child role playing at being a rebellious offspring (but keeping the car keys and the credit card) and the other plays at being a vexed parent (but still expects sex and laundry).

They shift roles while denying the implications of their new relationship. Acting out the roles of punitive, critical parent and impulsive, rebellious child will have enormous impact on family life. Not all of the tasks of the former adults will get done; many responsibilities will be neglected. But you can bet that all the privileges will be claimed. They may even switch these pseudo-roles. The fake parent may impulsively purchase something and blow the family budget into the red. Suddenly the acting out spouse is filled with righteous indignation. A new round of arguments and recriminations begins. Ignoring the impact of their behavior on their own interactions as well as the impact of their behavior on other members of the family is denial of change. How will their offspring get to be children, when their parents are being childish?

For all of the arguing and crying, the couple is strangely out of touch with their own feelings about this role switching. They have feelings about how the other behaves, but not about their own behavior. "What is it like being a 45-year-old naughty girl?" "How does it feel to father the woman who brings home a paycheck?" The couple *avoids experiencing their feelings* about relating in this way (see primary denial in Chapter 3). "What do you mean, how does it feel? I only do (this) because he/she does (that). You don't think I want to behave like that, do you? I really have no choice!" Crises, excuses, and problems continue. Family, friends, and even some counselors are surprised at how often and how long this excuse-making strategy is used.

Soon the people around the abuser may decline to offer help, but they can still see the panic and the pain looming behind each crisis. Eventually they come to see the user like the boy who cried wolf or someone who has to pay all at once for previous mistakes, someone who still wants to be treated fairly and to call on a level of belief and trust that has been exhausted. The family sees the whole string of broken promises to change and, focusing on the last event, lets loose a barrage of pent-up resentment. The user has an accident leaving a tavern parking lot. If he were in denial of change he might ask, "Why would anyone make such a big deal over one little fender bender?" He then dismisses the angry response of his spouse as "overreacting" or "hysteria." This is not an overreaction, however, if this accident is the one that makes him uninsurable, or if this DUI costs him his license, and losing his license costs him his job.

To avoid being too frustrated and punitive with a user (or an enabler) in denial of change, it is wise to remember that the old saying "The sins we commit two by two we pay for one by one" is not entirely accurate when applied to addictions. It is often quite the other way around, as anyone who has ever received a credit card bill can attest. The isolated "sins" of the addict always threaten payment, and they must be paid for all at once. One too many absences on Monday and suddenly the addict is fired. One "little" mistake with the law and the whole house of cards collapses. One puff of ill wind and a house of straw vanishes.

THE DENIAL OF FEELINGS

The final layer of denial, denial of feelings, is the exclusion of feelings from awareness. This form of defense differs from the preceding layers because it is wholly outside awareness or, as psychologists say, *unconscious*. Many psychoanalysts, such as Dorpat (1994), see the effects of blocking awareness as having far-reaching implications for cognitive development, symptom formation, and treatment. The other layers are wholly or partially conscious. A person in denial of facts is usually aware of what he is lying about and that he is lying. "I never saw that lid of dope before in my life." A locally notorious thief from

Chicago once told an arresting officer, "I don't know *nothing* . . . and I can *prove* it." The person in denial of implications is quite aware of the point he or she is trying to prove and the point he or she is trying to disprove. "I'm not an alcoholic; I never missed a day of work in my life." At the level of denial of change, people are aware of avoiding whatever point of blame is under discussion, even if they do not see that there is a pattern of avoidance. "You got to believe me this time. It really wasn't my fault that they fired me." All of these levels involve some conscious awareness. The NO is deliberately focused on someone or something outside themselves rather than being focused on preventing internal awareness.

Denial of feelings is different from other forms of denial because it is an unconscious process aimed at shutting off feelings. It will shut off ideas, memories, even consciousness itself to achieve that goal. Beneath this final layer of denial are not only the self-doubts, shame, and remorse of years of abuse, but also an open door to all of the secrets of the soul. We have come to the person in the middle of all those boxes. We meet the inner self as opposed to the public self—the sheltered part, which is rarely viewed in clear light or shared with others. This core contains peoples' sense of who they are and what matters most to them. It also contains the self-images accumulated from countless dark nights of the soul, about which we have our deepest feelings. It contains both conscious and unconscious attitudes and images. It contains both the shell of the *false self*, with its mistaken impressions of true identity, and the kernel of what is the *natural self* imprisoned in that shell (see Chapter 4).

If all that was in this inner box were experiences of self-worth and inner goodness, there would be no need for all the outer chambers—at least not such a fortress. Sure we need to protect our self-esteem from what Hamlet called "the heartache and thousand natural shocks that flesh is heir to," but that self would be clamoring for expression and seeking intimacy, not hiding from the view of self and others.

Abusers are often described as being "out of touch with their feelings" or using drugs to "mask" or "anesthetize" their feelings. Some writers, for example Levine and Zigler (1973), have tried to distinguish between those alcoholics whose lives were all right until they started drinking and whose internal conflicts and interpersonal stresses ended when they stopped using, and those who were demonstrably distressed (that is, had a diagnosable illness or significant conflict with society) before they started and were still miserable after they stopped. The issue is controversial among professionals who debate whether there is such a thing as a "pure" addict. AA handles the problem by advising its members, "There is no problem that a drink can't make worse." Some people say that the feelings are frozen from the first use. That's a big iceberg floating out there. Furthermore, it does not thaw quickly. That comes much later, if at all.

Denial of Feelings and Recovery

Which came first? The feelings or the denial? Was the addict in denial to escape painful feelings, and that is why he or she acted the way he or she did? As Father Joe Martin (1972) says, "If they weren't in so much pain, they wouldn't use so much painkiller." Were the painful feelings and conflicts generated by the abuse? The life of an active user is fraught with painful moments. A great deal of denial can go into resisting the fear generated by an "unmanageable" life. And that kind of denial takes a lot of energy.

While in denial of feelings, addicts are protecting themselves from feelings that are too strong. They may be moody and complain that they are uncomfortable, but they do it indirectly by complaining about something or someone who makes them uncomfortable. They describe the person or the situation, but will not express or acknowledge their feelings. "No, I'm not angry, my boss is a jerk." It takes a long time for them to really get in touch with their feelings, let alone become articulate about them and the internal conflicts that surround them.

The deep feelings that have been blunted by chemical abuse and have not been shared with significant others may emerge when the patient speaks for the first time in a group of other abusers about the way drinking and drugs have affected his life. This may happen in group therapy or in the process of "taking the first step." The feelings may not emerge until the patient is well along into recovery and working closely with a sponsor or counselor. The relationship with a sponsor or a counselor is often the first close honest relationship the patient has had in years—perhaps ever. While working a 12-step program, the patient is presented with several opportunities to explore his or her feelings. The feelings stirred by ideas such as "powerlessness . . . unmanageable . . . searching and fearless moral inventory" come up in just the first four steps. Typically, the first feelings to emerge are painful: shame and guilt, anger, despair, etc. Other feelings and internal conflicts may follow.

A full, rich emotional life does not develop the moment the user stops using. Some days feelings seem to pour out and the next day they are all gone.

Newly abstinent patients have the worst time. They may become moody, angry one day, sad the next, and then just as shut-off and unavailable as ever.

Frequently, patients who wept bitterly about the mess their lives were in when they entered treatment will leave treatment focusing their attention entirely on how much better they feel, how rosy the future is, and how everything is going to be fine now. They may express confidence that they will be okay because they have accepted the diagnosis and a rigorous treatment plan. They behave as though there is nothing frightening, nothing anger-provoking, nothing uncomfortable in the world they are responding to. In AA this phase is often called the "honeymoon." It is a clear example of the reassertion of the denial of feelings. The bad feelings seem to be gone, hopefully forever. In reality they are just being kept outside awareness once again.

Who wants to argue with a cooperative, confident patient? Who wants to make the patient feel anxious, perhaps have other powerful feelings that scorch the very heart of the addict, rattle his or her sense of identity, self-esteem, security, and place in the order of things? Certainly not the patient. The patient's denial system was designed to keep conflicts over these issues unfanned. When they flare, a great sense of dread floods the awareness. The wolf is through the door and at the hearth.

Several authors writing about the breakthrough of this final level of denial have noted its similarity to the grief and mourning process. Elisabeth Kübler-Ross (1969) and Ken Moses (1995) both begin their discussion of the process of responding to traumatic loss with a discussion of denial. Getting sober requires confronting one's own self-image. Staying sober means saying good-bye to some of the oldest and most deeply held beliefs about self and others. When the denial has been penetrated, grieving can begin. The feelings of that transformation are profound and they signal that the process is at work. Grieving involves a conscious struggle with guilt, anger, fear, and depression. The expression or even purging of these feelings is not an end in itself. The end is the transformation. Since these are the most soul-wrenching emotions, grieving is the most difficult task a human being faces—and the one from which they are most likely to seek the protection of denial—the struggle with grieving issues can profoundly influence the course of sobriety. Recovery takes a long time, a lot of talk, and a lot of action. Keeping sober, while facing the losses caused by one's addiction without retreating to denial's protection, is one of the greatest challenges to the person in recovery. The special dynamics of grieving will be discussed in Chapter 7.

3

Anxiety: Pressure Against the Wall of Denial

Anxiety and denial are opposites: Anxiety is a force for change; denial is a bulwark against change. Most of the time they are in a kind of balance; like centrifugal and centripetal forces they keep our lives moving, but in fixed orbits.

At times this chapter may seem to repeat itself and go around in circles. Because anxiety, addictive behavior, and denial are so inextricably intertwined, reading about their relationship may seem like riding a merry-go-round. For readers who are new to the field of addictions, seeing these cycles laid out will be instructive. For those who have been stuck on the ride, the chapter will explain how the machine works—and perhaps how to get off.

FORCES IN BALANCE

Denial as "NO" to Change

As we have seen in previous chapters, denial is essentially resistance to a demand to change behavior or to incorporate a life-altering truth. Denial enables and maintains life-threatening behavior patterns. It also holds help at arm's length. At the same time, it enables psychological survival and the

27

maintenance of our deepest values and beliefs about the world. The oppo-site of denial is adaptation and change. The addict, who, as the first of the twelve steps reminds us, has a life that has become "unmanageable," experi-ences both the external demand to change, and internal pressure to regain his or her lost "sanity." When external demands or internal pressure penetrate his or her denial system, the addict is said to "hit bottom." Ironically, the same anxiety that drove the denial system can then become the motivation to abandon it.

Anxiety plays a complex role in addiction. Like denial it seems to be both a cause and an effect. Many people use drinking (and other potentially harmful behaviors) as a way to reduce stress, to medicate themselves, or to escape from painful realities. "What a mess. I need a drink." Such a flight from anxiety is also related to denial. Being anxious is a kind of cue or trigger to go into denial or to do things that will later be covered up, rationalized, or denied. "If you had a job like mine, you'd drink too." The tension, the behavior, and the denial seem all of one piece.

Denial and anxiety intertwine before, during, and after acts of addiction. The addict who uses chemicals (or acts in some other way to reduce tension) must later cope with (or deny) the consequences of his or her addictive behavior. A life out of control generates a lot of stress, worries, and nameless fears. Who would be surprised to hear that a woman binged after her doctor told her that her weight had become a significant health risk and was creating a hypertension crisis? Nor would anyone be surprised that, when confronted, she said, "I couldn't help myself. I was so anxious." There they are, tugging in both directions at once: the sense of dread and the denial ("It's not my fault, I couldn't help it") for what she did about her anxiety.

Anxiety as "Must Change"

If denial holds us in old ways, then anxiety moves us out of them. It is a force for change in how we think, feel, act, and believe about our world and the experience of living in it. It covers a range from little nudges to alter our current behavior ("I better put down this magazine and check on dinner") to persistent nags ("Have I really saved enough for retirement?") and panics ("Oh my God, it's April 15th and I have not done my taxes!") to insistent demands to alter the structure of our lives ("Look at me. Everything is a mess. I've got to do something and do it now!").

Anxiety and Denial in Balance

Anxiety triggers denial. Denial protects the addictive behavior from scrutiny. However, behavior done in denial generates anxiety. So the cycle starts all over again.

Extremes of either anxiety or denial are unstable states, so we spend much of our lives vacillating between them. When there is too much denial, all four walls are up. We are deaf to the messages of threat and, like the little pigs, happy in our flimsy structures and complacent in our little orbit. Like Scarlett O'Hara, we are going to "think about it tomorrow." Too much denial produces inertia. Why change, if the threat is not serious? On the other hand, when there is too little denial, we are buffeted by any wind of fate. We lose the integrity of our core values and commitments and break faith with our core being. Too little denial means too much anxiety. We feel and act "crazy."

Too much anxiety is toxic. Paradoxically it can immobilize us rather than energize us. We are so busy coping with the anxiety and so distracted by its discomfort that we lose the energy to do anything about the life we are living. Anxiety becomes a threat on its own.

FORCES OUT OF BALANCE

Toxic Anxiety as a Disease

No one needs to have anxiety defined for them. Everyone, from little children to senior citizens, is anxious some of the time. We also know intuitively that either too much anxiety, or coping with it in disruptive ways, means that something is seriously wrong. The wrong is not in the thing being worried about, but in the way the worrying is being done.

When the normal cares of life immobilize people, we see them as struggling with the *toxicity* of anxiety. In the past, professionals called this struggle a disease and diagnosed it as neurosis. The term "neurotic," like the term "alcoholic," was both a diagnosis and an insult.

In 1980, the American Psychiatric Association completely revised the standards used for diagnosing mental disorders. The new standards of the *Diagnostic and Statistical Manual, Third Edition* (DSM-III), replaced the old term "Neurosis" with the new term "Anxiety Disorder." The authors noted that:

In this group of disorders anxiety is either the predominant disturbance, as in Panic Disorder and Generalized Anxiety Disorder, or anxiety is experienced if the individual attempts to master the symptoms, as in confronting the dreaded object or situation in Phobic Disorder or resisting the obsessions or compulsions in Obsessive Compulsive Disorder. (American Psychiatric Association, 1980, p. 225)

The term "Anxiety Disorders," and the essential characteristics of the subtypes of this group, were maintained in the most recent revision of the *Diagnostic and Statistical Manual, Fourth Edition* (DSM-IV). The condition called "Generalized Anxiety Disorder" is characterized by such symptoms as: restlessness or feeling keyed up or on edge; feeling easily fatigued; difficulty concentrating or mind going blank; irritability; muscle tension; sleep disturbance (difficulty falling or staying asleep, or restless, unsatisfying sleep) (APA, 1994, p. 436). That is surely a description of toxic anxiety. The emphasis on the management of anxiety by avoiding, ruminating, or performing ritual acts is part of the definition of an anxiety disorder. What if the obsession is a craving, or the compulsive act is intoxication? Then anxiety is also a description of an addict who is about to act out his or her addiction, or an addict with a shaky recovery who is on what is called a "dry drunk." A dry drunk is an unstable anxiety state about to tumble into the old orbit of abuse and denial.

Anxiety and Postwithdrawal Syndrome

Addictionologists refer to "postwithdrawal syndrome," or PWS. PWS is defined as a combination of anxiety, craving, and depression working synergistically and potentiating each other. Like a pair of figure skaters taking turns at using the energy of one partner to lift and propel the other through a dizzying series of spins, one symptom triggers the others, as well as making the first harder to cope with. Because the presence of one PWS symptom increases the potency of the others, each symptom multiplies the effect of the others, while its own toxicity is increasing. For example, depression, with its feelings of hopelessness, can flood the newly recovering addict with despair. "I'll never get really clean." Contemplating such a dreadful future can trigger anxiety, which in turn can drive the search for relief of pain. Enter craving, which is the obsessional thought about the relief that might be had by acting out the addiction. Now the addict may think, "What good am I if I'm thinking about doing it again? No good that's what! I'm just no good." Now he is back to depression, but this time self-depreciation has been added. Now he really needs a fix to feel better. Trying to resist this obsession triggers more anxiety. Round and around he goes. Typically, the discomfort of PWS is ended by relapse.

An irony about the use of alcohol to medicate anxiety and depression is that at low doses in nonaddicted people, alcohol tends to reduce anxiety and depression. However, at high doses, and in addicted users, alcohol often increases anxiety or deepens depression. The same thing can be said about most compulsive behavior. For example, Joanna is just a little anxious about leaving on a vacation. She stops in her driveway and goes back to check that her door is really locked. She is relieved and goes on. On the other hand, Joe has an obsessive compulsive disorder. He never leaves the house without performing an elaborate ritual, which includes checking every window in the house three times and the door four times. If he tries to leave without completing this ritual he will become very anxious and upset. He tells himself he should not do it, it's crazy, he has already checked twice. But he knows he will be a wreck if he does not check again. When he has completed the ritual he does not feel relief; he feels ashamed, and defeated. He has only succeeded in terminating the pain generated by trying to inhibit his impulse; the anxiety that triggered the incident is left hanging.

By the time users are identified as addicts, they have been through PWS many times. The old-timers say, "No one ever stops the first time; you stop a hundred times" and "I had to quit because I couldn't stop." If PWS did not trigger relapse, addicts could control their using. They could "cut down," "stay out of trouble," "drink like a gentleman." If they could, they would. But the triggering of the PWS, and the havoc of shattered self-esteem and ruined lives left in its wake, are terrible testimony to the toxic power of anxiety. And terrible testimony tends to be denied.

Can Anxiety Cause Addiction?

No. As powerful as it is, anxiety is not *the cause* of addiction. Addicts are no more or less anxious (as a group) then any other group (football fans, manic-depressives, or brunette bird-watchers). Addiction is not a subcategory of neurosis, nor a type of anxiety disorder. Addicts are not overmedicated neurotics any more than they are overindulged hedonists. Anxiety is not the cause of addiction. The problem is what addicts do when they are anxious: Their tendency (if not their outright goal) is to avoid feelings (including anxiety). The walls of denial they erect to keep their inner life secret also hold others and help at arm's length. The dynamic between their anxiety, their denial, and their symptoms is more a barrier to help than a cause of their illness. Anxiety does not cause addiction. It causes anxious addicts.

A similar chicken-and-egg question has been researched regarding early childhood experience and the etiology of alcoholism. The longitudinal study conducted at Harvard and reported in George Vaillant's book, *The Natural History of Alcoholism* (1983), found that just as many boys who had troubled childhoods grew up without drinking problems as later became alcoholics. Vaillant's data suggest that somehow in the course of a life, many troubled boys find ways to heal their wounds. Obviously some do not. The troubled boys who later became alcoholics may not have had access to the natural healing the other boys used. There may not have been significant others there to help with healing. They may have been present, but were kept outside the wall of denial. Some boys and, later, men may not have been able to utilize help because denial had created too many blind spots in their awareness. Some drank, others did not. The alcoholics-to-be were not alone in their pain. The pain does not explain the alcoholism. The active alcoholic who blames his disease on his "rotten childhood" has both his drinking and his pain intact. Denial is not the special province of alcoholics. Juvenile delinquents, adult sociopaths, and brunette bird-watchers use it too. Denial, however, alienates a sufferer from healing.

Furthermore, adopted-twin studies on the influence of genetics, for example McCord and McCord (1960) and Goodwin (1976), have shown that the chance of the son of an alcoholic father growing up to become an alcoholic is the same (about one chance in four) whether he is adopted into a nondrinking family or into a family with an active alcoholic. This kind of research leaves us with the impression that early childhood experience (good or bad) does not so much determine whether or not a person becomes an alcoholic, but what *kind* of alcoholic he becomes (anxious, depressed, antisocial, or parent-blaming). As one wit put it, "Now that I stopped drinking, I'm still the same jerk I always was. I just have fewer dents in my car."

Again, there is an almost circular relationship between denial and anxiety. Sometimes anxiety is a trigger to seek out a familiar comfort. Getting that comfort may trigger more anxiety and more denial. Our denial causes our blind spots and sets up the next ride on the terrible carousel. It is also true that anxiety is triggered when a threat or terrible truth is pushing into our awareness. When our denial system fails, anxiety wells up. At those times anxiety may become a goad ("I've got to get off of this merry-go-round!"), driving us to an encounter we have previously avoided. Perhaps an encounter with help.

Yes, denial causes inertia, but it is like the pause at the top of the roller coaster. Hold your breath; here it comes. Similarly, anxiety can immobilize its victims, but with all that pent-up energy, there will eventually be an explosion.

COPING WITH ANXIETY

Every "psychological" process is connected in some way to an underlying biochemical event in the brain. The brain is prewired to produce the biochemicals necessary to mobilize us for emergencies. This is called the "fight or flight" response. Alertness is heightened so that we are better able to spot the threat and energy is mobilized so that we can put forth as much effort as is necessary. This is the extra energy that got our ancestors away from the saber-toothed tigers.

However, as we have seen, if there is not enough anxiety, denial reigns. If there is too much we are, in the language of the nineties, "too stressed out" to cope. One way to look at the problem of anxiety disorders and addictions is as breakdowns in the internal guidance system that converts anxiety into solutions. Of all the techniques for reducing anxiety, the most important is problem solving. The best solution is to deal with the cause of the threat to our well-being. A voice inside tells us, "Get it done right," "Don't put it off," "Don't accept half measures or good enough for now." Anxiety drives that search for the *right* solution. One of its great benefits is that it helps us stay focused on the problem. We stay rattled until we find the answer. It keeps us on track. Another benefit of anxiety is that it mobilizes enough energy to overcome inertia and keep going until we get where we need to be.

Anxiety as a Signal for Problem Solving

At low levels, anxiety is a kick in the behind. At high levels it is a kick in the stomach. Anxiety is a knock on the door:

Who's there?
The wolf.
Uh Oh!

There is no question that anxiety is an energizer. It gets us up and moving, whether it is just pacing back and forth and worrying about our taxes on April 1st, or finally gathering up all the papers, forms, and records on April 14th. At its core, anxiety is a drive to find the right thing to do and the motivation to overcome inertia and do it. It is not the only human motivator. Love can get us to move mountains, or at least try to. However, in the grip of addiction, other motivations lose force. One stops searching for a better way, until driven again by anxiety. When the search ends with accomplishment or problem solving, anxiety is "beneficial," "useful," even "healthful" rather than toxic. This can be true, even when the level of anxiety is quite high.

At low levels it is just the thing to get us to do what people in 12-step programs call "the next right thing." The nature of anxiety is to drive us to look for the right thing to do. "Are the kids getting a good education?" "Should I be spending more time with them?" It keeps us from ignoring what is important and letting commitments and values slide in priority. If you are a little anxious about the kids, you might talk to your spouse. If you are very worried, you might talk to the teacher . . . or even the kid. Maybe the talk can wait. It's not that bad. Here comes a note home from the school. It's time to *do* something.

Often anxiety drives us to find solutions by pushing us to define the problem more accurately. When it does this it pushes against denial, particularly denial of implication ("If X is true, then Y and, *oh my God*, Z must be true too!") and denial of change ("I've really got to do something this time"). Anxiety that motivates necessary change can be beneficial, even at high levels. It is beneficial as a motivator when the time has come for a major reordering of priorities or values. Anxiety provides the drive to undertake that restructuring, to see it through and then act on it. Thus anxiety plays a central role in making major life changes, such as achieving sobriety or the transformations that follow a core level loss. Such monumental changes require high levels of motivation. Unfortunately there is always the possibility that at these levels we may take flight rather than focus and fight.

Old-timers in 12-step programs say that you get sober by changing your behaviors, and you stay sober by changing your attitudes and values. Consider the following internal monologue of an addict who has recently been discharged from his first treatment:

Well here it is Tuesday night again. I guess I should go out to the meeting this week. Jeez, look at the weather out there! Besides, its a good night for TV. I can miss a meeting or two. No harm done. Don't bug me. Where did I hear an argument just like that? Right. It was between Joe, that guy I was in treatment with, and that old geezer they fixed him up with as a sponsor. Yeah, that's what Joe was saying the last time I saw him. And the old man kept saying, "Keep coming back." Joe wasn't worried. Come to think of it he missed a lot of meetings before his slip. God it was awful too. Lost his job, damn near lost everything. What would I do if Peg and the kid left? Where would I get the money for the child support, if I got fired? Oh Jeez I couldn't handle that. I can't let that happen to me. I'm not like Joe. Yeah, but I'm an addict like Joe. Better get these bones to a meeting, before my stinking thinking gets me in any more trouble than it has already.

Anxiety accompanies pressure on one's denial system. As such, it triggers denial as well as all the avoidance and escape strategies at our command, which have a nasty way of being right up there at the top of our list of priorities. But anxiety also heralds a shift in denial when the dreadful truth emerges. When anxiety shifts to its role as a motivator to cope with such a truth, it performs its most vital function. That is the time we need the serenity, courage, and wisdom the Serenity Prayer asks for. We are held to the task of finding the place for this new truth by the force of anxiety. We are confronted with the inescapability of change. The old way crumbles and the extra energy of anxiety makes us diligent in the search for new and better ways.

Anxiety-Binding Behaviors

Tension cannot always be reduced by problem solving. Sometimes the problem cannot be solved, and sometimes the problem cannot even be identified. Sometimes we do not find the right thing to do. At these times, anxiety can quickly become toxic and move from minor tension to major stress in a hurry. We may become aimless, easily distracted, have difficulty concentrating, become "jumpy," or given to nervous behaviors or habits. We may misunderstand the threat, apply the wrong solution, or misjudge the critical values at issue. Anxiety is uncomfortable, it detracts from the quality of life and interferes with relationships. We try to talk about something that worries us. A friend says, "Calm down . . . relax." We say, "Yes, but you don't understand."

It is not always possible to solve a problem directly and sometimes it is not even desirable. At those times we need ways to *reduce* tension until the problem can be solved. Thus, again we have the definition of denial as a way to buy time. You cannot always march into the boss's office and deal with your hurt feelings about being yelled at. You are blocked because it is not the *smart* thing to do. Better cool off and talk to her on Monday.

Anxiety drives the search for the right thing to do, but there is no end of right things to do. Housework is never really done; not only is dust settling in the living room while you are doing the laundry, but the clothes you get dirty doing housework will have to be laundered. We have to turn off that pressure to *do something*. So we all need techniques for reducing tension when we cannot solve the problem. We relax, take vacations, exercise, read, knit, and so forth. The tension becomes part of the energy fueling these activities. The activities direct awareness away from the discomfort of the anxiety, tension levels go down, and we do relax. Sometimes relaxation makes problem solving possible. Many "eurekas" have come in the bath. In a psychodynamic model, such as the one being described here, activities that reduce tension without impacting the cause of that tension or solving problems are called *anxiety-binding* behaviors.

The concept of anxiety-binding behavior covers a lot of ground. It can be said to include the whole range of tension-relieving behaviors, including aimless pacing, nervous gestures, muttering swear words when frustrated. What is most important for our discussion is that it also includes such potentially dangerous behavior as drinking and drugging. That is quite a range. Sometimes we do things that are not well thought out, useful, or even in our best interest. We shout at loved ones, smoke, overeat, drink too much, drive too fast, etc. Some of these anxiety-binding behaviors occur rarely or only under extreme stress. Others are common or occur so frequently in a person's behavior that they are almost characteristic of that person. "You know Joanne, with that little nervous laugh of hers?" The nervous habits may be innocuous, but annoying (e.g., finger drumming), or only mildly injurious (e.g., nail biting or knuckle cracking). Others are potentially very dangerous (e.g., smoking, drinking, overeating). We may be only dimly aware of performing "nervous habits" such as biting our nails, drumming our fingers, or brushing away a fallen lock of hair, but they are there and they are part of the way we cope with anxiety. Furthermore, we bite, drum, brush (and drink) more in a crisis. The people around us may know we are anxious before we do. They may know we are tense just by observing us. In fact, even when they point it out, we may deny being anxious even with the evidence between our teeth, under our fingers, or in our glass.

Often we just want to escape, to get away from the tension. The power of learning how to escape tension is illustrated in a classic experiment, described in Hilgard and Marquis (1964). A dog was placed in a cage where a bell was rung and then an electric shock was administered. It was able to escape, or avoid the shock, by jumping over a barrier to the other side of the cage. The next time the bell was rung, the dog got very agitated and quickly jumped to the other side of the cage. It repeated this behavior every time the bell was rung. Once this response was learned, it was difficult to unlearn (or extinguish). The dog just did not stick around long enough to find out that the shock was no longer coming. It was no longer doing this to escape actual pain; just getting away when the signal came seemed to be rewarding in itself. The signal elicits something like an anxiety state, and the animal works hard to "turn off" that state. The dog learned to jump over the barrier placed in the cage. When the barrier was raised, the dog literally learned to "climb walls" in reaction to its anxiety. If the dog was tied down, it leapt over the barrier as soon as it was free, even hours later. If the dog was held down, the experimenter got bit. We might think this reaction was normal in a *dog*, even that it was justified; but many a spouse has been beaten (not bitten) for flushing the last gram of cocaine down the toilet.

Sometimes a variation on this conditioning technique is used with rats to test the efficacy of new tranquilizers. Others who are not scientists reinvent it every day. Each new generation of adolescents discovers the power of escape. A young street pharmacist described the role of drugs in escape learning with chilling accuracy:

> Sometimes it helped to talk to friends, if they weren't busy or something, or play a little ball or something. But then once when I was hurting, and this guy turned me on, and like I was out of there. You know what? I had the way out, you dig? You can't count on friends but that stuff works every time.

Some anxiety binding behaviors are left over from childhood, others were added in times of adult strife. As parents, we try to prevent children from annoying us with them. "Don't fidget!" We also try to prevent children from discovering the more pernicious ones, such as drinking and drugging, until they are older.

A person's repertoire of anxiety-binding behaviors is built up over a lifetime. New techniques are added and old ones drop out, but as a rule the repertoire tends to become fairly stable in adulthood. Perhaps this is another way of saying that people are set in their ways (including their ways of handling anxiety), or that anxiety-binding techniques are habits.

Behavioral psychologists tell us that habits that are frequently used and systematically reinforced tend to be stable over time. To understand habits we have to look at the issues of reinforcement (or reward) and practice (or repetition). They tend to link a response (the behavior that brought anxiety to an end) to the cues of the threat. Behaviorists have taught us that escape and avoidance are powerful rewards, and powerful rewards make for strong habits. Escape responses become almost instant habits. The tendency to repeat them is very strong and each repetition makes the habit more difficult to change — even though the threat itself is no longer there.

The irony is that behavior that becomes addictive can be such effective escape that those who use it come to prefer it to all others. Further, no anxiety-binding technique really works well against anxiety generated by a deep internal conflict that keeps on stirring up more and more anxiety. In the face of that kind of anxiety there may even be a search for new and stronger ways of turning off the tension. "I was such a nervous wreck that I called my doctor for a tranquilizer."

When Techniques Become the Problem

One person might call his habit "letting off steam"; another person might call it "making a fool of yourself." A counselor might call it "acting out." The phrase *acting out* is often applied whenever a person is trying to *feel* better rather than *get* better. It is a form of dealing with the tension, not its cause. It is a generic term for addictive behaviors of addicts. It has generalized from the actual drinking, drugging, sexing, debting, eating, raging, etc., to the whole range of behavior surrounding and supporting the active addiction or interfering with the recovery: feeling better not getting better.

Internal conflicts and emotional problems are often said to be "acted out" in the sense that they repeat the problem rather than solve it. Usually the acting out generates a whole new round of problems in the form of critical feedback of others. What was once a kitten meowing in a bag, is now a loosed wildcat, howling, running around, and causing havoc.

While the consequences of anxiety itself (such as the symptoms listed above: motor tension, autonomic nervous system hyperactivity, apprehension, vigilance, etc.) are usually within the individual, or intrapersonal, the consequences of acting out are often interpersonal. In fact the claim that no harm is being done is a basic form of denial of implications. "If I hit a tree on my way home from the bar, that's *my* problem." "That's between me and my bookie." "Prostitution is a victimless crime."

Acting out affects relationships. When people experience a threat and act in some way to reduce the anxiety, that behavior has an impact on those around them. The anxiety-reducing behavior becomes an interpersonal event. It is the pebble in the aquarium. When the behavior is irritating, odd, unusual, or restricted under some social code, the individual who engages in it will eventually face criticism, blame, or censure. Some ways of acting out may be tolerated, while others become the focus of relationship-shattering confrontations. The difference does not lie in the habits themselves, but in their impact, their interpersonal consequences. Drinking or drugging to reduce anxiety will have an impact on the relationships in the user's support system and, possibly, the whole interpersonal network of the individual. Some friends and loved ones will ignore the using, some will try to help. Still others may demand that the user change his or her ways or face the end of the relationship. The outer layers of denial (denial of facts, implications, and change) are meant to buffer the demands by outsiders for change. Like the turtle described in Chapter 1, they help us dive and survive the pressure to be different.

LEARNED HABITS OF ESCAPE AND PSYCHOLOGICAL DEPENDENCE

Human anxiety-binding behavior is learned to turn off anxiety. Any response that is made in times of stress and then is followed by a reduction in that stress gets a place in the response repertoire and tends to stay there. The ones that are used most often are the hardest habits to break. Such habit learning plays a major role in addictive behavior. Any analysis of the progression of addiction must acknowledge the powerful influence of emotional and behavioral habits. Anxiety reduction is a powerful reinforcer. Any behavior associated with a reduction in tension will be repeated and may become a habit (not just the drinking, but also "getting out of the house," "going to a bar, hanging with my buddies," etc.). Habits learned this way can become extraordinarily resistant to change. They are resistant because they help avoid pain. As long as we have the habits we use them and we avoid pain. The alarm may be false, but why take the chance? If we do not take the chance, we never learn differently.

Theorists used to make a distinction between physiological dependence (withdrawal symptoms) and psychological dependence (the rest of addiction phenomena). The distinction proved not to be helpful and was abandoned by the time DSM-III was introduced in 1980. If one thinks of taking a drink, placing a bet, or even treating one's self to ice cream as a way of escaping tension or anxiety, that behavior can also become a habit. What happens in the progression of addiction is that habit works its way up the hierarchy of responses until it is the first thing the addict does. In addition, the other habits of coping, problem solving, and tension reduction drop out. At that point the behavior has become the only way of coping, and the addict could be said to be psychologically dependent.

Recovery requires learning new habits, and the lessons can be hard. Even with the knowledge that the old habits are not working, the new ways offered by the program are just that—new and untried. They are risky. Going to one's first 12-step meeting, instead of using, is taking a chance. This new method of coping with anxiety might not work as well as the old. Miraculously, they sometimes do. Many recovering people report that they initially went to meetings because they just felt better and safer there. Going to meetings became a habit. They listened and participated; that became a habit too.

DENIAL AND THE ADDICT'S "LICENSE"

Anxiety and denial are both normal and pathological. All of us have used denial to deal with anxiety before, after, during, and (tragically) instead of change or recovery. There are great differences in when, where, and how often denial is used. Most of all there are great differences in the effects of using it.

In the film *Chalk Talk*, which is widely used in alcoholism treatment centers, Father Joe Martin (1972) observed an interesting way that denial interacts with acting out. He contrasts two confrontations based on smelling alcohol on the breath of a fellow elevator passenger. In one, a man who does not have a drinking problem (in our terms, is not in denial about his drinking behavior) is asked why he has alcohol on his breath. He explains how it got there; he shared a toast at a wedding. He is just as likely to say, "Never mind. None of your business." Ask a man who is hiding his drinking problem, and he will not only deny that he has been drinking but will probably hold his breath throughout the rest of the elevator ride. Father Martin calls this the "blue variety" of drinker. He, too, is just as likely to tell you to mind your own business. His nip was not a sip, but a gulp. His toast was not a celebration, but a necessity. His use of the rules for polite elevator riding was not an exertion of his right to privacy, but an expression of his need for secrecy. His denial is pathological to the extent that it protects his self-destruction rather than his autonomy.

When a particular behavior (drinking, drugging, sexing, eating, debting, raging, working) is a firmly established habit, the person acting out this way can easily come to see the behavior as a necessity for normal well-being. Not only does he or she see it as necessary to the reduction of anxiety, but also being blocked in performing it makes him or her anxious. So the anxiety multiplies itself. Then it becomes important to protect that behavior from the scrutiny, consent, or control of others. The protection is denial of facts, implications, and change. These layers of denial serve to deflect, blunt, or buffer the criticism of others. When a person uses these forms of denial, we often say that they are being "defensive." Addicts are notorious for being "touchy" in just this way. For example, a cocaine user had a date with a friend, but did not show up. She gives her friend an alibi to cover the missed date, broken promise, flubbed expectation. The friend feels twice burned; once by the original disappointment, and again by the lie which brushes her off and discounts her hurt feelings. The friend begins to grumble about the user behind her back. The user's use caused one problem, and her cover-up caused another. Her use of a buffer has been reacted to by others as a rebuff.

In part, our reaction to addicts' acting out depends on whether we see it as either symptoms of disease and as such out of their control, or as behavior that is wholly volitional and under their conscious control. We tend to look at the behavior called "social drinking" as just that, within social rules, under control, chosen. "Do you want a cocktail before dinner?" "No thanks. I'll order now." Substance abuse, on the other hand, is chemical use, which is not chosen or controlled. "She got so drunk, she threw up. What a damn fool thing to do!"

For those who are addicted, criticism of use is a threat to their entire defense system, and they respond accordingly. The whole system of excuses, arguments, and negations comes into play.

"You went to that damn adult book store again last night didn't you?"
"No I didn't!"
"You're lying!"
"Shut up!"

The rest of the denial system functions to protect the user's rights. Unfortunately, that circle of rights is drawn wide enough to include the using itself as if it were a protected civil liberty. If the demands of others cannot be fended off, and one is forced to surrender the behavior, he or she is thrown back into an anxiety crisis. The anxiety mounts, and behavior gets desperate.

As the anxiety mounts, it is possible that the primary denial system itself might fail. If primary denial fails, one can become aware of conflicts which are by definition intolerable to awareness. That is the reason the so-called "license to use" is defended so strenuously. Understanding this point is necessary to understanding the fearsome energy that goes into defending the behavior. Addicts are not so much protecting this drink or that episode as they are protecting what they take to be their very *right to be protected at all*. Often they do it without knowing why they feel they must, aware only that it is vitally important to do.

Oddly enough, the wall of denial, which so often seems like an impenetrable slab of granite, sometimes falls like a house of cards or a string of dominos, tumbling down, one after another. Because these layers depend on one another, they can sometimes come tumbling down all at once. The domino-like structure of a denial system is like the child's nursery rhyme:

> *For the want of a nail, the shoe was lost.*
> *For the want of a shoe, the horse was lost.*
> *For the want of the horse, the rider was lost.*
> *For the want of the rider, the battle was lost.*
> *And for the want of the battle the kingdom was lost.*
> *And all for the want of a nail.*

This is why users "make a big deal out of everything" or are "touchy all the time." They are rigid and inflexible because so much depends on this drink or that pill—more than the observer/critic can imagine, or the user is willing to imagine. They cannot be talked out of it, punished out of it, or manipulated out of it. For them it is a matter of life or death. Here again is the paradox of anxiety: It can provide the motivation to change this false belief about who they really are and what is necessary for their survival, or it can drive them through the cycle one more time.

In fact, whether or not a person can be flexible when a favored way of dealing with tension is blocked is important information about their mental health. The non-driven behavior of the social user can easily be manipulated. They ask for a second highball before dinner; the host refuses, and they demur. The alcoholic causes a scene.

ANXIETY AND THE UNCONSCIOUS

Filters on Awareness

When denial was discussed in Chapter 2, it was defined as protecting awareness. Awareness can be divided into three levels: consciousness, preconsciousness, and unconsciousness. In the simplest sense, consciousness is the data of current awareness. Preconsciousness is that which we can be reminded of or bring to awareness with a little effort. It may include old telephone numbers, the names of schoolmates, noises out in the street which have melted into background noise while we concentrate on a conversation, and so forth. It may also contain the embarrassing details of the last acting out episode. Unconsciousness is that which cannot, under ordinary circumstances, be brought to awareness, even with effort. It differs from simple forgetting or biochemically mediated lapses (blackouts) because it is kept from awareness for a reason. It is denied access to awareness by means of a series of filters, because it is too painful to experience or recall. One could almost think of these filters operating like some television censor clipping out movie scenes that are too graphic to be broadcast to "younger or more sensitive" viewers. Ordinarily we are only aware of that which we need to know. Irrelevant, troubling, unrecognizable, or unmanageable material is kept outside awareness in the preconscious. Unconscious material that is too threatening to know either does not enter the preconscious at all, or is not moved from there into awareness.

Denial operates at all three levels of awareness.

- Denial of facts is a wholly conscious protection. Change the TV channel to avoid some graphic war news, or leave the room when your mother asks about the twenty dollars she is sure was in her purse yesterday; it is a conscious act. You know what you are avoiding. Denial of facts includes outright lying. Such and such information simply is not so; such and such event did not happen.
- Denial of implications is also conscious. One is quite aware of the argument or conclusion one is fighting against. In addition, this level of denial sets a limit in the preconscious by keeping other inferences from that conclusion (and the implications of *those* inferences) back in the shadows.
- Denial of change also operates at both the conscious and preconscious level. The desire to escape consequences is quite conscious. "Hey don't blame me; I tried." However, the root of the struggle with responsibility lies in the addict's negative self-image. The pain of his or her life-long struggle with a sense of inadequacy resists being dragged into the light.
- Denial of feelings works at the preconscious or unconscious level.

Sometimes, if pushed or encouraged, one might admit being "a little upset," but the roots of those feelings may run too deep to be admitted into full awareness.

The 12-step programs say that the path of recovery requires "rigorous honesty." In this context that means constant pressure to bring the preconscious into full awareness, to avoid yielding to the comfort denial affords by keeping truth hidden.

Normal Filtering

The mechanisms of denial allow for the normal filtering of experience. Without them we would be flooded with all sorts of remote associations, distant memories, urges, and admonitions. It would be William James's "booming, buzzing world." One needs only to observe an overstimulated two-and-a-half-year-old to be thankful for the smooth operation of these filters.

One place where the filters are suspended is in our dream life. Dreams are an experience of the disorganized welter of images and feelings sloshing around in the preconscious. Freud said that dreams were the "royal road to the unconscious." They are not, however, the unconscious itself. Dreams symbolize, disguise if you will, those processes in order for them to gain entrance to awareness. But if the conscious mind is unable to cope with those issues without denial, the disguise is not penetrated; note the following example.

A man tells his friend about his dream. In the dream there is a white-haired woman on a staircase and he is trying to strangle her. He says he awoke very frightened by his hostility. His friend is an amateur psychologist. He suspects the dream may have something to do with his friend's family conflicts. The dreamer always talks about how "lucky" he was. After his mother died, his father remarried right away. He had a new home to go to and did not have to go to an orphanage. The dreamer grew up but still lives with the now-widowed matriarch. The home is not peaceful. They quarrel often. He stops at a tavern every night "to prepare to go home." The would-be Freud suggests that the dream might be about his unconscious hostilities. "I think the woman on the staircase is your *step*mother. Get it?" The man looks at him blankly and says, "I don't get it. I got to go home. Mom is holding dinner. Although I don't know how I can eat with this headache."

Perhaps the amateur psychologist was right about the dream, but he was wrong about his friend. Even though the dream allowed his friend to suspend the constraints of reason and the inhibitions of denial, it is only safe to do that in a dream.

Unconsciousness

The unconscious is the untamed part of all of us. It obeys no rules, not even logic. It is irrational, surreal, and every bit as maddening to the conscious mind as Alice's trip to Wonderland. Psychologists say it is dominated by "dream logic," which is no logic at all. It contains every urge, terror, memory, and dream. The contents of the unconscious go beyond symbols to the issues and the conflicts themselves. "Uncivilized" is probably the best word for it. The urges to grab what we want, smite our enemies, be all-powerful and above good and evil all dwell there. According to Freud it also contains the ogres, goblins, and furies which first taught us right from wrong by terrifying us with punishment. These fears are as nonlogical as the urges they suppress. Jung talked about the "shadow" in the unconscious: the Mr. Hyde within each of our Dr. Jekylls.

Nonetheless the unconscious is not all evil. The wellspring of life itself is there, albeit uncivilized and unharnessed. It demands existence at any cost and suspects all inhibition. Artists, mystics, and creative people seem to have a special window into this world and they often seem to pay a high price for that access. The rest of us live with rare moments of great passion, creativity, or mystic insight. We rarely experience the great highs or lows that are created when the full force and energy of our lives bursts forth or clashes with the rules of civilized behavior. It seems safer to content ourselves with watching movie heroes and heroines struggle with their passions than to feel the full surge of our own.

The wellspring is always there. The primary sense of one's own life has its roots in the unconscious. It comes from a time of true innocence, when being and doing were one and the same. The right to be, the drive to grow—to become—flows from these primal springs. In civilizing our young and socializing them to live with others, we must curb and channel this force. Paradoxically, the drive to live must be harnessed if the child is to survive. Sometimes those lessons are too harsh and leave scars on a child's sense of self. The harder the parents find the child to tame, the more punishment is heaped on its spirit. Rather than channeling the spirit, they seek to stifle it. One thinks of the cowboys of the old West, who spoke of taming wild horses as "bronco busting." Frustrated or overwhelmed parents may resort to harsh punishment or repeated shaming to control their young broncos.

Perhaps the most pernicious legacy from this time is the accumulated sense of shame about the free self built up in this domestication. Surely one of the most *unsafe* feelings to have stimulated and *not filtered* out of awareness is the fury and terror of having one's spirit broken by shaming. In the next chapter the role of shame in the development of the adult's self-concept will be discussed. Here it is dealt with in conjunction with the adult addict.

Pressure from the Internal Sense of Shame

Most interpersonal denial of addicts is aimed at the avoidance of shame. People get very anxious when they think they are about to be blamed for something. Denial of facts, implications, and change (particularly the latter) deflect, buffer, or discount attempts by others to get them to change behavior or see themselves in a way they abhor. It is blame, not really responsibility, that is being shunned. Blame is avoided to prevent an overwhelming sense of shame from boiling up from the inside.

Responsibility differs from blame in several ways that relate directly to denial. Responsibility is a commitment to achieve an outcome or to maintain a status quo. When I accept responsibility and then fail to meet that commitment, I may owe you an explanation (not an excuse; see Chapter 2) of what happened. Even as I explain, I ought to reaffirm the original commitment to you, rather than seize on my failure to escape the obligation. In the words of 12-step programs, I owe you an "amend."

Blame is a primitive form of punishment. Using it means asserting that all of the bad feelings for the disappointed expectation, both the guilt and the frustration, are going to be dumped into the psyche of the one who misbehaved. When I accept blame, I affirm that all of the bad feelings *both of us* have about this thing that happened are to fall on me. I am supposed to feel as bad as you do, or worse. It is my punishment and I deserve it. I lose the right to object to the punishment or to argue with (in program terms) your "inventory" of my "character defects." I failed you and I *deserve to be ashamed of myself*.

Often these criticisms and demands resonate with painful childhood experiences of parental shaming. When parents use blame and shame as primary disciplining tools, they subject their children to a systematic pattern of abuse. Usually the children develop a deep internal sense of shame. That painful sense of worthlessness, ineptitude, and general "badness" lasts a lifetime. The struggle to keep such toxic shame from flooding awareness becomes one of the most basic internal pressures against which primary denial (see p. 49) is marshaled.

Remember how bad you felt when you were punished for some childhood misdeed, say, making a mess while mother was out of the house? The worst part was not the "licking" but the lecture:

> I can't trust you for a minute, can I? You're nothing but trouble, aren't you? You're just no good and this proves it. Who do you think you are? I'll tell you. Don't just stand there, answer me! Don't interrupt!

Blaming is shaming the core self of the guilty one. The message is designed to penetrate all the layers of defense against assaults on self-esteem. If you tried to use denial of facts, you were told, "Don't lie to me. I caught you." If you tried to use denial of implications, you heard, "This means I can never trust you alone in the house again as long as you live." If you tried to use anxiety-binding techniques, you were told, "Don't say you are sorry. Sorry doesn't fix anything." And if you were not already crying from the punishment meted out so far, your parent demanded that you feel remorse. There was no denial of feelings allowed: "You should be ashamed of yourself!"

That is a phrase to chill the soul: "be ashamed of your self"—not sorry for what you did, but sorry for *being who you are*. How does one accept that kind of blame? Which chemically dependent person, however, does not feel that he or she is constantly being asked to accept just that sort of blame?

Several contemporary writers, such as John Bradshaw (1988, 1988a), have discussed the effects of toxic shame on the psyche and ways of healing from that shame. One part of that healing is coming to understand how a nonblaming parent responds to a child's mistakes. Ann Landers once listed ten rules for living with other people. Halfway through the list was this one: You broke it, you fix it. That is a simple statement of responsibility without blame. You could almost hear her responding to a child's mess when she came back home:

"Look at this mess. Boy am I angry. Clean it up now. Later we will talk about ways to play neatly and safely."

Getting help for chemical dependency is a way to stop making a mess and begin cleaning it up. No blame, just responsibility. Recovery in general and 12-step meetings in particular deal with what some people call "secondary shame": the shame of being addicted. What about primary shame acquired from too many injunctions to be ashamed of your *self*?

The deeper level of healing requires an understanding that shamed children develop a false sense of self based on these negative messages. They are told to identify themselves with the bad, and they do. "You're rotten . . . no damn good . . . can't do anything right . . . stupid . . . evil . . . " Unable to resist the insertion of this false data into the core of their self-concept, the children accept this characterization (see the discussion about attribution in the next chapter) as their true identity. Unfortunately, that also means that any time they behave well, get complimented, or feel good about being themselves, they are forced to discount this experience as false, misleading, and untrustworthy. In fact, they may even hear the same parent who originally abused their self-concept tell them that they are "phony, just a con artist, manipulating, dishonest, and deceitful." In case they should ever be inclined to forget or reject this message later in life, the addict gets to hear, "I told you that you'd turn out no good. You'll always be a bum. No one is going to believe this sobriety garbage."

The conflict created by the struggle with one's shame and negative self-image often presents difficulties in recovery and the working of a 12-step program. As one participant in Overeaters Anonymous said:

> I always had trouble with the part of the sixth step dealing with the removal of defects of character. I thought, if all my character defects were gone, there would be nothing left of *me*. That's all I was.

A member of Sexaholics Anonymous said:

> The shame messages were painful, but the acceptance-on-a-string messages were really worse. I heard, "You're really no good, BUT you could be tolerable if you did more to please me." It confused me completely. What's love? What's manipulation? Is it better to be a puppet or a person? Later I wanted to be the one pulling the strings. For me, the third step, turning my life over, was hard. It seemed like going back to being a puppet.

DENIAL AS THE BASIS OF
PSYCHOLOGICAL DEFENSES

In Chapter 2, denial was described as a series of walls protecting awareness. Anxiety accompanies both the building up and the tearing down of those walls. The innermost wall, denial of feelings, serves to protect awareness from the flood of painful emotions. It protects and stabilizes the deepest convictions of the inner self. In that chapter we looked at the walls of denial from the outside and examined how they function to stabilize the self. This section will now look at the walls from the inside.

Denial of feelings protects awareness from feelings we believe to be too terrible to bear. We read about some tragedy in the newspapers and say, "God, if that ever happened to me, I don't know that I could bear it. I'd go nuts, kill myself. I don't know what. I just couldn't go on." The phrase "I'd go nuts" is more than a cliché. It reflects the sense that living in a nightmare is intolerable. The unconscious is a nightmare. It must be kept out of awareness for us to be sane, and to be able to cope with "reality." If denial is what makes it possible to go on, then one of its most basic functions is to protect us from dread, terror, and paralyzing fear of the sort that might elicit just such a collapse. It literally keeps us sane. That is why the basic form of denial is the blocking of feeling.

Repression and Primary Denial

Psychologists attribute blocking of awareness to the operation of defenses they call *repression* and *denial* (e.g., Dorpat, 1994). In its simplest sense repression is the defense that pushes powerful feelings and memories below conscious awareness. Repression forms a seal over the flames of unconscious emotional turmoil. It functions unconsciously, passively, and without any effort we are aware of. The memory is just gone, like last night's dreams. True repression is the psychological equivalent of the biological phenomenon called blackouts. When psychologists use the term denial, they are referring to the defense used to prevent material that is already conscious from reminding us of material that is unconscious. When this narrow sense of the word is meant, the term *primary denial* will be used to avoid confusion with the larger, multilayered sense of denial.

Cues from current experience could create a gap in the barriers we have erected. We could always be reminded by some chain of associations of something we intended to forget. So we must erase the immediate memory *and* the memory of the events immediately surrounding it. Sometimes people will not only forget a horrible car accident, they will also report that they do not remember anything that happened that whole day. They have erased the tape of the event and the events that preceded it, because memory of those events might cue the tape to roll again. They *could* go on erasing; they could lose the memory of ever driving that damn car, ever having ridden in a car, seen any cars, or ever knowing someone who saw a car. This could go on until they had complete amnesia. If they absolutely *had* to be unable to recognize cues, they would also have to start erasing data that *might* remind them of the accident. Then they would also have to become unaware of things that might remind them of reminders. Then they would end up deaf, blind, aphasic, and insensate. If not, any reminder or association to this forbidden topic that came to mind could open the lid of Pandora's Box.

Relying on repression is too costly, because so much needs to be repressed. The Victorian era illustrates this process. In Victorian times it was deemed necessary never to think about sex. Chairs no longer had "legs," they had "limbs." Eventually upholsterers developed "skirts" to cover these "limbs."

Today we cannot afford to miss seeing or hearing things going on around us. We need to be alert crossing streets (even if struck by a car as a child) and remember to lock our doors (even if robbed and frightened last year). What we need is a mechanism that will allow us to think about today and react to these new experiences and ideas without being flooded by the feelings attached to them in the past. Primary denial provides a way out of this problem by preventing current ideas and information from being linked with the pain associated with that data in the past. Primary denial is the separation of feeling from perceptions, ideas, and memories; it allows us to think about the ideas without feeling the feelings. In its acceptable form it is called *being objective*. In its unacceptable form it is called *being a robot*. When this latter form of denial is operating, associations (that is, chains of ideas) are deflected away from painful feelings; the individual has no sense of any emotional response to ideas, memories, or sensory experiences related to old emotional conflicts.

Primary denial and repression make a powerful combination. One or both of them are involved in what we call "getting over" a trauma, or "putting it out of our minds." Without them we would never recover from the pain of an automobile accident or the agony of a loved one's death. These defense mechanisms work outside awareness or, in classic psychological terminology, *unconsciously*. It may not seem very efficient to have this going on where we cannot monitor it. But as with a septic tank or a sewer system, we would just as soon it did its job and not remind us of what its job is.

In order for the protection afforded by primary denial to be effective, it is necessary for this part of the defense system to be buried in the unconscious. If you become aware that you are denying, you come dangerously close to knowing what you are denying. A legend about a great Russian writer illustrates this point. It is said that Tolstoy and his friends once invented a very exclusive club. It was so exclusive that no one could pass the initiation rite. In order to be a member, all one had to do was to stand on a busy street corner in downtown St. Petersburg for an hour, and never think of bears. This may seem to be an easy task, but successfully completing it is difficult. An attempt to join this club will soon meet with frustration because purposefully *not* thinking about bears turns out to be impossible. One either becomes aware of what it is one is trying *not* to think about or becomes aware of thinking about something else, say camels, and aware that one is thinking about camels in order *not* to think about bears, which leads to the awareness that one has actually thought about bears.

Other Defenses

One defense closely allied to primary denial and repression is *dissociation*. Sometimes, when people experience severe trauma, they lose all memory of the traumatic event or events. Sometimes they have to use massive doses of denial just to survive the ordeal. They may destroy or filter their experience of the event even as it happens. "I felt like it was happening to someone else. Like I was off in the corner watching it happen but feeling nothing." This splitting of awareness is dissociation. If the trauma is chronic or repeated (as in child abuse), later stress may trigger dissociation again.

When people dissociate they disconnect parts of experience. If a trauma were just too big to repress in one place in the unconscious, it is taken apart and buried in separate places: a frightening sound over here, a terrible vision over there, and, way in the darkest corner, the stifled screams.

Repression and denial form the basis in the general system of defense. From these two primary tactics, other defenses develop, such as *projection* (attributing an unwanted thought or impulse to something outside the self), *reaction formation* (proclaiming positive and laudable attitudes and behavior as a way of managing unacceptable feelings), *undoing* (using penitent behavior or attitudes in a magical way to compensate for hostile or aggressive impulses), and *sublimation* (converting unacceptable impulses into energy to achieve acceptable goals). None of these more sophisticated defenses will work if the underlying feeling breaks through into awareness. But as we saw in Figure 2.1 (p. 13), which examined denial from the outside in, a single layer of denial is not adequate; denial of facts alone, for example, does not work, because we cannot always turn the TV channel fast enough to avoid seeing some tragic scene, or talk fast enough to avoid being ticketed for improper driving. The same thing is true when looking at the system from the inside out (as we are doing now). As good as primary denial and repression are in shielding awareness, they are not good enough. The other three layers of denial are necessary for the system to work effectively.

The psychological defenses discussed in this section operate outside awareness. They protect the conscious mind from destabilizing intrusions from the unconscious mind. In one form or another, they are present in all of us. Whether we have been traumatized in infancy, or just became civilized enough to learn the lessons of kindergarten, we have all profited from having these tools in our armamentarium. It is not pathological to have and use them. Like anxiety, they do not cause addiction; they are part of the denial system of the *person* who becomes an addict.

ANXIETY AS A WARNING

Life assaults us with new experiences and reminders which fan the smoldering coals of our inner emotional lives. Sometimes the defenses provide enough insulation, and sometimes they do not. New fears, guilts, or angers stir old memories. Associations or insights pierce the shield of denial, so more protection is necessary. However, augmenting primary denial presents a problem. One cannot know from moment to moment how well the shield is working, because by definition it (as well as the painful conflict) is outside awareness. One cannot, for example, check with one's unconscious during a heated argument:

> Let's see, am I still repressing the memory of being abused as a child? I am? Good! Then it is safe for me to displace this anger on my brother-in-law.

In the heat of such a battle, internal system checks are impossible, and at such moments the recovery of repressed memories would be disastrous.

Thus, we are in the rather uncomfortable position of needing the defenses to work, and yet not being able to know if, in fact, they are working. A flooded basement is a terrible way to find out that your sewer system is not working. Because conflicts and defenses are both kept outside awareness, we would only know something was wrong when it was too late. If the primary defenses did not work under stress, we would have two problems: dealing with the current crisis causing that stress, and dealing with the flood of old feelings. In order to continue to function under the constant threat of such dual crises one must have a warning system that will sound an alarm when the primary defenses are under stress. This warning bell could be *conscious* while the original conflict and the primary defenses remain *unconscious*. In a psychodynamic system, that alarm device is *anxiety*. We become anxious when there is stress on, or a threat to, our primary defense, but we experience the anxiety, *not the conflict beneath it*.

A comparison can be made between this warning process and the thermostat on an automobile's cooling system. An automobile's engine is, after all, a controlled gasoline explosion, which releases enormous amounts of heat. This would damage the engine, the car, and the driver if they were not protected by an adequate cooling system. The cooling system is like the wall of primary denial. This entire mechanism is under the hood and outside our awareness. We could conceivably drive along with our toe sticking through a hole in the floorboard and touching the engine block to determine if it were overheating. The more functional alternative is the thermostat with a gauge mounted on the dashboard which warns us if the cooling mechanism is not functioning adequately enough to protect the engine. This warning mechanism, with its various buzzers, blinks, or needles serves to alert us to impending danger. It is a warning that the "defenses" may not be adequate, and we had better do something to cool the engine.

Many people find that warnings are intrusive, uncomfortable, and obnoxious. Consider the buzzer-seatbelt system in most late model cars. The buzzer warns us that the seat belt is not connected, letting us know that we are not adequately protected. Many of us respond to this warning by shutting it off. Early models of this system were later changed to soften the sound of the alarm. Even so, legislation was passed in many states prohibiting disconnecting or bypassing this system. Why do such laws exist? Why would we avoid or reject this life-saving warning? We prefer not to know how vulnerable we are. We do not want to deal with our illusion of invulnerability. The warning is threatening and we shut it off without experiencing the dread of death and dismemberment. In driver's education classes students are taught to put on their belts before starting the engine. Some of us older drivers, I am afraid, put on the belts to turn off the buzzer.

Anxiety can also be a noisy, obnoxious alarm. Like an alarm it is a dreadful demand to do something. Initially, anxiety can make us more tense. We become tense about being tense, and the entire experience can quickly become intolerable. There is an old parody of Kipling's poem "IF" which says, "If you can keep your head when all about you are losing theirs . . . you obviously do not understand the gravity of the situation."

Anxiety is the feeling that you have to do something. The newly recovering addict described earlier got very anxious thinking about what relapse would mean. He did something about that anxiety: He went to a meeting. Worried about an exam? Study! Worried about your job? Work harder! Anxiety energizes problem solving. Don't put it off. Do it *now*. And if you successfully solve the problem you do not have to be flooded with the feelings that might follow failure to solve it.

When there is an external problem to be solved, anxiety provides the drive and energy to solve that problem. When there is no external problem, the need to do something is just as strong, but there is nothing to fix. We are led to do things which have reduced anxiety in the past. We might have a cup of coffee (even though it is bedtime), look at our watch for no apparent reason, or nibble on something when we have just eaten. Often we go from one to another randomly. Other times we repeat gestures or rituals, twist a lock of hair, drum fingers, hum a long-forgotten tune. The anxiety seems to exist for no apparent reason. But there it is, demanding that we take action even when there is no obvious action to be taken. There is no conscious problem to be solved. We just feel uptight. We fidget and pace. Our behavior vacillates, we can't concentrate. We go from task to task without accomplishing anything or reducing the tension. We have what psychologists call *generalized anxiety*. In the face of such anxiety we are not efficient problem solvers. We don't focus the energy. Our behavior is more like the rattle of the lid on a boiling pot than the whistle of a tea kettle. It is the result of general rather than focused pressure.

Another Paradox about Anxiety: It Is Not the Future We Worry about

There is an old saying that goes, "If it weren't for bad luck, I wouldn't have any luck at all." There are many variations on this theme, such as, "I don't worry; nothing is going to be all right," and so forth. Newly recovering addicts are told that they must learn to stop worrying, to "turn it over," and "take it one day at a time." Relief from worry is a great aid to sobriety, so the advice works both ways. Turning it over will get you sober, and getting sober helps teach you how to turn it over.

In the present context, however, learning how to stop worrying has a specific meaning. Worry is not just the projection of negative outcomes or catastrophes, it is also the projection of the negative (that is, shame-filled) self into the future. It turns out that we not only think the worst will happen, we expect to be at our worst when it does. The problem is not the accuracy about the prediction (you might get fired, get sick, lose a loved one), but the unchallenged assumption that the one who will deal with it is the one whose true nature is "rotten . . . no damn good . . . can't do anything right . . . stupid . . . evil . . . etc." It is not the future we worry about; it is the past we insist on reliving. It is our false beliefs and our untrue self-image we dread, but still cling to.

This takes us back to the original discussion of denial. It protects our deepest values, truths, and commitments. When they are challenged we feel the deepest kind of anxiety. Can we find a truth that will last a whole life? Can I ever form a final, lasting self-image and be assured that it is not false? Is safety ever more than a temporary illusion? The origin and development of this false self will be discussed at length in the next chapter.

THE FAILURE OF DEFENSES

Flashbacks

Repression does not always work completely. You can run into someone you have not seen in years and suddenly recall the pain of your last encounter. Victims of trauma may have vivid nightmares (or even "daymares," called flashbacks) in which they relive all or part of a horrible experience.

People experiencing flashbacks stop processing experience in the normal way and behave as if in a trance. They may have no idea what triggered this state, and be unable to account for why they feel such panic. All they know is that they saw or heard something and the bottom dropped out. They feel terrified and crazy. Try as they might to regain their sanity by solving the mystery, repression keeps the whole truth hidden until it is safe. Since the original experience itself was fragmented, it is difficult to recall the experience as a whole. Pieces of it (just one sound or a single visual image) emerge unbidden to haunt them, while the meaning of that memory fragment eludes them in the mists of the unconscious. When something stirs our worst memories (or fragments) we need extra protection from those intrusions. Then, the defenses of repression and primary denial become more active.

Hitting Bottom

The next chapter will discuss therapeutic interventions that are designed to get behind the walls of denial. Even without the intervention of professionals, this can come about naturally; this failure of denial is called *hitting bottom*. Often the crises in an addict's life overwhelm all the defenses, and the terrible truth of his or her addiction gnaws at awareness from within. The anxiety accompanying this breakdown may drive an addict to change. In Chapter 7 we will examine a related kind of bottom, which is hit when a shattering loss such as a death or other trauma occurs. That chapter will discuss at length the role that anxiety plays in mobilizing and motivating those who grieve for the task of transforming their lives.

ANXIETY, DENIAL, AND THE
DEFINITION OF NORMAL

Anxiety is normal and necessary, as is denial. They are biologically wired in by means of neurochemicals, such as adrenalin and endorphins. Both processes, however, can go haywire and pose significant threats to the existence they are designed to protect and enhance. Furthermore, the dialectical relationship between these two processes is fundamental to our existence as human beings.

Anxiety is a response to a threat to existence itself. That is why existentialists speak of *angst* as being our response to the awful awareness of our vulnerability, aloneness, and lack of power in the universe. Standing before the awesome, indifferent fury of a great storm, one has to feel the terrible vulnerability of one's existence—even though one is in no actual danger at the time. "Angst" is used to distinguish the *authentic* fears and present dangers from the overriding fear basic to existence itself—the awe felt in the face of the storm. This fear can then be distinguished from the dragons (or wolves) of our own manufacture. We need to find a way to manage this terror, a way to convert it to something over which we *do* have power (or at least think we do). Thus superstition, illusion, and self-deception become part of being human. To resolve these feelings with phobias about lightning or rituals to propitiate the gods is to convert the energy of angst into what the existentialists call *dread*. The conversion of angst to dread enshrines all sorts of mistaken beliefs about the world and false images of self, beliefs that must be shed to find one's real identity and path in the world. Somehow it is all manageable if I get Daddy's approval, enough money, enough cocaine, chocolate, or sex.

Anxiety is also our warning that all these dread-manipulating techniques might be failing. It is an alarm that the gates to the bedlam of the unconscious may open. So it is not surprising that when a core-level loss occurs or when one hits bottom, that one must reconvert the energy bound up in dread back to its natural purpose. Nor is it surprising that all too often such a confrontation with dreadful realities drives people into denial and preestablished survival strategies with greater resolve.

No defense system can work indefinitely in the presence of alcohol or drugs. The more they are used, the more tolerance to their effects is developed. One of the side effects of this process is that one learns how to operate at higher and higher levels of intoxication. The more physiological tolerance developed, the more likely one is to engage in offensive behaviors. These terms have direct analogies in other addictive behavior. One can see the operation of tolerance in the progression of a sex addict from pornographic magazines to peepshows, from topless bars to prostitutes. One can see it in the behavior of a workaholic who buys a cellular phone so that she can "spend more time with the family." The progression in addictive behaviors will require more denial. With such behavior increasing, sooner or later strains in relationships develop. Less and less can be talked about, and fewer and fewer people are present to talk to.

Sooner or later systematically choosing drugs (or other addictive behaviors) will lead to crises (health problems, DUIs, job pressures). One of those crises may land the addict in treatment. Once in treatment, the patient learns how to become "normal" (i.e., relate without denial, problem solve, use a variety of coping methods) again. He or she learns behavior that is less driven and more chosen (see Chapters 2 and 4 for discussions of the relationship between choice and denial).

Being Normal, Being Healthy

Some critics of the American health care system have observed that the system is really about illness, not health. Instead of being described positively, health is described negatively, as the absence of disease. Being "normal" seems to mean the absence of disease, disabilities, or psychopathology.

We could define "normal" as the absence of addictive behavior and denial. There are two problems with this negative definition. First, "normal" does not mean the absence of denial. Quite the opposite. When you are normal you have all four layers in fine shape, thank you very much! You have the defenses to protect your resources. Second, we need a positive definition of health, wellness, and recovery.

With these admonitions in mind, I would like to offer three approaches to a wellness theory of normalcy that incorporate the natural presence of anxiety and denial.

1. *Health as wealth*. "Normal" people have a whole *range* of problem-solving techniques—a wide variety of coping techniques. If one method is blocked or challenged there is another that can be substituted. Bar closed? Okay, let's go to a movie. If you have a range of problem-solving techniques *and* a wide range of tension-relieving techniques you will not have to stack up a whole lot of denial to protect the single vital one. Mental health is having an adequate set of alternatives. It is not so much the absence of denial as it is the presence of choice.

2. *Health as relationship*. The second characteristic of mental health is the presence of healthy, supportive relationships. There are people behind your wall of denial, preferably more than one. These relationships provide alternative ways of expressing impulses, ambivalence, and anxieties without engaging in the objectionable behavior. Healthy people have more things to do and more people to talk to.

3. *Health as a path*. There is an awareness of, and active engagement in, the task of being human. It might be called growing up, actualizing one's self, finding one's path or mission or spiritual progress. Whatever it is called, it is an active project that takes effort, concentration, and honesty. It is by no means free from anxiety. On the contrary, it asks the hard questions and deals with the truth of the hard answers and copes with the anxiety which accompanies the discovery of life-changing truths. It does mean an ongoing struggle with our own denial. We are all on this path, shedding illusions, finding new dreams, grieving lost ones, following our path. Perhaps what is "normal," after all, is the human spirit and frailty which attend that path. And on this path we can only, as they say in 12-step meetings, "claim progress not perfection."

4

Successful Treatment of Denial

THE THINK/FEEL/ACT MODEL OF RECOVERY

William Glasser (1965), the founder of reality therapy, concluded that mentally healthy, responsible people (that is, sober people) are "response-able." This is more than simple competence or the ability to meet the expectations of self and others. It demands the ability to integrate thought, feeling, and action into one's responses to life. If one or more of these elements is missing, or mismatched with the other components, the response is incomplete or incongruent. Denial depletes the repertoire of addicted persons in all three areas. They cannot be responsible because denial keeps them from being "response-able."

Most human experience can be placed under one of three headings, *thinking*, *feeling*, or *acting*. These terms are not meant to be exhaustive or mutually exclusive, but are convenient because they match our common use of them in everyday speech. The term "thinking" refers to such mental activities as perceiving, remembering, problem solving, and, of course, thinking. These cognitive processes range from creative problem solving on the one hand to ruminating, obsessing, and the unique logic of the addict called "stinking thinking" on the other.

The term "feeling" covers such diverse elements as energy level, emotions, moods, affect, and feelings. These too can vary in quality. They can be neurotic or authentic, and certainly they can be mixed or ambivalent.

59

"Acting" includes behavior, verbal communication, and nonverbal communication (such as body language and voice tone). Here too one can construct continua such as moral to immoral, effective to ineffective, etc. Actions can fit the circumstances in which they occur, or be manifestations of distortion, delusions, or compulsions. For the sake of illustration, think, feel, and act can be arranged in the form of a triangle, as in Figure 4.1.

Addiction attacks all three corners of this triangle. Perceptual distortions are part of the definition of intoxication. Such symptoms as blackouts (episodes of amnesia), which distort memory, and the peculiar logic of "stinking thinking" help define addiction. Similarly, emotional outbursts and exaggerated mood swings during both intoxication and withdrawal are basic phenomena in the experience of substance abuse. Drugs alter behavior drastically, but the life style imposed by any addiction changes the addict's behavior, mood, and whole way of being in the world. Who is higher than a gambler on a winning streak, or lower than a bulimic after a binge? As abuse grows, behavior associated with obtaining, using, hiding use, and recovering from use dominate the day-to-day life of the abuser. And, as dependency grows, the capacity to perform other daily tasks, meet expectations of others, and even perform essential self-care diminishes. Although this chapter will focus on the abuser, it should be kept in mind that the collapse of the think/feel/act triangle and the problems of restoring it are identical for *all* recovering persons, regardless of the condition they are recovering from — dependence or co-dependence — or the setting in which the recovery takes place.

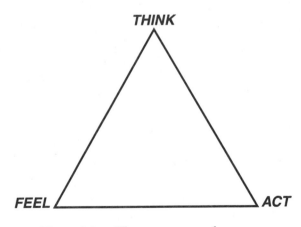

Figure 4.1.   The components of response.

The three components of responding are presented as a triangle to emphasize the need for integration of those components for healthy, sober responding. When one achieves the ideal of sobriety, the components are integrated. When one is using or in denial, the triangle seems to lose one or more of its components or completely fall apart. Disintegration, or incongruence, of this basic unit is another way of defining denial. For example, when an angry feeling leads to a hostile act with no thought to surrounding circumstances or later consequences, the actor is in denial of change. Denial of implications is a distorted thinking process and, of course, primary denial is denial of feelings. Since all of us, not just addicts, use the protection of denial, all of us experience the breakdown of our triangle. All of us are incongruent from time to time.

When we observe the behavior of someone who has lost a part of the triangle, we notice that something is missing. Something is wrong. We may not be able to put our finger on it exactly, but we are aware that there is something "off" about the way the other is responding. As a rule we characterize these partial responses negatively. In fact, we often reserve the harshest judgments and cruelest names for our own incongruent responses. A response that seems to go from feeling into action without thinking will get the label of "impulsive," "moody," or "irresponsible." Similarly, ideas that are spoken directly (from think into act), without incorporating feelings may get labeled as "cold," "intellectualized," or "robot-like." People who speak that way are usually judged to be "out of touch with their emotions." Lastly, having a good conceptual grasp on one's emotional problems without being able to behave effectively will lead to still other judgments of nonhealth. People who feel but do not act seem to be helpless "victims" of their lives. They never seem to be active decision makers in the face of the challenges life presents them. These persons who think-feel, but do not act may get called "weak," "unmotivated," or "childish." They seem stuck. Their "can't" may really be "won't"; but most of all, they just "don't." They are talkers, not doers.

Figure 4.2 shows the ideal relationship of thinking to feeling, feeling to acting, and acting to feeling. These relationships also represent three basic existential tasks, or challenges, of living a full life. Meeting the challenge of these tasks is hard enough when times are good. When the wolf is at the door the performance of these tasks suffers. Under acute threat or chronic stress we lose integration. We use denial to buy time and protection until we can find the safety or resources necessary to reintegrate ourselves and return to the tasks interrupted by the threat or stress.

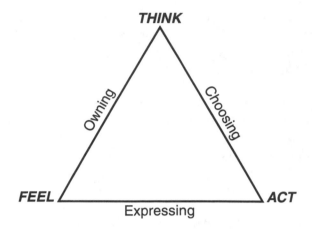

Figure 4.2. The existential tasks that integrate responses.

STRIVING FOR OWNERSHIP:
ACHIEVING INSIGHT

The disconnection of thought and emotion is the basis of the whole denial system. It is the inner box in Figure 2.1 – denial of feelings. Establishing and maintaining a connection between think and feel is a critical part of health and recovery, so the discussion will start there.

The task of integrating thought and feeling is called *striving for ownership*, which depicts the existential task of dealing with one's emotions. When people are response-able and not in denial, they are *aware* (the perceiving part of thinking) of what they feel, and they *know* (the cognitive part of thinking) what has gone on inside them to generate these feelings. It is a three-part chain connected by awareness: awareness of events, awareness of interpretation of those events, and awareness of the emotional reaction following those interpretations. If the chain is broken, ownership of the feeling is lost. When the task of ownership is being performed, the chain is solid. Performing this task leads to a special awareness, the experience of *insight*. Insight *illuminates ourselves to ourselves*. It is an experience of self-awareness. "Yes, that is *what* I truly feel, and *why* I feel it." It is an "Aha" experience. Striving for ownership keeps one on the path of self-knowledge and acceptance. "Know thyself," Socrates said. It is a life-long journey, with many detours and aimless wanderings in the cul de sacs of denial.

Here is a simple example of the chain being broken and restored.

Alice arranged to meet Jane for lunch before going to a 12-step meeting. Alice did not arrive. Jane waited for a while, then ordered in anger. At first she told herself that Alice was just late, "You know how she is." Then she told herself, "She forgot!" By the time the salad arrived, she was saying, "How rude! She has no right to treat me like that. Who does she think she is? Who does she think I am? I can't let her get away with that; I'm angry!" Out of this internal monologue came a feeling, and the feeling was anger.

Jane might have said, while she was stabbing her lettuce, "I'm not mad." That would clearly be denial of feelings. Saying "she made me mad" keeps her in touch with her feelings, but breaks the chain of awareness, because it goes from Alice's behavior to Jane's feelings and skips the part where Jane interpreted Alice's actions. It is not so clearly denial, but it does distort reality. It is not the whole truth. Jane might instead say, "Boy did I burn myself out about that missed lunch!" That internal statement maintains the connection; it is part of the striving for ownership, but, as we shall see, not all of it. What Alice did was to miss their date; what Jane did was to say some things to herself that made her mad. Later, at her 12-step meeting, Jane talks about her anger in a different way. She realizes she had high expectations for the lunch. She wanted to tell her old friend about her new recovery. She realizes that while she was muttering, "Who does she think I am?" she was also thinking, "She thinks I'm just the same old who-cares-Jane, the same old she's-probably-drunk-anyway boozer I used to be. Have I really changed all that much, if Alice does not see it? Wait a minute. Who am I doing this for? Who do I need to prove something to?" Jane realizes she had been struggling with her own doubts. Once she recovers that link in her think/feel process, she has an insight into herself, an "Aha moment."

Feelings do not just happen to us. They are created by us. We are the ones who connect what we perceive to what we tell ourselves those perceptions mean. Between the events we perceive and the feelings we perceive come the interpretations we place on those perceptions. When ownership is lost, feelings seem to come from outside us (outside our personal triangle) and are not connected to us anymore. If he, she, them, or it causes our feelings, we become victims rather than creators, the ones acted on rather than the ones acting, at risk rather than at choice. The prize for keeping ownership of the feelings is insight into, and ownership of, the self. If Jane tells herself, "She made me mad," then Alice is responsible for Jane's feelings. Suppose, instead, Jane says, "*I* made myself mad. *I* did it, when *I* interpreted her behavior. *I* was the one who told myself what her behavior meant." Then she, not Alice, is responsible for her feelings. She may tell herself, "Boy we alcoholics are a touchy lot, ready to take offense at the drop of a hat . . . or a lunch for that matter."

Jane has more power to change herself than to change Alice. Freedom and choice come from this sort of insight. There is freedom for Jane inside her own triangle. She cannot alter Alice's lateness, and probably cannot make her be more prompt in the future. She cannot control whether or not Alice thinks of her as "just the same old Jane she used to be." She *does* have control over whether or not she thinks of herself that way. She can choose when and why she views herself that way. That gives her freedom and choice she does not have when she is focused on Alice.

We may sense several feelings from a given experience. Which feeling will dominate will depend on the particular conclusions we draw from that experience. For example, sometimes criticism generates anger, and sometimes despair. The same criticism may be interpreted as, "He only said that because he thinks I'm a fool," or it may be experienced as, "I messed up again; I can't even do this right." Yet another interpretation might be that the critic is the one with the problem: "What's the matter with him?" Whatever the internal experience, trouble comes when people who are facing criticism are unaware of the interpretation they are using. The feelings will seem to happen to them. Then they will feel buffeted and controlled by the feelings. Many people experience powerful mood swings. When they are down, everything is black. They perceive and process negatively because the feelings drive the thoughts. For them it is an important discovery to learn that their feelings are not facts. Feelings change; facts do not.

It is difficult to be around people who habitually discuss their feelings without owning them. When the cause of their feelings is attributed to outside forces, their feelings seem to be inevitable; they seem to be helpless victims of those outside forces. It is hard to offer them help. They may see themselves as helpless and out of control, but we observers may see (label) them as "dependent," "regressed," or "childish." If we use these labels, we may also find ourselves refusing their requests for help. "You just need to grow up!" Most of us think of emotional control under the heading of being grown up, or being responsible. When feelings are owned rather than attributed to outside forces, responsibility for those feelings is maintained. The individual is seen as more adult, more competent, and, ironically, more deserving of help.

Ownership is diminished when we pass judgments on our feelings. "I shouldn't be angry. It's not fair/justified/right." Such judgments may apply to the thought process that generated the feeling, but not to the feeling itself. Indeed, it may not be "fair or just" for Jane to say about Alice, "She's selfish and doesn't think about my feelings." It probably is not even accurate, but Jane's hurt, angry feelings are real, present, and powerful. Some people might say it is morally wrong for Jane to attack Alice for being selfish, but it is Jane's execution of revenge that should earn judgment, not her feeling of anger.

Ownership is affected by other layers of denial. Denial of facts starts out the sequence by closing off awareness of the events; denial of implications blocks awareness of the thought process generating feelings; and, of course, denial of feelings truncates ownership and precludes insight.

The use of what are called attributions has a negative effect on ownership. An attribution is an interpretation, judgment, or label that one, the perceiver, places on a person or object but treats as an intrinsic trait. By treating the attribution as an intrinsic trait rather than a label projected and stuck on it, the perceiver distorts the truth in two ways: first, by asserting that the person or object has some quality that is, in fact, not part of its essence; and second, by asserting that the perceiver had no role in creating the attribution and is therefore not accountable for the act of interpreting, judging, or labeling. This latter distortion means that the perceiver can claim the right to be in denial; to avoid accountability for the attribution; to avoid ownership of any feeling of his or her own is being expressed by the attribution or that the act of interpreting, judging, or labeling has consequences that were chosen.

Attributions can work at all four layers of denial. Since they basically argue that a statement has nothing to do with the speaker and therefore does not allow any conclusions to be drawn about him or her, they usually function as denial of implications. They can, however, function as denial of facts, "I didn't say that, don't put words in my mouth." They can be used to protect the speaker from the consequences of his or her act, "Heh, don't blame me, that's the way it is." Lastly they involve denial of feelings. "I am not angry, you are being hostile." Attributions about character and motivation are among the most pernicious forms of double lies. They are labels, not truths, and they are accompanied by communication-distorting denial.

LEARNING TO CHOOSE:
GAINING ACCOUNTABILITY

The process of choosing one's behavior is the critical connection between thought and action. When one is "at choice," one feels competent, effective, and response-able. In a healthy (or sober) person, behavior is chosen on the basis of the impact it is expected to have and a willingness to be accountable for both the intention and the impact. Unwillingness or inability to accept responsibility is part of denial of accountability. Learning the art of choosing requires exercising three human rights: the right to have alternatives and select among them, the right to have an impact on one's self and outside one's self, and the right to be accountable to one's self for that impact. If one is going to be accountable to someone else, that contract should be a choice *both* participants make, not one that is made unilaterally by either. These rights are not permanently lost because powerful others (including abusive parents or spouses) arrogate them. Nor are they lost through the misuse or disuse of them in addiction. Exercising them is learning to choose. Mastering this art leads to the experience of accountability.

This task, like the ownership of feelings, is a life-long existential task. In childhood, the emphasis is on matching intent with outcome. "Can I hit the ball when I want to?" "Can I get good grades?" "Can I make people like me?" In adulthood there are many expectations and acquired responsibilities to others. "Can I be a good friend, spouse, or parent?" "Can I be successful?" In old age the capacity to act diminishes, and "having a choice" becomes a critical issue in maintaining dignity.

Making excuses for behavior (the hallmark of denial of change) is a way of saying, "I did not pick *that* consequence, so I *should* be excused." An intoxicated spouse comes home with half his week's pay and says, "All I did was to stop by the tavern to cash my paycheck." His wife knows better. There were several other ways to get that check cashed or deposited safely. The point is that he picked one way that was not safe. Abusers often claim that last night's incident was not really their fault. They did not choose to act in that way. The evasion of the responsibility for these consequences is a sign of a broken link between the head and the hand, between think and act. When people say their behavior is not the result of choice but of accident, fate, or coercion, they are telling us that the behavior is not integrated or congruent.

Disclaimers of responsibility are repeatedly used as the desperation and denial of addiction increase. Soon, the people around those in denial start to call them "undependable" or "irresponsible." In fact, they are in denial, and the denial is maintained by blocking the process of choosing from their conscious awareness. As we have seen, those in denial of change describe events as happening to them, and their own behavior as accidental, inevitable, or excusable—anything other than as chosen by them. Although the actions come with a disclaimer, the consequences are still out there and they may be profound. They can impact directly on the chemically dependent person (e.g., toxicity and tissue damage), on his environment (drunken driving), and on his relationships (co-dependency).

EXPRESSING PASSION:
EXPERIENCING VITALITY

The remaining leg of the triangle is the relationship of feeling and acting. It is labeled *expressing* to reflect the very human need to express feelings behaviorally. The need is always there, even when something or someone (including ourselves) seems to prevent us. When feelings are congruently expressed, one experiences one's own aliveness and *vitality*. Life is lived fully and passionately.

It is not only sometimes that we need to "get our feelings out," but all times. Feelings that are not expressed or acted on in some way become a source of stress. Acting one way and feeling another does not provide relief from stress; it causes it.

Personal expression is also an existential life-long task. Anyone who has raised (or is it civilized?) a two-year-old knows what a struggle it is to harness someone's impulses—and what a relief it is for everyone (including the toddler) when this mastery is achieved. Many tears are shed while that mastery, which Erik Erikson called "autonomy," is being learned. The task does not stop then. As the feelings get more complicated, the rules get tougher. Adolescence explodes in the psyche. Maturity demands intimacy. Old age means loss. Expression becomes ever more varied, subtle, complex, even poetic—but always essential.

Unexpressed (or stuffed) feelings may come out. The harder it is to find a way to let them out, the greater the stress. Of course, one way to deal with this dilemma is to break off awareness of having those feelings (to deny them). Another way is to express them indirectly in some form of behavior that is similar to what you really want to do but is directed at a safer target. There is an old *Saturday Evening Post* cover illustration by Norman Rockwell that depicts a boss scolding a man, who in the next picture is shown scolding his wife, who then scolds her son, who then scolds the dog, who sits forlorn and confused. Feelings can be displaced into another setting rather than onto another person (as when angry feelings are turned into aggressive driving). Substitute or symbolic behavior often has the same impact as congruently expressed feelings, but is disavowed as innocent of the intention.

"Joan, why are you playing so rough with your little brother?"

"Aw Mom, we were just playing cowboys and Indians."

"Well you untie him right now! And how many times do I have to tell you not to play with matches?"

Another problem occurs when feelings have been repeatedly stuffed. A reservoir of unexpressed feelings can suddenly come tumbling out. For example, a couple's argument can start over a trivial cause. Suddenly, deeper anger and stifled feelings come pouring out. One party stoutly denies that there was any hostility in the burnt toast or the forgotten birthday, but the other is furious. Then the old resentments emerge. Now there are hurt feelings all around.

Not every feeling needs to be acted out or inflicted on others. Friends and loved ones (let alone strangers) do not need such afflictions. This is even more true with neurotic emotions. For example, one might be driven by a need to please one's parents and tortured by neurotic guilt about not doing it right. This in turn could send one off on a quixotic search for the *perfect* Christmas present. Do those feelings need to be expressed at all, let alone in that way? Does a spouse need to *understand* them, let alone squire the knight errant to the shopping mall?

Congruent expression of authentic feelings gives rise to the experience of vitality. Genuine authentic feelings need tongue, ear, and hand. They are the energy and the power of life. They move us on our journey, and are the essence of our vitality. Some of the most powerful experiences of life occur when one expresses one's commitments passionately. In those moments we feel completely alive and truly ourselves. It is not enough to care about people, values, life-work, etc. One must express that passion in the way one lives; it is the heart of being fully alive.

CONGRUENCE: INSIGHT + MASTERY + VITALITY

Congruence is a special term for the integration of the think/feel/act model. It is an awareness of self—of what it is like to be one's self, without the distortion of denial. This awareness is made up of the experiences of insight, accountability, and vitality. When these experiences are present in awareness all at once, one has the clearest awareness of who one truly is. This is me truly being me: my thoughts, my feelings, my deeds. The tasks of integrating them have been accomplished, and the sense of self emerging from the integration of these tasks is extremely powerful.

The awareness that derives from the performance of existential tasks tends to be potentiating. It reinforces and enhances each of the experiences that come from performing these tasks. As one gets greater ownership, the resulting insight into one's self makes congruent expression of one's feelings easier. The vitality that comes from expressing one's passion makes the selection of an action to express that feeling easier. This in turn potentiates the sense of accountability. The experiences and the performance of the tasks can come in any order, flip back and forth, or even come all at once. Thus, congruence is a way of experiencing life and learning from it while living it. Few of us are congruent all of the time. Truly congruent experiences, when it "all comes together," are precious moments. In those moments we *know* ourselves deeply and *are* ourselves fully. Owning, choosing, and expressing are hard work. The experiences of insight, accountability, and vitality make it all worthwhile, especially for people in recovery. Figure 4.3 shows the congruent model and the core experiences of congruence.

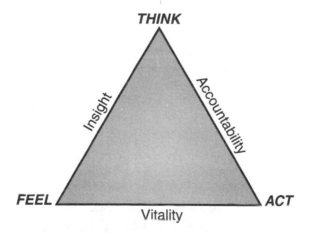

Figure 4.3. The core experiences of congruence. The shading pattern inside the triangle represents the way that performance of existential tasks and the awareness of self arising from that performance interact with each other to potentiate the movement toward congruence.

The goal of addiction counseling is to achieve congruence for the work of sobriety (working the steps, relating to one's sponsor and the fellowship, giving and getting help). Congruence is both the prize of sobriety and the path to it: the means to the end and the pay-off for getting there.

Furthermore, as we have seen, congruence and denial are negatively reciprocal and self-potentiating. Being in denial means not having congruence; being congruent means not being in denial. As such, the degree of congruence in a recovering person's responses are a measure of his or her progress toward recovery. The more sober they are, the less denial there is; the less denial, the more congruence.

BEYOND SIMPLE CONGRUENCE

Before we leave the triangle model, there are three more points to be made. The first is about *truth* in the triangle. The second is about interpersonal *impact* and the *power* of congruence. The third is about an internal gyroscope called *believe*.

Truth

THE POWER OF THOUGHT

The nature of truth is an old philosophical problem. We can never know for sure that our perceptions are accurate, or that our conclusions about events are valid and correct. In terms of the triangle, this means we cannot rely on truth coming out of the think corner. We may misperceive events or misconstrue their meaning. We can, however, go back to our direct experience, away from the words, ideas, judgments, and attributions (see p. 65) and back to the sights, sounds, etc. A degree of truth is to be found in the analysis of direct experience. From that starting point a congruent triangle can be constructed. Only a *degree* is necessary to *start* the process, because even a degree improves the integration between think and the other components of responding. It makes doing the tasks of congruence easier. Since the awareness that derives from performing these tasks is self-potentiating, clearer integration of any pair of elements has a tendency to move one toward greater congruence.

A special place in the triangle is reserved for the power of thought. We are the authors of our own emotional realities. We cannot change the events that impacted on us in the past, nor the feelings resulting from those events. No one can replace a lost parent, or change the pain of that loss. Our power lies in that we are free to think about those events and what we choose to learn from them. We may not be able to pick our teachers, but we can choose our moral lessons. We can change how we think about the world, even when we cannot change the world itself. People in recovery are fond of saying they are powerless over people, places, and things; they can only change themselves.

THE VERACITY OF FEELINGS

Feelings are another matter. It can be said that we really are feeling what we feel. It is honest-to-God anger when we are enraged, and fear when we are terrified. But there are problems using feelings to identify or validate reality. Feelings are not the facts of events, they are the facts of one's reaction. For example, one does not so much *feel* threatened as one *thinks* that someone or something is acting aggressively.

Some people say there are only two honest feelings: love and fear. Others say there are four basic feelings (sad, mad, glad, and scared) and all other terms are disguised judgments or evaluations about the events we are responding to. Having evaluated the intention of the other as threatening, we may become frightened, angry, or even pleased. Consider a scene in which a father and his son are wrestling. The boy becomes engrossed in the action. The father backs off, and evaluates the meaning of the interaction. He may say, "That's my boy! What a tiger!" Then again, he may say, "How dare you try to hurt me?"

There can be more than one feeling at a time. One feeling may temporarily mask another. Close observation of emotional reactions suggests there is some sort of connection between fear, anger, and sadness. If you are feeling one of them, then one or more of the others may be close at hand. Some people get aggressive when they are frightened, some are fearful when they have had a loss, others may cry when they are angry. The thought process connected to those feelings may be flawed, but the feelings are real. Feelings are not justified, right or wrong, they just are. It may be a childish, paranoid, or neurotic reaction to events, but the feelings are real sensations, just like the perceptions of sound and sight. There is always a source of truth in the feel corner of the triangle because feelings are direct experience. But that truth depends upon ownership to produce insight about the self or the world.

THE IMPACT OF ACTION

There is no absolute truth in act either. We cannot be sure that our chosen course of action is right. An antacid may relieve gastritis, but it is the wrong thing to give for appendicitis. Honesty only qualifies as a good policy. When one is being mugged, it is not a good time to express one's opinions on gun control. When the baby cries, is it time to feed it, change it, or play with it? Congruence, like honesty, is also a good policy. Since congruent acts are expressions of feelings that are being owned, they provide a road back to direct experience and the think and feel corners. A spark of truth can begin in any of the components of a response, but only through diligent pursuance of the existential tasks connecting these three elements can one come to stand on solid ground.

Actions have special significance. They create something in the world and outside our heads: an *impact* on self or others for which we must assume accountability. The impact that changes our lives and the lives of others is primarily in what we do and say, not in what we think or feel. In the end, others are helped or harmed by deeds, not wishes. Sobriety is rarely achieved through the good wishes of others. Efforts at recovery may be supported or sabotaged by what is communicated (overtly or covertly) by our actions and how those actions are reacted to by others.

When one acts, the intrapersonal processes of thinking and feeling become interpersonal events. Behavior becomes part of the world others respond to. It sends a message. When one acts, a window to one's inner world opens and others react to what they see (or think they see) through that window. Behavior becomes part of the world others respond to. When we act, something is being "said"; whether we wish it or not, a message is always being sent. It becomes communication; all behavior (physical as well as verbal) communicates. Whether we are aware of it or not, what we do ranks with what we say. It becomes part of our relationships, whether it is a "slip," a forgotten birthday, or the statement "I love you." Our communication becomes the proverbial pebble dropped in still water, but this still water is not an open pond. Someone is out there, reacting to it and communicating back. The relationship of an interpersonal act to its consequence inside a relationship is more like a pebble dropped in an aquarium than in a pond. The effects do not ripple away to distant shores; they bounce back.

We may not even know the intended audience for our communication. "What's he trying to prove? Who is he trying to prove it to?" Many people are still trying to please parents and proving points to people who left their lives years ago. Sometimes the message and the audience are easy to identify, but not always. The message may be obscure or even coded. "I thought you knew yellow roses meant I was thinking of the day we met." Sometimes the message is confused, mixed, or garbled. "Do what I *want*, not what I *ask*." If we suspect someone of deliberately sending a mixed message, we will say he or she is "playing games," and get angry at them.

Behavior that is not congruent for feeling sends a mixed message. "Your mouth is saying 'No, No, No,' but your eyes are saying, 'Yes, Yes, Yes.'" Mixed messages complicate relationships, since the responder does not know which is the "true" message. Should she respond to how you behave or how you are feeling? How does she know what you are feeling? It is no wonder that such conflicted communication can easily be spotted and labeled as fraudulent. In an addicted individual, the inaccuracy will be picked up by both those who support the addict's stopping use and those who want to encourage his or her use for their own reasons. The drinker announces he is on the water wagon. Instead of congratulations, he hears, "Yeah, you make that resolution every New Year's afternoon."

People who are addicted often fracture the feel-act axis when they promise to stop acting out their addiction. They are saying one thing and feeling another, and whether or not the mismatch is obvious to them, it is observable to others. The incongruence is read as denial, and the response to the promise is cynicism rather than support. On the other hand, the recovering person cannot afford to merge with an addictive urge just to regain a false congruence. One solution is to make no promises. Just do it, "one day at a time." Another is to talk about the recurring desire to use (the "craving") in meetings and with other recovering people. There, the user can reestablish a truer congruence and get support for talking about his or her urges rather than for acting on them.

Behavior is most effective when it is a congruent expression of feeling; when it comes from a feeling (or motivational base) that matches it. In AA, they say the program will help someone who wants to stop drinking, but will not help someone who only wishes he wanted to stop. Behavior is least effective and least believable when it comes from fragmented, stuffed, or unowned feelings. Such persons who are "trying to stop" may find themselves in dangerous situations simply because they are not congruent for feeling and action. For example, a cocaine user who has disconnected acting from feeling says she wants to stop, but she spends time with the same friends with whom she formerly used. Eventually she relapses, which is painful enough without hearing the inevitable, "You only made a half-hearted effort." Behavior stemming from unowned motivation is contaminated. Such motivation undermines attempts to perform promised or expected behavior. An example would be a man making an appointment with a counselor only after his wife threatens divorce.

Sometimes troublesome and unbidden feelings can trigger postwithdrawal syndrome. A woman was working on her compulsive overeating when she suddenly uncovered buried incest issues that had been eating away at her since childhood. She has a difficult congruence problem: how to make the feelings those issues generate congruent with the tasks of working on her Overeaters Anonymous program. Again, it is safer for her to work on those issues with others who have "been there." It is safer for the same reason it is safer for the cocaine addict to talk about cravings with others who have "been there." Both will profit from the experience of identifying and choosing this option over old patterns of coping with stress. Exercising one's right to have options and to select among them is practicing the art of choosing. Choosing on the basis of accountability for intent and impact diminishes denial. Support, encouragement, and even confrontation from others may help pull both of them from being victims of their feelings into the congruence of sobriety

Acting/communicating opens us to feedback. When a person is not in denial, feedback can bring about change. When denial is in effect, the efficacy of communication as an agent of change is compromised in several ways. The one behind the wall is not congruent for think/feel/act, and thus is in denial about ownership, expression, and/or choice. "I know I promised, honey, but you've got to understand . . ." The one outside the wall experiences the frustration of having his or her message ignored or distorted. (The next two chapters will discuss how addiction counseling uses the dynamics of communication to effect change).

Congruence

AUTONOMY AND BOUNDARIES

When the think/feel/act model is intact, the individual can also be said to be truly autonomous. Autonomy refers to successful individuation of the psyche, and the sense of mastery over the internal forces governing one's life. It emerges developmentally in toddlerhood, as the infant comes to know that he or she is a separate entity from his or her mother. Each of them has a separate triangle. We speak of those with a stable sense of autonomy as having "good boundaries." They know where others leave off and they begin. Mastering ownership, expression, and choice is the way those boundaries are formed.

When they break down, one feels that he or she is an extension of another, who controls his or her thoughts, feelings, and actions. This sense of self is called *merger*. Merger differs from healthy adult interdependence (which is a conscious choice to make a quid pro quo tradeoff with another response-able adult) and from the mystical sense of unity with the beloved, which Erich Fromm called "fusion." Merger is more than a temporary suspension of boundaries; it is the dissolution of them. For some people, merger may feel like the ultimate safety, the comforting lap, the soothing breast. To others it may feel like the ultimate terror, smothering or stifling the will, or the loss of self. Still others seem to carom wildly between these two responses, alternately grabbing onto people and pushing them away.

The sense of being self-controlled, separate, yet still safe and loved, is a great developmental victory. It comes along with a sense of mastery over impulse and will. The toddler is as pleased as its parents with its first successful steps. Loss of autonomy is associated with loss of control, with being a victim of raging internal storms, and with the intrusion of shame (see Chapter 2).

PERSONALITY AND CHARACTER

The last point to be made about the think/feel/act triangle is that it does not represent the whole of human experience. A simple triangle is a model of a single slice of the psyche frozen in time. We are more complex than that. It is a gross oversimplification to say that there is only one triangle in a person: one perception, emotion, or desirable course of action. A breakfast cereal company runs an advertisement in which a big burly lumberjack proclaims, "The grownup in me likes Frosted Flakes because it meets all my nutritional needs." Then the picture dissolves to a young boy wearing the lumberjack's clothes, who says, "But the kid in me loves the sugary taste of Frosted Flakes."

Furthermore, a single triangle does not connect the individual to anything beyond immediate experience. It does not address the patterns and configurations of experience (conscious and unconscious) that emerge over time and shape the selection of meaningful experiences out of the three corners of the triangle. Against the background of external stimulation, there is an internal continuity, a figure against a background of change. This entity has been called self, personality, or identity.

In the first chapter, we discussed how denial worked in a positive way to protect and stabilize the inner core of self. This inner core is formed, nurtured, and protected beneath all the layers of denial. It is the me to which the experience happens. It is the fabric of meaning in my life, the internal guide that keeps me on course, and the center from which the dreams of the future are spun. This self, which is continuous over time, is the point of interaction with the outer world. Self-image is abstracted from many exchanges with the world. It cuts across and transcends current experience.

This idea may seem to belong in a philosophy text rather than a book about denial, but the inner core of self has direct relevance to the problem of addiction, disease, and recovery. For sobriety to be stable and rewarding, the recovering addict must integrate this recovery into his or her self-concept. The real self must be sober, not a hypocrite putting on a phony act. The change must be radical and total. As AA's *Big Book* says (in the chapter titled "How it Works"), "Some of us tried to hold onto our old ideas and the result was nil until we let go absolutely." Recovery, then, requires radical change in self-concept, core self, or personality. This idea is also addressed in the psychiatric literature; see for example, Frank (1961) and Levin (1991).

In DSM-IV, the American Psychiatric Association identifies personality traits as "enduring patterns of perceiving, relating to, and thinking about the environment and oneself that are exhibited in a wide range of social and personal contexts" (p. 630). These patterns of reacting to life are so enduring that they are the means we use to identify each other. "What's the matter with Edith? She's not herself these days."

Personality traits are a kind of constant of experience. They are internal beliefs held about experience. Collectively they can be said to make up our personality. We do not experience our personality traits directly, but we do have a sense of what we hold to be the real meaning of our lives. These beliefs are directly related to assumptions people make about what they are *going to* experience as well as the way they relate to what they have *already* experienced.

The DSM-IV goes on to say, "Only when personality traits are inflexible and maladaptive and cause significant functional impairment or subjective distress do they constitute Personality Disorders" (p. 630). Users seem to have exactly this sort of rigidity and maladaptive self-system. Despite years of research, no addictive personality pattern as such has been found. Nonetheless, addicted persons often seem to themselves as well as to others to have something "wrong" with their personalities, and that something is more than just a reduced response repertoire in terms of think/feel/act. The thing that is wrong seems to be connected to the addicts' world view. They seem to have a world view that not only fostered the development of the disease; it also hampers recovery.

At the time Bill Wilson was writing, the psychiatric community used the term "character traits" to refer to what are now called "personality traits." Wilson recognized the need to alter these patterns and addressed this right in the middle of the 12-step program; step 6 speaks to the removal of these "defects of character." In fact, the middle third of the program, steps 4 through 7, outlines the process of making these radical changes.

Part of the addict's world view is his or her self-image, which in turn is directly related to the unique set of thoughts and feelings called "self-esteem." We often speak of addicts as having low self-esteem, or negative self-image. In more clinical terms, self-depreciation and negative self-image are symptoms of depression. Addicts are often described as suffering from mood disorders as well as addiction. They can indeed become despairing about who they think they are, have become, or are destined to be. They may also be guilty, frightened, or angry. These feelings are directly related to who they take themselves to be, what they expect in relationships with others, and ultimately their whole philosophy of life or world view. That world view and that self-concept must change if sobriety is to be stable and rewarding. Paradoxically, that concept, that inner self, is at the core of the four layers of denial. It is what denial protects and shields from the winds of change.

Believe: Adding Self to Congruence

The feelings most protected by denial, the acting-out behavior deemed most necessary for survival and, most of all, the cognitive process habitually used to mediate perceptual experiences, are directly connected to our fundamental beliefs about the world in which we live. The beliefs go beyond direct experience to become a framework that shapes our thoughts, feelings, and actions in that world. Underneath all of our denial is a set of beliefs about who we are and what *it* (reality, the world, life, etc.) is.

Several writers in and out of the addiction field have written about this enduring sense of *self-in-relation-to-others*. Most recently, writers have discussed the idea in terms of the roles that emerge in a dysfunctional family (hero, scapegoat, lost child, etc.). These roles are the accumulated expectations about what one is supposed to do, think, say, or feel. These expectations become adopted as models, and are like theater scripts which prescribe (and therefore limit) the actions of the persons assigned to those roles. The theater analogy has an interesting linguistic irony. The word "personality" has its roots in the Latin word (*persona*) for the mask a character wore in a play. It means the same thing as role. Step outside the script and everyone else in the play is thrown off. Violate the expectations of your assigned role and you are "misbehaving," or "disappointing" someone else. In addition, each role carries with it an expectation of how others (or life itself) will treat one and what will happen if one acts in this way. "I never get a break." "Others are depending on me." "Don't let your feelings show." These roles, like the APA's personality traits, can become rigid and maladaptive. We have no specific psychiatric name for this disorder, but we do have one for the family systems in which such fixed roles evolved. We call them *dysfunctional families*. Of course, roles emerge in both healthy and unhealthy families, as do personality traits, but dysfunctional families are pressure cookers. Their chronic stress, unrelenting denial, and consequent abuse/neglect/exploitation create exactly the conditions that force those roles to become rigid rather than flexible, maladaptive rather than growth-oriented.

Eric Berne (1961) and the transactional analysts have also written about people developing "scripts" which they seem to be following in their lives. We often play out these scripts and roles in simple or complex interactions called "games." It is hard to tell winners from losers because the games have tricky rules which are never mentioned nor allowed to be discussed. Adlerians, for example Mosak (1979), have written about people forming "mistaken beliefs" about their world. They speak of people guiding and governing their thoughts, feelings, and behaviors by these concepts of themselves.

These concepts about beliefs can have a negative or pathological connotation, but not all writers have taken that approach. Existential psychotherapists, particularly Frankl (1963), talk about the human need to "search for meaning," and about the personality as the process for generating meaning out of experience. Erik Erikson described enduring personality traits as being shaped by a "sense" of the world and as being derived from attempts to master emotional conflicts in both childhood and adulthood. Jung (who is widely quoted as the author of the depiction of alcoholism as a "spiritual" illness) had much to say on the issue of beliefs. In the larger context of his writings, Jung addressed the timeless symbols and struggles of all human beings, which he called "archetypes." Jungians often speak of people as having "missions" in their lives.

Few of us are familiar, let alone comfortable, with such grand themes in everyday life. When examining biographies of writers, artists, and other great individuals (including those thought to have had addictive disorders, such as

Dostoyevski, Van Gogh, or Hemingway), one often reads of their lifelong quests, missions, or struggles. Somehow these terms rarely show up in drinking or drug abuse histories of average clients. One does not hear such lofty ideas being applied to ordinary persons, and that may be our loss as helpers. The concept of unifying themes connecting across a lifetime or the generations of a family, village, or country could broaden and humanize our approach to humbler folks such as ourselves, clients, and their families. The concepts of "spirituality," "mission," "sense," and "script" can all be grouped under the heading "believe." It captures both the psychological and the spiritual connotations of living, and brings them into the work of recovery.

The work associated with integrating a healthy belief system into a sober, congruent think/feel/act triangle will be discussed later in this chapter, and again in Chapters 6 and 7.

THE SELF, THE INNER CHILD, AND BELIEVE

In Chapter 2, the layers of denial were described as a series of nested boxes that protect the inner core of identity. Figure 2.1 depicted this core as a small child, surrounded by the walls of denial. The image of a child as the embodiment of our deepest beliefs about the world and our place in it illustrates a major feature in the dynamics of the fourth point in our model; believe, the contribution of childhood experiences to the formation of the self and the many masks, roles, and personae which surround it.

The true self can be contrasted with any number of false identities or mistaken beliefs about the self. The self can be thought of as the part of you that transcends and unifies all the roles you play and organizes your experience into a coherent, congruent whole. It is the actor inside the role. The self is the part of you that recognizes when you are not being yourself. Around it are your personality traits, your assigned and assumed roles, and your character defects. It is the absolute center of your belief system.

None of us got to be adults without learning the lessons and enduring the struggles of childhood. The record of these lessons is a personal history, a mental family album. We all carry one, even if we have not consciously looked at it in years. Unlike a typical family album with its pictures of vacation spots and posed relatives, our mental albums hold the vivid souvenirs of our most formative experiences. Their personal meaning to us is written on our young faces. We are looking at life, not at the camera, and often we are not smiling at all. What the children in these pictures think and feel about the world is forming the basis of their belief system. Right or wrong, true or false, we take these images as our gospel.

These inner certainties often turn out to be misjudgments and bad decisions made in pain, confusion, and isolation. Once, hot-eyed with crying through a dark night of the soul, we plumbed the depths of the universe. We found its secret. We decided our place in it, and set out on the path of our lives. We found those verities while we were still little children. We survived by acting on them, and in so doing enshrined those younger selves like holograms in our psyches. In the right light, they live again and run our adult lives. Any later situation, problem, or crisis for which their truths *might* be the answer will automatically animate them. Whether their truths are right for this time and this place will not matter in the face of their insistence on being heard and reacted to. Their way must come first, with no second thought, no question whether or not their assumptions still hold. Run! Fight! Cry! Hide!

Their world views are not necessarily reflections of our true selves. We may have grabbed onto distorted perceptions (a face glimpsed in a funhouse mirror that made one look like the biggest and fiercest boy in the world) or the jibes someone selected for their cruelty rather than their veracity (an ugly name never is shaken off). These images were once taken for real. Once they solved a great mystery of who we were or why things were the way they were. They offered the promise of invincibility or balm for great pain, but they also may have misdirected us about our true identity and sent us on a lifelong journey under the aegis of a false self.

On our way to becoming who we are/will be, we get many glimpses of our identity. Yet, we are often tempted to select the wrong perception, to cling to a false self, and devote our lives to the protection of that image.

Inner Children

The intrapsychic holograms of belief form the core of our sense of who we are in the world, our fate, what the universe is all about, and our place in it. Although the basic structure of this belief system is laid own in childhood, the collection of what the DSM-IV calls personality traits (which make up one's personality, and in this context what can also be called self-concept) are stable over time. These ways of being oneself can be grouped under three headings: the *natural self*, the *hurt self*, and the *adapted self*. Each has its origin in childhood and each incorporates experiences throughout one's life. The hurt self and the adapted self differ from the natural self in that they are rigid, inflexible, and, over time, maladaptive.

The natural, authentic self is both the place from which we start as infants and the way of living existentially toward which we strive. People are born with certain givens; we do not come into the world as blank tablets. Among the existential givens at birth are specific DNA codes, and one's biological heritage as a primate. Genetic codes create both possibilities and limitations. As primates, people are born with biologically mediated instincts and drives. As mammals they will suckle and bond. We will form families, create organized groups, establish social hierarchies, mate, and rear young in the midst of complex relationships. Biological determinants will lead us to be both territorial and cooperative, aggressive and nurturing; to be sexual, to attach, and to grieve.

The way one's sensory-motor system is organized, and how one orients toward pleasure and away from pain are also basic elements of one's natural self, as is temperament. One human being will be quiet and shy from birth onward, while another will be outgoing and adventuresome. The unique manner in which people value and organize sensory data, process information, and learn form experience appears to be established at birth. Neurological capacities that are wired in from birth influence who has a talent for music, who is athletically gifted, and who thinks abstractly.

The circumstances of the family into which an individual is born are also given at birth. The family may be rich in material resources, but impoverished emotionally, or vice versa. Some children are born into the middle of war zones, others into golden ages. Some are born with AIDS. All children, however, are born into cultures, social systems, and family structures. These systems may be child-centered and nurturing or completely dysfunctional. Nonetheless, these systems affect a child's upbringing, and then affect whether or not the child is welcomed, ignored, or discriminated against as an adult.

All children are also born into developmental tracks. Their sensory-motor systems will mature. Following their own internal clocks, they will move outside the world of the crib and the lap. Compelled by inborn drives, children venture forth, discovering themselves and their universe, guided by an existential imperative to be and to attach. This is the natural state of children before their instincts are socialized, their drives frustrated, or their will challenged by terror.

Developmental tracks include age-based changes in the way the child will be treated by those around it. First come weaning and toilet training, then at about age five, every culture in the world begins formal training. This social-ization/education prepares the child to become a member of society (Erick-son, 1964). With time and good fortune, adolescence will burst forth and ripen into adulthood.

The universe, with its physical laws, cultural demands, and inherent threats, forces children to confront pain. The most protective and nurturing caregivers cannot protect children from the pain of physical injury, the distress of illness, the anguish of loss, or the stress of denied gratification. In the best of families, ice cream cones are dropped, mothers called for in the night do not come, illness strikes, and strangers frighten. Some children experience traumas of tragic proportion: critical injury, neglect, abuse, or the atrocities of war. For developing children, the nature of their encounters with their own frailty and the fallibility of those on whom they depend confront the limits of their own power and those around them. Their trust can be violated through accident, carelessness, inattention, or malevolence. For this reason, Erikson (1964) called the first developmental crisis a struggle between basic trust and mistrust.

All children discover that their very existence can be threatened. At times they are terribly vulnerable. Pain and suffering can be unavoidable, and at times inconsolable. All children are exposed to the fundamental anxiety arising from human vulnerability. The sense children make of this pain becomes the basis for the meaning they attribute to the universe. Out of their understand-ing of this pain comes a new sense of themselves—who they are in this universe of pain. This is the beginning of the injured self—the hurt child. Along with this sense of self, and in response to its developing world view, a third entity comes into existence—the adapted self.

THE NATURAL CHILD

Our lives create the frame for the expression of our own capacity. That capacity can be called our "natural" or "true" self. It is a way of being and is there from the beginning. Thus, the first inner child is a *natural child*. This way of being has certain characteristics; it is spontaneous, creative, relational, curious, and joyful. In his* world, playing, working, loving, and being flow

*This aspect of self is so unique and personal that only a singular pronoun seems appropriate. Using "they" to get around the problem of gender distorts the uniqueness of this aspect of self. Alternating between he and she to achieve some sort of balance would be confusing. Using an impersonal "it" would be ugly. Since *my* natural child is a boy, I have taken the author's prerogative to refer to this aspect of self in the masculine. I could have gone all the way, and used "I, me, mine" throughout, but my natural child is not that brave.

seamlessly into one another. He is secure in the center of his own world and therefore relates openly and undefensively with adults, animals, other children, and God ("Suffer little children unto me . . . for such is the kingdom of heaven"). The natural child lives directly in experience, without reliance on a philosophy of life; he just lives it. This capacity to live in direct experience is highly prized in an adult. In psychology it is called many things such as presence, authenticity, centeredness, or congruence. In discussions of spirituality, it is seen as the result of enlightenment or as a precondition for spiritual rebirth ("Unless ye become as little children . . . ").

Nonetheless, we are talking about a real child, not an angel. He gets angry, sad, scared. Those experiences rise and fall, come and go. Feelings are not held in awareness after the experience is gone. A natural child takes the healing kiss on his skinned knee and climbs right back on the swing. He is the center of the universe and sees that it is good.

These natural children are not featureless and identical to each other. They are unique and individual. They have individual talents, tastes, and temperaments. This one is energetic; that one, reserved. This one is introspective; that one, gregarious. These conditions, along with such existential givens as the sociocultural circumstances of one's birth, genetic code, and the influences of the family of origin, preexist individual experiences and histories. When these givens are understood, they can provide valuable information about the natural self of the adult. They provide the sort of inner sense that leads people to say something like, "You know, I've always enjoyed working with my hands. I think in another life I was a carpenter."

THE HURT CHILD

The natural child lives in a world that is surrounded by the care and protection of his parents. He gives no thought to this protective bubble that separates him from harm. Sometimes that bubble collapses and he is confronted with unbuffered reality. This vulnerability in the face of awesome power requires a totally new way of coping. Tomorrow will not be better. There is no healing kiss for this injury. It may be the death of a beloved grandparent, which neither the child nor his seemingly omnipotent parents could prevent. It may be an accident or an illness, or it may be the chaos, abuse, neglect, or exploitation of a dysfunctional family. When the bubble collapses, the child is still a child. He has only those resources he has already mastered with which to solve the mystery of what happened to safety and love. Children, particularly young children, have very few options for dealing with pain. They can go inward or outward. They can withdraw or they can protest.

If, or when, a child is set upon by massive trauma, chronic abuse/neglect, or random violations of his autonomy, a sense of self as hurt/pain/injury emerges. This way of being is called the *hurt child*. The hurt child is the original messenger carrying an awful truth. "You are not safe. This is not Eden." The hurt child is the first lesson in grief.

The hurt child shares the narcissistic legacy of the natural child. He, too, is the center of the universe, but instead of being bathed in light, he has been plunged into darkness. The sun has gone out and he has divined the meaning of the eclipse. The hurt child "knows" why he has lost the circle of love. He "knows" what this pain means. It means he is not loved. It is his fault. He made it happen. He is the center of all cause and all blame. Because he is born in violation of the natural child's autonomy, he is powerless and without esteem. He "knows" that the pain is about his unlovableness. He "knows" this condition is immutable and unalterable; he believes it to be his true self. All his conclusions must be true because his pain is real, and his pain becomes the core of his new self.

He has found the meaning of pain, and this revelation ("It's all about me") is a great victory, so great that he will not relinquish it or rethink the problem — ever again. His power is in this "truth." Affirmation of his truth is more important than comfort. He will not let go of pain for that is his identity. So, paradoxically, the hurt child will not stop crying. He will not be soothed. He wants to be noticed as one who is suffering. But if he accepts comfort, he might lose his right to it, and most importantly his grip on being itself. When caregivers become exhausted, frustrated, angry, or leave him, it only proves he was right.

Shame is the special province of the hurt child. The fire of shame is an improvement over the dark void of pain. The shame gives form and meaning to the pain. "It is my fault and I know why." He is still the center of the universe. The vortex is better than the void.

There are few boundaries in a hurt child's world. It is a world of incomplete triangles and porous self-concepts (see earlier discussion of merger). He has no clear idea where he stops and his caregiver begins or vice versa. If he gets angry, the caregiver gets angrier. Who owns that anger, who caused it? Does his crying cause the diaper change? When there is fear between them, he has no idea where it comes from — unless and until he claims all of it. He sees the caregiver's feelings as being shared rather than owned or contained in one or the other of them. Thus he is as responsible for mother's anger as she is.

There are three reasons for this boundary problem:

1. The hurt child is born in repeated or traumatic violations of his autonomy. Often his self-concept is literally dictated by the shaming of intrusive, punitive, exploitive, non-nurturing, or abandoning caregivers. The child hears hostile slurs masquerading as truths. They are delivered by the same people who are teaching him to tie his shoes, "You little bastard! Who do you think you are? I'll tell you! You're a nasty, sneaky . . . " In this context, the attributions are more than simple linguistic distortions; they are violations of the child's autonomy backed by the abusive use of power by the caregiver.
2. The hurt child usually emerges during early childhood, when one is struggling to form boundaries and achieve autonomy. At that time, children are just learning how to differentiate their feelings and behavior from the ongoing stream of experience. They are just starting his existential tasks of ownership, choice, and expression, just beginning to connect the lines of the think/feel/act triangle.
3. In a dysfunctional family the parents (and siblings) have a vested interest in maintaining merger. They feel the need to hold others responsible for creating and maintaining their happiness or suffering.

The characteristics of inner children are contrasted in Table 4.1.

THE ADAPTED CHILD

The hurt child cannot be comforted from the outside, yet he can only call upon a child's resources to fix his world. These resources include three indelible impressions from the collapse of his bubble. The first is the scar of the injury and its never-to-be-forgotten lesson, for example, "Men are dangerous," "Abandonment means death," "Love hurts." The second lesson depends on the dynamic of whatever developmental issue the child was working on at the time. If he was working on autonomy, then the secret of the universe for him will lie in mastery of power and control. If he is struggling with the school-age issues of industry, or the adolescent issues of identity and independence, the dynamics of these issues will dominate his world view. The third permanent truth comes from whatever sense of good and bad parenting the child had

Table 4.1
The Characteristics of Inner Children

Natural Child	Hurt Child	Adapted Child
Center of a safe and loving universe	Center of an unsafe, unloving universe	Center of a world that can be made safe and loving through playing a role
Spontaneous	Restricted, fearful	Reactions restricted, to roles, and missions
Creative	Reactive	Reactive, compliant, or manipulative
Sees self as the maker of joy	Sees self as the maker of pain; causing it, responsible for preventing it or fixing it	Sees survival as depending on avoiding dreads of ambiguity, abandonment, blame, and betrayal
Curious, in awe of life's mysteries	Frightened, superstitious	Knows all the answers
Relational	Fearful, withdrawn	Creates barriers to authentic relating; relates to others in terms of scripts and games
Joyful	Sad	Triumphant when games are working; sad, fearful, or angry when they are not
Secure boundaries	Born in autonomy violation(s)	Tends to merge with others, be a victim or perpetrator of boundary violations
Consolable	Inconsolable	Only happy when compliance, manipulation, or reactiveness is successful
Momentary fear, anger, guilt, sadness, pain, etc.	Obsessed with pain; knows that pain means his true self is worthless, bad, weak, unacceptable to others; he knows he is basically unlovable	Uses emotional behavior to get his way

(Continued)

Table 4.1
Continued

Naively grandiose	Powerless	Obsessed with interpersonal power and its use
Confident	No self-esteem	Develops self-image in terms of role; gauges worth in terms of the reaction of others
Flexible	Deals only in blacks and whites; focuses on inevitability of impending doom; never alters world view	No tolerance for ambiguity; deals only in blacks and whites; focuses on avoidability of impending doom; never alters world view
Hopeful, confident	Pessimistic	Never gives up mission

developed at the time of the injury. Since his primary relationships are with his parents, this sense will frame the definition of closeness, love, and intimacy. If Mom and Dad are stern disciplinarians, he may come to view this as the cardinal virtue of good parents. On the other hand, he may come to crave "freedom" at any price. He will take these views into all his relationships, including his choice of a mate and the way he will parent his own child.

Thus, the *adapted child* emerges to make survival possible, to fix the world, and to diminish the pain. The adapted child is above all a protector. He is the one with a world view. He is the one with a plan for gaining safety and fixing things. He is a savior, a champion, a magician, a fairy godperson, a knight in armor. His adaptation shields the hurt child and it preserves the natural child. Although his intention is to protect and make the future (as he sees it) possible, he builds the fortress that imprisons the natural child/self.

The adapted child is the center of a universe that can be made safe and loving. He does it by magic. He develops a mythology and a mission in life (fixing, pleasing, tricking). He figures out what he has to do to survive and preserve his chance at happiness. Unfortunately, his kind of happiness is a substitute for the real thing. It is a counterfeit happiness. He has absorbed the hurt child's sense of being damaged goods, so he knows he must settle for second best. "I cannot have bliss, so I will take gratification. Bliss is for others, those who are allowed to love and be loved. The bastards!"

He develops manipulations, tricks, and strategies to get what he wants. They are not games for amusement; they are undertaken in deadly earnest. As far as he knows his very life depends on being right. Because this is a life-and-death struggle ("Everything depends on . . ."), the adaptive child has no tolerance for ambiguity; everything has to be black or white. No compromise is possible; all urges are insistent, imperative, and dictatorial. Like the mottos on the shields of medieval knights, his slogans are fighting words by which to live or die. "Never let them see you cry." "Security before everything." "Keep them laughing."

Claudia Black (1982) once listed the three ground rules for surviving in an alcoholic family: Don't talk; don't trust; don't feel. Survivors of such families are surprised when they discover that not everyone lives that way. For the adapted child these hard-won truths are eternal. They are his shield and ultimately his undoing. A knight's armor was the perfect protection for jousting; but off his horse he was clumsy and vulnerable. When gunpowder changed warfare, the knight in shining armor became the proverbial sitting duck. Again, the image of the self in a fortress of denial comes up; and as was observed in Chapter 1, a fortress and a prison look a lot alike from the outside.

The survival solution the adapted child discovers will depend on the circumstances surrounding his emergence. The nature of his injury, the developmental issues (with their previous mastery and successes), the expectations of parents, the roles assigned by the family, the alternatives available, and his existential givens all play a part in the solution he finds. It usually takes the form of a role—a pre-set, well-rehearsed cluster of actions and reactions to his world and the people in it. Above all, this role is an assumed identity, a disguise, a false self. After all (he assumes), if people knew what he was *really* like, they would surely reject, abandon, exploit, or harm him. And he must guard against that vulnerability at all costs. The child first plays this role in the family, and then in the larger world.

The roles of victim, enabler, addict, as well as hero, clown, trickster, are tried out with parents and siblings. If the audition succeeds, he studies the role in earnest. Once learned, it is not easily abandoned. Very admirable qualities, such as "strength" and "determination," can come from his grip on his truth. Survival itself may hinge on the cleverness he brings to his performance.

The adapted child is the one who learns the basic rules of the family. He carves out a niche for himself, learns his lines in the family script, masters his role in the melodrama. The generic roles are the pleaser/fixer/complier, the trickster/performer/manipulator, and the reactor/rebel/malcontent. Every adapted child knows how to do all three. We usually think of ourselves as doing just one of these, but we are really quite adept at all of them. If one of the roles is blocked, we switch to another in the blink of an eye. The variation in roles is not limited to the characters familiar to those active in Adult Children of Alcoholics groups: hero, scapegoat, mascot, lost child, and clown. There are older roles, the archetypes discussed by Carl Jung and Joseph Campbell: hero, king, Madonna, magician, etc. We have regenerated these roles since the garden of Eden. Children often learn aspects of these roles in fairy tales and fables. *Cinderella, Jack and the Bean Stalk, Beauty and the Beast,* and *The Snow Queen* are all stories of the transition from natural to hurt to adapted. Unfortunately, the lesson they teach is often that the adaptation is the route to living happily ever after. Sometimes, as in the story of Dumbo, the message is mixed. Yes, the hero learns to let go of the feather to which he has falsely attributed his own power of flight, but he is only accepted by the others in the circus when he saves them all from fire.

The hero is no safer from the dread of blame than is the rebel or the scapegoat. He is only one victory away from the approval that would allow him to relax, and only one failure away from rejection. The fixer and the pleaser never believe their jobs are done. No amount of success ever seems to be enough for the adapted child. He is like the actor who knows that the audience is not applauding him, but his acting. Because the kudos come for the performance, they go to the performer; not the person.

The adapted child cannot truly win, much in the same way the hurt child cannot be comforted. Suppose he gets what he goes after. The first problem is that any victory of the adapted child is inherently hollow. A loving cup is not love. The adaptive child's goal is a substitute for the true nurturing and love he feels is lost to him. So when he gets whatever he wants, the taste is bitter. Furthermore, he is getting what he wants, not what he needs. He has a future, but no future orientation. Today's junk food binge is tomorrow's health problem. He neither knows nor cares about nutrition. The second problem with the adapted child getting what he wants is that it only reinforces the hurt child's negative self-image. Getting second best proves you are second best.

The third problem is that his adaptations do not change over time. They become rigid and maladaptive. Like the dog who learns how to escape being shocked (discussed in Chapter 3), he is not going to wait around to see what would happen if he did not react. The light goes on, and he acts the way he knows works. His boss is not his father, but if he is replaying the scapegoat role, he will inevitably find himself being blamed for something he did not do, yelled at inappropriately, and unjustly fired.

These fixed habits of perceiving and reacting to experience are called "defects of character" in 12-step programs, and they form the basis of what DSM-IV calls "personality disorders." The adapted child is stuck because both winning and losing prove the kid's point. "Did you smile after I said something cute? I'll keep it in the act. Did you frown? Quick! I'll find a better trick." He will never pause to wonder if the other's disappointment came from seeing a clown instead of a person. "Become a better clown! If the act fails, try again, harder, longer, try it with someone new; change the act, but never think of changing costumes." That is why he is called "adapted" not "adaptive" The natural child learns and changes; the hurt child and the adapted child are frozen in time and never change. The hurt child cannot be comforted and the adapted child will not grow up.

The hurt child and the adapted child are quite different. The adapted child is active, manipulative, and absolutely clear about what needs to be done. The hurt child is passive, overwhelmed, helpless. The adapted child does not feel out of control or "crazy," no matter how much trouble his behavior gets him into. The hurt child is undone by a broken shoelace and abhors punishment. He withdraws and waits while the adapted child insists and demands. One family member may call the adapted child "irresponsible," "spoiled," or "impulsive"; another may call him "amusing." In a dysfunctional family, the attribution may hinge on the degree of sobriety in the house. It may be years before he figures this out. By the time he does (if he ever does) he will already have spent years thinking that he caused these reactions. Ironically, the adapted child's response to both positive and negative attributions about his character is, "They don't understand." He may be into plots, the enactment of myths, avoiding pain, or gaining pleasure, but he is curiously without an internal sense of control. He is reactive, rather than proactive. For all his take-charge attitude, he is only doing this because they are doing that, and "If they would only . . . " is a constant refrain. When the adapted child discovers drugs, sex, gambling, etc., he can quickly learn how to "run" an addiction. There is no doubt that he is the one who says, "What problem? If I had a problem I'd stop." They don't understand: It's not the problem; it's the solution.

The adapted child often seems quite social, but he is not. For all his involvement with others, he *feels* alone; he *is* lonely; he *knows* he is a loner. He craves and fears the intimacy he has never known. He engineers and manipulates relationships to maintain a pattern that he hopes is not too threatening. Maybe it will work this time. How he selects sexual partners, friends, or enemies may seem mysterious to others, but they are all part of the master plan that he keeps secret, even from himself.

The adapted child's world is one of blame, rather than shame. His denial system is more evolved than the primary denial of the hurt child. He has all four levels to operate from. If he gets away with something, he gets to have another try. He will cover his tracks (denial of facts). He feels permanently deprived. He expects to get in trouble when his father comes home, so he has only a short time to crowd in his fun and set up his excuse (denial of change). He will get punished—he always does. When Dad points out all his failings, he will reluctantly admit them and then say, "Yes, but that doesn't mean . . . (denial of implications)." His punishment is a ritual from which he will never learn self-discipline. He will be held to blame for his father's anger (and even for his father's shame at being unable to form a relationship with his son). The proof that he is to blame is that he *has* done something wrong, or disappointed an expectation (which may have been inappropriate or never even articulated). He lied, disrespected his mother, or left the workshop in a mess. It is always something and it always points toward accepting a negative self-image as real: "lazy," "stupid," "just no good." He lives in the dread of this blame. It is the guiding principle of his life. This is also true for adapted children who guide themselves by the philosophy of the fixer/pleaser/complier. Their aim is to be so helpful, pleasing, faultless that they can win affection. It takes a lot of control to be perfect. The slightest flaw "ruins everything."

HOW TO TELL WHERE YOU ARE COMING FROM AS AN ADULT
Table 4.2 compares what it is like to have one's consciousness dominated by one of these three children. When people are dominated by their hurt child, they feel overwhelmed. A dour mood engulfs them in a dark cloud and all they can think of doing is running, hiding, or protesting in reaction to this feeling. Acting on a feeling to change it, or doing anything else at all is out of the question for the hurt child. The tone of this mood is helpless/hapless/hopeless. Although these terms are usually associated with depression, they are qualities of the hurt child's mood even when he is angry or protesting. No matter how intense this pain is, it is nonetheless familiar. "Here I am, *again*. I know what this is about." As noted, shame is the special province of the hurt

Table 4.2

Characteristics of Consciousness Dominated by the Hurt, Adapted, and Natural Selves

Hurt Self/Child	Adapted Self/Child	Natural Self/Child
Concern with developmental issues of preschooler such as trust, autonomy	Concern with developmental issues of latency (industry)	Concern with developmental issues appropriate to age
Affect dominated by depression, fear, and rage	Avoids anxiety/dreads; reacts to situations without ownership; "He/She/It made me feel"	Affect full owned
Passive, reacts to self more than others	Reactive to others in pursuit of roles and missions	Proactive, creatively finds his own way in the world
Finds pain familiar, distrusts joy	Sees both pain and joy as dependent on externals	Finds meaning in both pain and joy
Dependent; feels helpless, hapless, hopeless	Counterdependent or manipulative; knows what others must do next	Independent or interdependent
Feels shame	Focuses on blame	Strives for ownership and accountability
Says "I can't"	Says "I won't" or "I should/shouldn't"	Says "I could" or "I ought"
Interacts on basis of his own feelings	Interacts on basis of others' feelings; content oriented and goal-directed	Interacts on basis of interpersonal process, being in the moment with the other
Merges with others	Plays roles/games	Strives for authenticity and intimacy
Past-oriented	Future-oriented	Here-and-now oriented

child, so the feelings of hurt and shame are clues to the takeover by this child's belief system. Similarly, the overwhelming desire to hide or strike out are clues to the hurt child's presence.

The adapted child can be identified by the clarity with which he sees the solution to all his problems. Since the clarity comes from an intolerance of ambiguity, there will inevitably be distortions, exaggerations, and deletions. The need to do it "my way" is a strong indication that he is running the show. A further sign is the sense that the disagreement of others proves you are right. The adapted child has the full range of denial levels, so defenses beyond primary denial are another clue. Since blame avoidance is a major goal of the adapted child, denial of change is a dead give away. Again, it does not matter whether the "Don't blame me" is coming from an in-your-face rebel, or an overwhelmed fixer. It is still a claim that one is not accountable for choosing things this way. Some people in recovery talk about the days when they were active in their addiction with phrases such as "my addict used to . . . " Their addict self is a full grown adapted child.

All this can be contrasted with what it is like to be in touch with one's natural child, or to be coming from one's natural self. Those are the times when one feels intuitive, instinctive (without being impulsive), gracefully congruent, natural, centered. The natural child is not in denial. He has no problem with owning or expressing his feelings and being accountable for his actions.

Another contrast with the hurt child and adapted child is that the natural child knows that he belongs in a relationship and that he is safe and loved there. Therefore, comfortable intimacy in primary relationships is a sign that one has adequate contact with one's true self. So too is comfort with alone-ness—solitude. The natural child is *not* relationship addicted. Another sign is full involvement with work and leisure activities. Both are enjoyed, rather than labored over. Activities are done for the sake of doing them, rather than as a means to a different end. Playing the game is more important than winning. Intimacy and cooperation are more important than power and success. No one is keeping score. Pleasures are enjoyed for themselves. They are not substituted for other goals. In contrast, pleasures are a means to an end in the hurt and adapted self. They are a balm for the hurt child's pain and the prize that life conspires to deprive the adapted child of. Perhaps the simplest definition of an addict is one who pursues a once pleasurable sensation when he or she does not want to. Lastly, coming from the natural self means living congruently; think, feel, act, and believe all match.

INNER CHILDREN AND THE ABUSING ADULT

When people discover their inner children for the first time, they are often shocked, then disappointed, then angry. Their hurt child seems like a liability. He is childish, dependent, emotional. His reactions complicate things. He makes them feel unacceptably vulnerable. They view their adapted child as obnoxious, a trouble maker, a fraud. His errors in judgment "mess everything up." They want to dissociate themselves from him, get away from him, or just get rid of him. The natural child is, sadly, a stranger; and precisely because his characteristics are child-like, he is greeted with the same distrust and suspicion as his unattractive siblings. Once again he is pushed into the wings.

Escaping from the hurt or adapted child is another name for denial. Many people have been doing that for years. Without knowing it, they have spent decades denying that such feelings, thoughts, and experiences ever happened, let alone that they have been shaped by them. They have been running pell-mell from their childhood. Like a dog with a can tied to his tail, the harder they run, the more racket there is.

Sadly, the first response of many people to their own hurt child is an impulse to neglect, abandon, or abuse him, often in ways that are shockingly similar to the mistreatment in their own childhood.

Others discover their hurt child and immediately want to give him all the cake and ice cream he can eat. They react like a guilty divorced dad who is going to make up for years of neglect by indulgence. The hurt child and his big brothers, the adapted child protectors, do not need to be pampered, exploited, or spoiled any more than real kids do. They certainly do not need to be bribed or bought off. Nor will they tolerate it. They need boundaries, and that means structure and limits as much as nurturing and "love." They need to be *disempowered*, not given free reign. You wouldn't give a nine-year-old the keys to your car—why let him run your life?

It is often said that people who were abused in their childhood grow up to become abusers as adults. That is an oversimplification; it does not happen that automatically. When it does happen, it is not a sudden flip from victim to abuser. Between childhood and adulthood is the flight from the hurt child. The denial of him means an estrangement from the natural self. The fortress formed by the walls of denial are a prison for the natural child. Their attempts to suppress the hurt and adapted child have resulted in reinjury of them. This time the injury is occurring at their own hands. They are the enemy, the abandoner, the exploiter. The victim/abuser relationship is internalized. The first acting out is not with others (or with drugs) but against the self. The first abuse follows years of self-abuse and self-exploitation.

Believe and the Higher Power

The word believe is selected to match the words used in the triangle, like think, feel, and act; it is a verb, an action word. Verbs are used to reflect the dynamic way all four of these points interact and effect one another. The concept of believe is used here to cross-reference to all the connotations of role, self-image, personality, mission, and world view. It is also intended to include one's expectations about relating to others and one's sense of the meaning or mission of one's life, which includes powers "greater than ourselves."

For many people "a power greater than ourselves" or "higher power" are familiar parts of the 12 steps (particularly steps 2 and 3). For others it may seem an odd note to be sounding in a discussion of denial. Nonetheless, experience has proven that a sense of oneness with, alienation from, or absence of a "higher power" plays an important role in the basic structure of the psyche. That which I take to be beyond me plays an important role in defining basic meanings in my life.

People who learned about God in religion school and promptly filed the idea away in the back of their minds feel no influence on their world beyond what they see, hear, and touch. Others are even more influenced by the sense that there is nothing beyond, or greater than, themselves. Yet, faced with serious illness or difficult recovery, most people find their sense of alienation from, or relationship to, a higher power being evoked. For them, recovery includes the quickening of spiritual awareness. In our terms, recovery involves changes in the deepest beliefs about self and the highest beliefs about God.

INTEGRATION OF BELIEVE INTO
THE THINK/FEEL/ACT MODEL

When this fourth point is added to the think/feel/act triangle, it changes the shape of the configuration. That fourth point can be placed on a plane above the first three to denote transcendence of this dimension. How would it look? If you picture a camera on a tripod, you can see the three legs touching the ground to form the corners of a triangle. Those tripod legs touch the ground at the three points of the think/feel/act triangle (Figure 4.4). The legs connect to the camera at the fourth point where the camera sits. The camera sits at the point called believe. Direct lines can be drawn connecting all four points to each other and forming a shape called a tetrahedron, a kind of three-sided pyramid (see Figure 4.5).

Another way to think about this figure is to see it as a tecpee-like tent. Image a belief system at the top. Poles anchor this system in one's everyday life of thought, feeling, and action. The canvas wraps up a private world. Inside it, all the elements reinforce each other. Standing in this tent, one is on

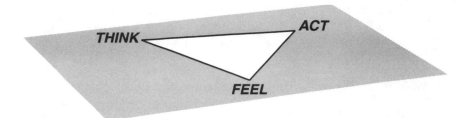

Figure 4.4. The think/feel/act triangle as a base for a four point figure.

what Jim Bugental (1987) calls one's *pou sto* (Greek for "here I stand").
Archimedes once said, "Give me a lever long enough and a *place to stand*, and
I can move the world." Martin Luther said, "Here I stand; I can do no other."
Congruence is standing on the *pou sto* of the natural self. It is not, of course,
the only world, nor the only sense of self that we can dwell within. The
addict is in a different teepee. When one is wrapped up in the belief system of
the hurt child, or under the aegis of the adapted child, the *pou sto* is very
slippery ground.

The existential demands of identity require that one's beliefs be congruently
integrated into the think/feel/act triangle. With believe at the apex of the
figure, three additional existential tasks form the legs of the tripod. Believe is
connected to act through *committing to values*; it is connected to think through
searching for meaning, and to feel through *daring to dream*. The struggle with

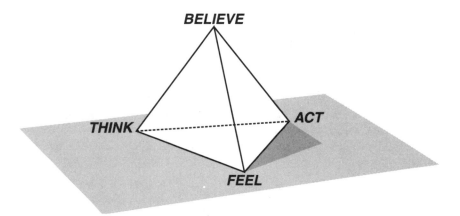

Figure 4.5. The think/feel/act/believe tetrahedron.

these tasks yields three more kinds of experiences which deepen awareness and extend congruence: *guidance*, *understanding*, and *attachment*.

The Believe/Act Connection: Committing to Values; Generating Guidance

Beliefs are deeply held perceptions about the nature of the universe and one's place in it. Who one takes oneself to be has a profound influence on the course of action chosen in any given situation. Faced with a challenge, the hero will strive; the clown, perform; and the victim, weep.

As we become who we take ourselves to be, we develop an internal guidance system. This is the gyroscope that keeps us on our path or mission. The peak experiences of life are often those involving the passionate expression of one's values. Life has purpose and meaning when one's internal morals, ethics, and compassion are put into action. As it has been said, "If you don't stand for something, you'll fall for anything."

Existentialists call this congruent expression of self "authenticity," living passionately in the world. They say it is *mauvais fois* (bad faith) to live life on the basis of an externally directed mission, role, or false identity. In our terms that would mean letting anyone other than your natural self run your life.

When you play out your role in the drama of life, you are (for better or worse) putting your value system on the line, living your truth. There is an awesome ring in the words of the relapsed addict who says, "What do you want? I'm just a junkie. That's all." Not only is he or she trapped in denial of change, and thus estranged from the experience of mastery born of choosing; he or she is also embracing a false identity and alienated from his or her true self. The false self provides a script. It is driven by rigid, fixed beliefs (credos) and plays a role. When one connects one's actions to the natural self, however, one has the experience of discovering one's path. One develops an intuitive sense of when one is straying on that path or straying from it. It is like having a reliable inner compass or gyroscope. This is what is meant by the experience of guidance.

The Believe/Think Connection: Searching for Meaning; Finding Understanding

Victor Frankl (1963) called our search for meaning the essence of existence. The experience of understanding arises out of connecting thoughts and beliefs. It arises from the search for meaning. We are about this task from the first day of our lives to the last; it is deeply satisfying. For decades, developmental psychologists have been documenting how infants learn about their environment, organize their experiences, and react to moments of discovery. Mothers who have observed babies discovering their toes confirm the finding of Rovee-Collier and Hayne (1987): When infants make a connection about themselves and their world, they spontaneously smile.

The sense of what is important and why is determined by one's beliefs. Conversely, one's perceptions and interpretations of the world provide the feedback that shapes those beliefs. Driven by the search for meaning, one seeks out, repeats, or deepens experience. Again, a contrast should be made between the meanings attributed to experience by the hurt and adapted selves on the one hand and the natural self on the other. When the search for meaning is connected to the natural self, an understanding of one's true nature and one's place in the scheme of things emerges that is not distorted by the *a priori* assumptions of the other inner children.

The Believe/Feel Connection: Daring to Dream; Risking Attachment

Beliefs are the source of our drive to create our own future as well as to understand it. Through dreams, and visions of the natural self (and the fantasies, distortions, and illusions of the hurt and adapted selves), we imagine a future of feeling and move toward it. Dreams, in this sense, are a vision of a fulfilled self. Dreams are the medium for bonding and attaching to people, ideals, and such institutions as parenting, work, friendship, marriage, and religion. Dreams embody one's deepest wish to feel. They are a kind of rehearsed expression of love. When one dares to dream, one allows one's self to be committed to people and attached to life itself. "The courage to be," as Paul Tillich (1952) called it, is facing the vulnerability of caring. Dreams are an imagined future in which core aspects of the self-image are fulfilled. Because deep longings carry great vulnerability with them, there is risk in dreaming. As Buddha said, "The cause of suffering is attachment." To love is to be vulnerable to loss. For that reason, the connection between feelings and beliefs comes from finding and empowering one's dreams.

Attachment is a special kind of loving which is felt toward persons (or symbols) who are believed to be necessary for one's well-being. The bonding/attachment process plays a critical role in the early development of an infant. Later in life, attachment connects us to our own children. The enactment of these special feelings can be seen as the pursuit of a dream. The dreams we pursue and the means we use to cherish and cling to them say more about us than anything else.

Dreams are often pursued mechanically, without reflection on their meaning or the feelings connected to them. Some people chase fame, fortune, excitement, or pleasure, without asking why. Some people attend church out of habit. Some people hope for parental approval long after they have grown up and had children of their own. One can adore one's beloved whether that be money, mother, or Buddha; but if one's behavior becomes a ritual without access to one's feelings, the experience is incomplete. Life without attachment is meaningless and isolated. Without this connection, life itself is incomplete. In fact, this incompleteness relates directly to the spiritual aspect of the 12-step program. Figure 4.6 shows the tasks of integrating believe into the think/feel/act triangle; Figure 4.7 shows the complete awareness that comprises congruence.

Beliefs, Loss, and Denial

Change in one's belief system does not come easily; it is brought about because some traumatic loss has shattered a core level attachment dream. In the development of inner children the natural child loses Eden and the belief system of the hurt child is born. Then the adapted child spins his daydreams of safety and power. The hero, lost child, trickster, and scapegoat all have dreams, dreams that can script a life. Addiction is the great spoiler of dreams.

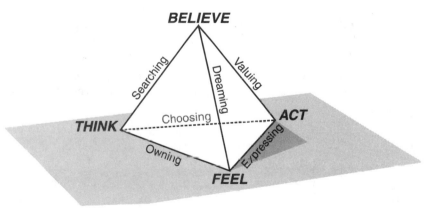

Figure 4.6. The existential tasks integrating thought, feeling, action, and belief.

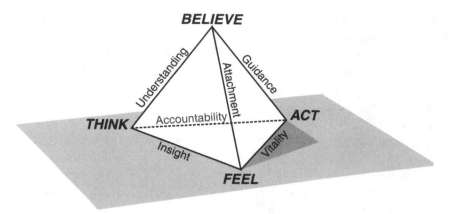

Figure 4.7.   The self-awareness resulting from congruent integration
of thinking, feeling, acting, and believing.

When loss occurs through trauma, death, separation, or failure, the initial
response is shock and denial. The walls of denial are erected to protect the
dream against the truth that "it cannot be." The belief system that spun the
dream may be buried deep within the psyche behind layers of denial. The
repression of belief leads to the loss of experiences generated by living those
beliefs. Meaning is lost; guidance goes awry. Without the stabilizing influence
of believe's gyroscope, one stops living authentically. The existential tasks
(owning, expressing, choosing, valuing, searching, and dreaming) are put on
hold; so too is the awareness that is critical to congruence (insight, vitality,
accountability, guidance, understanding, and attachment). The protection of
denial causes a general breakdown in congruence. In this chaos, addictions can
flourish. By the same token, addiction will eventually strip the addict of all he
or she values, shatter every dream, and destroy self-esteem. As one alcoholic
put it, "You know that vodka that says it leaves you, 'breathless?' Well it will
also leave you homeless, penniless, and loveless."

The most familiar aspect of loss-induced shock is that feelings are cut off
from awareness. When all of the basic connections between thinking, feeling,
acting, and believing are unglued, responses seem impulsive, disorganized, or
self-defeating. Moods swing and emotions flood, buffeting the senses relent-
lessly. People who are suffering loss move about in a daze, seem unable to
"make sense of things." They seem purposeless, detached, and uncaring.

Ironically, although addictions and loss swirl around each other and alternate between cause and effect, the losses from addiction can lead to what is called "hitting bottom." Hitting bottom is a loss that leads to a life-changing transformation in the addict's identity and belief system. It is the loss of a dream that finally "wakes up" the addict.

CONGRUENCE AND RECOVERY

When actively abusing, an addict has a static or fixed think/feel/act system; an addict always has the same thoughts, feelings, and actions. Counselors are in the business of helping people create changes in the components of their response systems. In particular, the treatment of addictive disorders is designed to affect the client in two ways: first, to move toward more congruent responses; second, to alter the content (thoughts, feelings, and actions) of those responses.

Moving Toward Congruent Responses

Recovery can be thought of as a special kind of congruence—congruence for the work of staying sober. Compliant behavior alone is not enough to sustain recovery. Behaviors must be connected to attitudes and feelings related to that recovery. Feelings must be owned and expressed. Acts must be chosen. To be congruent, these acts must integrate both feeling and thought. One must say what one means and mean what one says. An addict expresses feelings one way when he or she is using, and quite a different way when fully sober. Acting sober changes an addict's life; it quite literally "cleans up the act." These changes cannot be permanent while feelings are isolated, however. Acting from feelings one is not aware of—feelings that have been disowned or kept unconscious—can lead to relapse.

Some counselors make a distinction between being "sober" and being "dry." "Dry" is used to connote behavioral change (abstinence) only. When a person is dry, all of the thoughts about abusing, and the images of self and others, are still operating in the same old way; they are just isolated from the using behavior. Feelings are not owned, and such "white knuckle" abstainers are not at choice about their behavior. They see themselves as victims. They will say, "I can't drink," which implies that there is no choice on their part. They are being forced by their spouse, their boss, their liver, the law, etc. The experience of self is not complete, congruent, or integrated.

The term "sober," on the other hand, implies a level of self-awareness and responsibility that closely resembles Glasser's concept of "response-ability." "Sure I could start again . . . and maybe get away with it for awhile . . . but you know, given a choice, I'll pick sober over high any day . . . any night . . . and particularly any morning after. That's what I have power over, the choice, not the alcohol."

Sober usually denotes participation in a 12-step program of recovery. In terms of the think/feel/act triangle, a person who is trying to think and feel sober without doing specific sober acts (going to meetings, working at a program, etc.) is still in denial and, therefore, still actively ill, even though the abuse part of the illness has stopped.

Successful treatment of addictive disorders requires many changes in the life of the client:

1. The abuse itself must end. For substance abuse disorders this means detoxification and abstinence; for other disorders, such as overeating and compulsive spending, an analogous form of abstinence must begin.
2. The endless stream of crises generated by the abuse (legal difficulties, medical emergencies, etc.) must be resolved.
3. An active program of recovery must begin.
4. The behavior and attitudes that will support this program and continuing recovery must replace the habits that previously dominated the client's life.

All four of these changes require a more basic change, a change in the denial system. It is the denial system that binds the person to addiction. All of these changes are interrelated; what relates them is the changes in the denial system of the person. While the user is in full denial, treatment cannot begin. Until denial of change is worked through, neither participation in a program of recovery nor life-style changes will be sustained, and relapse is an immediate threat. Until the denial of feelings is worked through and the emotional conflicts associated with sobriety are resolved, delayed relapse is a nagging threat.

The client is not alone in the disease, and not alone in the recovery. Spouses, family, friends, and even employers are involved in the changes of recovery. The closer one is to the client, the more one needs a recovery program of one's own. That means changes are in store for all of the client's significant others, and those changes mean working through their own denial, just as the user must work through his or her denial. The focus here is primarily on the changes that the addict will make in treatment. Occasionally, these changes will be compared and contrasted to the changes in store for the significant other, but because the need to change the denial system is common to both the addict and the co-dependent, the term "client" should be thought of as referring to both, despite the focus on the addict.

WHEN RECOVERY STARTS

A crisis usually starts treatment. This crisis is a fact which is not to be denied, even if the implications of it are. One first deals with the crisis by getting into treatment. "My God, I got to do something or else . . . !" The consequent treatment is sometimes called "primary care" and is often in a hospital or clinic setting. Increasingly these days, clients are seen in what is called "intensive outpatient" treatment, where the clients live at home, go about their customary work during the day, and attend a very concentrated form of treatment at night. Determining whether or not hospitalization is required can be a medical decision, but often it is decided on the basis of what resources are available.

Once treatment begins, the initial focus is on complete assessment and accurate diagnosis of the problem. Although it would seem that treatment should begin after assessment and diagnosis, this is not the case in addiction treatment. As soon as clients are physically able (and often before they feel very comfortable), they are expected to attend lectures, eat with the other clients, participate in meetings, etc. This is not really an atypical practice. When patients are admitted to a coronary care unit, they too are started on certain standard regimens. An internist may say to a new outpatient with a physical complaint, "I'm going to start you on antibiotics while I run some tests." For addicts, however, the mere fact of being a client is part of the confrontation with their addiction. They may be in complete denial, but neither the staff nor the other clients will be persuaded by the claim "I'm just here for a check-up."

The major goal of the assessment process is to establish a set of facts supporting the diagnosis of the disease. Other problems are often discovered at this time (for example, dual addictions, medical complications, co-existing mental or emotional problems); ignorance or denial of these problems could hamper recovery and contribute to relapse. Again, the history taking and assessment process establishes the facts necessary to cope with the denial surrounding these problems. When the client participates in gathering and validating these facts, the wall of denial is bridged. Even while gathering this data, the staff begins helping the client accept the disease. This process involves educating the client about the disease process. Education and counseling help the client get a grasp on what has happened to him or her (and his or her family) and what it means, and bridges the denial of implications.

Therapy will then focus on building a program of recovery and relapse prevention. Clients will be expected to begin activities that will support their recovery. They will be given assignments to work on problem areas that were identified during the assessment, work on the first four or five of the 12 steps, make contacts with members in outside 12-step groups, etc. They will also be expected to learn about relapse and work with staff to identify effective countermeasures.

As the primary care phase comes to an end, plans are made for what will happen after treatment, including participation in support groups (Alcoholics Anonymous, Narcotics Anonymous, Overeaters Anonymous, Sexaholics Anonymous, or similar programs) and whatever form of counseling (individual, group, family, combinations) has been selected as most appropriate. The client is then discharged with a full schedule of activities to perform, and a well-designed recovery program to put into effect.

In the aftercare program, the client's progress is monitored and he or she is provided access to professionals to help with the adjustment to "living sober." After several months of this kind of care, the active monitoring ends. Counseling and support group participation continue. The greatest work on denial of change takes place during the aftercare phase. It is during this time that the client accepts (or resists) taking responsibility for staying sober.

Recovery for co-dependents also often begins around a crisis. Although inpatient treatment is rare for co-dependents, the combination of professional counseling and participation in a support group is quite common. In addition, co-dependents will be encouraged to participate with the addict in couple sessions and support group activities with other families in treatment at that time. Co-dependents' denial may take the form of resistance to working on themselves. The same assessment and education process that is designed to bridge the denial of facts and implications for the addict will help bridge co-dependents' denial surrounding their situation. Much of co-dependent denial is organized around the insistence that the problem lies completely with the abuser: He or she is the one who changed; all will be well, if he or she changes back to "normal." The counselor works to establish the facts of the codependence or the co-dependent's facilitating.* The facts of co-dependency include rescuing, making excuses, shifting family responsibilities, and gradually centering life around the addict/dependent person. It is a bad day if he or she is having a bad day. It is a good day only if he or she does not use.

Once the facts have been gathered, the counselor helps the co-dependent see how he or she and the addict have lost control over their lives. Then, the implication of a family disease and co-dependence are established. The co-dependent is given literature, introduced to other recovering persons, shown films educating family members about the disease concept, and encouraged to discuss his or her reactions with other co-dependents who are also in recovery. Homework assignments may even be given to enhance education about the family disease concept.

The co-dependent's aftercare program overlaps with the client's. Membership in support groups after the client has left treatment is mandatory, even though the co-dependent may be tempted to drop out. The problem is not over "now that Charley has stopped drinking." This could be denial that Charley was all that ill to begin with (minimization or denial of implications), but it is certainly denial of the need for sustained change on the part of the spouse (denial of change).

The addict's or the co-dependent's dropping out of counseling or finding excuses for missing meetings is a sign of relapse. Relapse for the co-dependent means going back to old patterns of thinking and reacting to the client, the family, and most of all to him- or herself. The risk of relapse is particularly high if the addict returns to using.

DENIAL AND RELAPSE

Denial sustains abusing. Return of denial signals impending relapse. That is why congruence is a necessary part of the recovery process. The return of denial or the breakdown of congruence is sometimes called a "dry drunk." The fear is that a dry drunk will get "wet" and the client relapse. The symptoms, such as isolating self, moodiness, reduced participation in prescribed

---

*"Facilitating" is probably a better term than "enabling." To facilitate means to make it easy to do something; enabling means to make it possible. To say that a spouse made the abuser "able" to be addicted sounds too much like he or she caused, or is responsible for, the patient's actions. Nothing could be farther from the truth. Enabling does not cause addiction; it makes it easier for it to grow.

activities, blaming, excuse making, impulsiveness, all have the clear look of incongruence and denial.

Anytime a recovering person retreats behind the wall of denial, there is a danger of relapse. This is true even when denial may be a necessary coping device, such as in an emergency. For example, a newly recovering person will be discouraged from traveling alone to a distant city to attend a funeral; there will be too much isolation from support and a lot of emotional stress. Some old-timers in AA tell newcomers not to make any changes in their lives during the first year of sobriety. Don't change jobs. Don't move. And above all, no new love relationships or sudden divorces. Why? Because radical changes put the newcomer at risk for denial, if for no other reason than they take the focus of sobriety onto the problems generated by the change.

The layers of denial distort the contents of awareness and isolate thinking, feeling, and acting from one another. When they are isolated, the result is impulsive or maladaptive behavior. People behaving that way cannot be said to be psychologically healthy. Incongruence (denial) is a major symptom of illness. The addict cannot be said to be choosing the behavior of alcohol or drug use. The behavior is engaged in incongruently (without acknowledged feelings or acknowledged responsibility); it is a symptom because it is surrounded by denial.

The conceptualization of denial in terms of congruence also relates the illness of addiction to the therapy used to treat it. Recovery from chemical dependence requires reduction of denial. Not only must clients accept their disease, they must also accept the treatment and fundamentally alter their behavior. The change, again in Glasser's terms, is to behave "response-ably." Recovery is more than the behavioral change of stopping drug use; it is an integration of a sober life style. This integration is not possible while the client is still in denial. It is difficult, if not impossible, to make the behavioral changes permanent while isolating one's feelings.

When abusing, addicts typically alternate between little or no expression of emotion, and sudden disruptive outbursts of it. These continue for some time after active using stops; there are a lot of ups and downs in early sobriety. When fully sober, the expression of emotion becomes more regulated, the swings of mood level out, and affect is more congruent. The client's expressive behaviors are selected from among several alternatives. One behavior is chosen because it is both an effective expression of a feeling and an ethically acceptable behavior. Behavior so selected is congruent for thinking, feeling, and acting. Not achieving this congruence may signal possible relapse.

ONGOING RECOVERY

An addict can be said to be successfully recovering when the signs of active drug use are absent and denial does not interfere with participation in the recovery process. The client not only attends meetings, goes to counseling, etc., but he or she also is not in denial while doing so. Clients are their whole selves (perhaps their old selves), in touch with their feelings, responsible for their actions, and thinking about the world in a rational fashion. The word that old-timers and treatment personnel use to describe this change is "sober." The word means substantially more than the absence of intoxication. It means a change in denial and a change in life. Since the change is designed to be permanent, and the work to sustain and enhance this sobriety requires ongoing effort, people are said to be "recovering," rather than "recovered." As any dieter knows, one does not lose weight once; one works to keep it off, or one starts all over again.

What does sober mean for the co-dependent? Again, both abstinence and change are required. The co-dependent must be abstinent for enabling behaviors, but also must change the thinking that sustained these behaviors. Above all, sobriety for the co-dependent means taking (or taking back) responsibility for his or her own life.

Psychologically, sobriety can be thought of in terms of integration, the very sort of integration addiction and denial prevented. In therapy, the walls in the denial system are opened up so that the symptoms of addiction, the scope of the illness which those symptoms imply, the responsibility to change, and feelings which were previously denied are all connected to each other and admitted to awareness. The experience of self is opened to include a new existential awareness, which derives from performing the existential tasks of connecting think/feel/act/believe. The awareness of insight, vitality, and accountability are applied to the larger task of clarifying the perception of the natural self and its path in the world. One spends more time on one's *pou sto*, and less time under the belief system of the hurt or adapted self. These belief systems do not change or vanish, they are just less compelling. This is the core change necessary for complete recovery. As clients progress in recovery, their psychological system becomes integrated or congruent. They develop insight into themselves; they experience the attachment, guidance, and understanding which comes from the natural self rather than from the adapted or hurt self.

Altering the Content of Responses

THINKING

The second goal of treatment is to change the content associated with all four components of the think/feel/act/believe system. For example, education about the disease impacts thinking. Reading pamphlets, watching movies, and, above all, discussing addiction with staff and other clients provide new data and new ways of thinking about old experiences. And, as mentioned in the previous discussion of denial, learning about the disease process alters the denial of implications which has been shrouding awareness. In addition to shrouding awareness of the implication of one's symptoms, this type of denial has also been blocking the think-feel connection. Co-dependents profit from the same education, and frequently utilize the same materials. At first this is done separately from the abusers, in groups of other co-dependents who, like themselves, are beginning recovery. Later, they will work together and in groups of couples. Some of the methods associated with this aspect of treatment are discussed in Chapter 5.

FEELING

Individual counseling and group therapy impact on the feeling component of responding. These human encounters behind the wall of denial open feelings and provide the experience of sharing them. Special emphasis is placed on working with the feelings associated with ending the old denial pattern, and integrating the new feelings which arise from the existential awarenesses of congruence. Again, co-dependents will work on the same issues. The dynamics of these therapeutic encounters are discussed in Chapter 6.

ACTING

Homework assignments (such as writing out one's drinking/drugging history in one's own words) and therapeutic exercises (such as role playing the situation of being offered a drink) along with occupational and recreational therapy provide a kind of jump start to a new way of behaving. These techniques impact both the act part of the triangle and its connection to the other components of responding.

Many therapists will advise their clients, "It is easier to act yourself into a new way of thinking than it is to think yourself into a new way of acting." This idea is captured in the AA slogan, "Bring the body long enough and the mind will follow." When we do new things, we have new experiences. It is the newness that makes change in old attitudes possible. Acting differently has tremendous impact on our self-concept. Talking about this impact (precisely because it is a radical departure from the previous habit of secrecy and denial) extends that impact to its maximum. Therefore, treatment often repeats a series of alterations between performing some new behavior (sober, non-denying, behavior) followed by discussion (often called "processing"). The discussions help the new behavior become more congruent by providing a healthy outlet for the feeling. The new sober behavior provides something important to work on. If clients only think about sobriety, or only express their feelings about sobriety, they often find it difficult to sustain the behaviors that will insure sobriety once outside the hothouse of primary treatment. It is important for the newly recovering addict to translate attitudes and feelings of the treatment into behavior as soon as possible and as often as possible. Acting the opposite of one's previous denial helps strengthen recovery. One could call this "counterdenial" acting. The tradition in AA and other 12-step meetings of introducing oneself by saying, "My name is— —, and I'm an alcoholic (ad-dicted to— —)" is an example of counterdenial behavior for the new member. Using the word "alcoholic" runs counter to the years of hiding and denial. Another example is seen in working the fifth step (" . . . admitted to God, ourselves, and another human being . . . "), and so on throughout the steps. Since the support groups for co-dependents use the same steps, the significant others walk a parallel road in their own counseling and support groups. It can be just as hard for the co-dependent to say, "My name is— —, my lover is addicted to— —" as it is for the addict to get his or her mouth around the words. Chapter 5 also addresses behavior change in treatment.

TAKING OWNERSHIP

Many therapies address this problem. And during the course of treatment the client may encounter several approaches to reconnecting thinking and feeling. It was the Gestalt therapists who began speaking about "taking ownership" of one's feelings. They help their clients become more aware of their feelings by concentrating on undisturbed perception of those feelings. Cognitive therapists help their clients understand the relationship between their thoughts and their feelings by helping them focus on the interpretations they are placing on their experiences. They help their clients (both dependent ones and co-dependent ones) see how these interpretations generate emotional responses. Other forms of counseling (rap sessions, family therapy, etc.) are designed to help the client get in touch with feelings about everyday events ("How do you feel about telling coworkers you are not using any more?") as well as emotion-laden topics within the family.

EXPRESSING

While still using, the incongruent abuser rarely has the opportunity to express his or her feelings. The fear, anger, and despair that abuse generates finds few direct outlets. Nothing can be talked about. Everything ends up in a scene about the way he or she has acted. Treatment teaches that the answer to emotional conflict usually lies in talking.

This problem is just as acute, if not more so, in the life of the co-dependent. Those around the abuser find their experience of expressing has been blocked as well. Again, therapy or a support group (Alanon, Narcanon, Families Anonymous, etc.) can assist in reestablishing congruence and vitality. These venues address this emotional blunting directly. Recovery for the co-dependent, just like for the abuser, requires reduction in denial and reestablishment of congruence. Over and over, the recovering person is encouraged to put his or her thoughts and feelings into words, with a counselor, a sponsor, in a meeting, or all three. In treatment clients learn to talk about their feelings rather than acting on them. For some this is a whole new world of expression. Raising a voice rather than a fist is a new way of dealing with anger. Instead of an outburst leading to greater isolation, the addict discovers new ways of establishing congruence and connection.

CHOOSING

While in primary care, clients are given many assignments to carry out, for example, to write out the first three steps in their own words, or to arrange for the whole family to come in for a counseling session. If the client is having a hard time with the existential task of choosing in general, he or she will probably fail to complete the assignment. The client will not refuse to do it, but will fail with an excuse. "I forgot I was supposed to have the history by today." "I left the telephone number of my brother-in-law in my other purse." The counselor can confront this denial directly by reviewing the steps the client took to handle the problem, and in so doing, illuminate the choice points that were ignored. This confrontation of denial of change can take place while the client is still in the protected environment of primary care.

Later, in aftercare, the assignments will be harder to perform and easier to find excuses for. "I didn't make a meeting this week; my car didn't start."

BELIEVING

Changing a life-long belief is the most difficult thing a person can do. It requires two things. The first is a very special relationship with someone so far inside one's wall of denial that images, feelings, and memories that have not seen the light of day for years can safely be taken out and reexamined. The nature of this special relationship will be discussed in Chapter 6. The second condition for changing a belief is undergoing the painful process of separating from the representation, or manifestation, of that belief in one's life. Such separations come with the great losses in life; the process of separating is called *grieving*, which will be discussed in Chapter 7.

THE INNER CHILD: NEW WAYS OF VALUING, DREAMING, SEARCHING

As therapy proceeds, a new awareness of self emerges. Clients learn how to separate their hurt and adapted selves from their natural self. As they catch glimpses of the natural self, they experience moments of congruence and the existential awarenesses that go with it. The primary method for helping with this work is individual and group counseling. While clients may be assisted with literature and films that illustrate these points, it is only by directly experiencing new ways of being in the world and with other people that lasting change is likely.

Table 4.3 compares hurt, adapted, and natural selves in terms of therapeu-

Table 4.3
Therapeutic Approaches for the Hurt, Adapted, and Natural Selves

Hurt Self/Child	Adapted Self/Child	Natural Self/Child
Long-term individual psychotherapy	Twelve-step programs	Any form of therapy; makes good use of both insight- and enrichment-oriented therapy
Successful therapy often guided by self theorists such as Kohut (1971), Levin (1991)	Successful therapy often guided by confrontation theorists such as Berne (1961), Johnson (1980)	Successful therapy often guided by humanist/existential theorists such as Rogers (1961), Bugental (1989), Moses (1995)

tic approaches. Those individuals whose experience is dominated by issues and concerns of their hurt self do well in long-term individual psychotherapy, with this caveat: Sobriety itself must first be stabilized. These clients are often referred to as having a "dual diagnosis." Regardless of the diagnosis, treatment is not a matter of one problem being more important than another. Both must be worked on simultaneously. Severely depressed patients are in danger of relapse; they are also at risk for suicide, or such severe isolation and withdrawal from interaction that they are unable to participate in recovery activities. Treatment should proceed on both fronts. This can be accomplished by focusing the work on depression, thought disorder, severe anxiety, etc. on the way it impacts participation in recovery. How will the distress affect going to meetings, maintaining contact with one's sponsor, keeping counseling appointments, etc.? Many clients find referral to MIRA (Mentally Ill Recovering Alcoholics Anonymous) very helpful. Since the world of the hurt child is dominated by concerns and issues from early stages of development, such theorists as Kohut (1971) and Levin (1991) can provide helpful direction.

Perhaps the majority of clients seeking treatment struggle with adapted-self issues. They tend to fare better in a group setting than do those who are centered in their hurt self. They are ideal candidates for 12-step programs which confront both the behavior of the addiction and the world view underlying it. They tend to respond well to counseling techniques that are based on challenging "games" (e.g., Berne, 1961) and denial (Johnson, 1980).

When one is thoroughly grounded in recovery and the actualization of an authentic self, it would seem that counseling would not be necessary. Indeed it usually is not, although spiritual work with a guide, and growth enhancement experiences with someone adept at the practice of some creative art or consciousness expanding skill can be useful. More importantly, living fully and congruently requires daring to dream, and brings one inexorably into intimate relationships. The natural self is not isolated from loving and being loved; thus the trauma of loss is inevitable—grieving is inevitable. Since the process of grieving (see Chapter 7) can only unfold fully in the context of a relationship with another person who is willing and able to be *authentically* present (i.e., not in denial) it is often useful (although not necessary) to have professional help in working through the life-wrenching changes brought about by loss. Since the humanist/existentialist theorists, such as Rogers (1961), Bugental (1987), and Moses (1995), have explored the issue of authenticity in the helper (see Chapter 6). These approaches seem best suited to helping with the crisis and struggle of grieving. Further, these approaches take a strong antipathology stand. Since they are more likely to view the bereaved's struggle with loss as a natural, necessary part of existence rather than an aberrant affective state to be medicated, fixed, or put behind one as soon as possible, they seem better suited to working with the crisis of loss than others who use a more medical model.

5

Joining the Client Within the Wall of Denial

The first chapter offered the house of the third little pig as an analogy to denial; like the walls of a house, the walls of denial have several layers. As anyone who has tried to hang a shelf has discovered, it is hard to tell by looking at a wall whether or not there is lathing under the plaster . . . or where the studs are located.

Similarly, the addicted person often presents a smooth facade to outside observers. "Everything is fine!" At first the therapist has no way of knowing what is beneath the client's initial statement. There may be highly developed protection at several layers. One might think one was dealing with a simple wall of plasterboard and studs only to find out that it was the main load-bearing wall. There will be hard going before the therapist and the client see daylight. Many clients put up a fight at each of the four layers of denial, making each step of recovery a struggle for themselves and their therapists. Others may be relying on only one layer. Without the protection of that one level of denial, their system collapses. How does one get behind that wall?

It is tempting to try to just break through the wall, to stack up so much evidence that the client must accept the truth being presented. It is tempting, but may be disastrous. Denial does not yield to truth; it is a protection against it. Denial buys time until a resource critical to the client's sense of well-being can be identified and accessed. That resource is either an internal strength or an external support, that is, some knowledge, skill, or asset not previously

114

identified, or some person who offers a better alternative than remaining in denial. Both types of resource offer help and, importantly, hope. Where one can see help, one can see hope. The *knowledge* that people *can* get treatment helps. The skills of a good sobriety program helps. Meeting others who have "been there" may help most of all. People, help, and hope are all in the same place at the same time. In the end, it is a relationship with someone who is trusted within the wall of denial; a relationship free of the distortion of denial offers a renewable source of that help and hope.

FACING THE WALL OF DENIAL

It is not surprising that the wall called denial has generated forceful, aggressive images such as "breaking down," or "cutting through" denial. Such phrases connote force used against the willful resistance of the client, and such connotations pervade the terminology of the addiction treatment field. Most family members and friends feel the urge to use force. Some therapists even identify their therapeutic style as "confronting." Confrontation means "bringing face to face." It denotes a "show down." A "successful" confrontation seems to be one in which the client was brought face-to-face with the truth-bearing therapist or friend, was forced to see that truth, and not permitted or able to turn away. This show of force is perceived and reacted to by the person in denial, and the reaction is usually more denial, not less.

To "confront" implies being outside the client's denial system and arguing against it from that external position. The image is that of running up against a stone wall with enough force to knock it down. With a lot of power, one can bulldoze the wall down. Ironically, a confrontational approach is the very attack the wall was constructed to defend against. In terms of the three little pigs, confrontation makes those of us on the outside of the wall into wolves. If we succeed, we are the "big bad wolf." If we fail, we are the "blow hard wolf." Not surprisingly, clients who are coerced into treatment rarely get close to, or accept help from, the therapist who applied the critical pressure which brought them there. No matter what that wolf says later, he is still the one that wrecked the house. Because strictly confrontational approaches did not prove to be very successful with persons in denial, counseling techniques have been developed to "soften" the adversarial connotations of confronting.

Supportive counseling (even the therapeutic technique called "client-centered counseling") has also proven to be ineffective with people in denial. It is hard to support someone in denial. First of all, you don't want to agree with their way of dealing with the world. Second, they often seem to reject you and your help.

If neither support nor confrontation has a good chance of working, what does? Offering the client a better alternative than living with denial. That alternative must be both better and believable. It must be believable, or there is no hope; it must be better because false hope is worse than no hope at all.

Some therapists use a style called "intervention" (Latin: "come between"), to soften confrontation. Intervening implies entering into a process, somehow getting between the person and the denial system. Intervention is preferred to confrontation because it does not connote arguing, and can include being supportive. It offers something to the person behind the wall. But that offer comes with a price. The price is giving up the denial. Intervention still implies force, which is used to change the denial system, presumably by interposing the therapist between it and the client. The change is the loss of, or stripping away of, that denial. It is hard not to suspect a trick when someone is taking something away and saying "trust me" at the same time. People feel strongly about giving up their secrets and having them used as weapons later. If the message is, "First give up your denial, then I'll give you something back," the client might not feel the gift before he or she feels the loss.

The ideal form of addiction therapy would be one in which the client feels the help and the hope before (or at least at the same time) he or she is surrendering the protection of denial. That therapy would differ from pure confronting, supporting, or intervening, because it would integrate all three of those approaches. Such an approach might be called *intravention*. Intravention is the term coined to denote this process of *coming within the wall* and *joining* the client, rather than *coming at* the client. In such a therapy, the therapist begins work by becoming willing and able to join the client behind that client's wall of denial (as in intervention). However, the therapist's task is to come within (*intra-*) rather than to come between (*inter-*). The therapist begins this process by offering a relationship to the client as an alternative to the destructive defense system and the abuse which attended it. In terms of the three little pigs analogy, imagine two people talking face to face in a room, warming themselves by a fire, and talking about the wind and the howling wolf outside.

The therapist offers something of value to the client, for which the client might be expected to change his or her defense system: a relationship in which the client's needs are met without the distortion of denial. Once behind the wall, the therapist responds to the client's need for relationship and growth.

The image is of leading the client away from denial rather than attacking either the client or the defenses. The therapist offers healing rather than fixing. Healing implies a return to a natural process. Fixing connotes patching things up, making things manageable again. Fixing connotes survival, not change, and could collude with the client's denial system by accepting the non-change goal of feeling better rather than getting better. Immediate relief is not an intravention goal.

Intravention-oriented therapists use a variety of techniques, depending on their assessment of the disease process and the client. The therapist may behave supportively or not, confrontively or not, saying, "Yes, I understand" or "No, I do not understand." The choice of the response is made from an understanding of the denial and the client's relationship needs.

The choice of technique is not a simple expression of the value system of the therapist. Instead, it is a choice to behave in those ways that create and enhance a relationship with each client by meeting his or her growth. The choice is not, therefore, based on the needs of (nor for that matter to any great extent, the personality of) the therapist. The therapist may enjoy being seen as a "good guy," but that does not affect the choice of a response; the therapist's desire to be seen as warm, accepting, or empathic is secondary to the determination of whether or not it is useful to the client to be interacting with a "good guy." Similarly, the therapist may wish to be seen as being "wise to all the tricks," but the style of "not taking any crap" is chosen for the consequence of confronting client's interpersonal manipulations—it is not chosen to demonstrate that the therapist is too smart to be fooled.

The intravention therapy relationship is formed *with* the client and accepted by the client from behind the denial system. It looks, sounds, and feels different from other relationships because of the presence, authenticity, and congruence of the therapist, and because it is designed to evoke those qualities in the client. This process advances with the agreement and concurrence of the client. Often the client accepts the relationship, and feels relief and gratitude that he or she is no longer alone behind that wall. Together, therapist and client work on the imprisoning walls of the client's denial system from the inside rather than confronting them from the outside. With both of them on the same side, clients experience one of the rare partnerships in their lives.

One last word should be said about this "ideal" form of therapy. It is not something that exists only in theory. It is a very real attitude of respect, caring, and toughness that is built into most treatment programs. These days, most treatment programs have several therapists working as a team to help clients.

Today the client may get support in individual counseling from one therapist, and some pretty tough confrontation from another one in group therapy. Tomorrow the roles may reverse. As a unit, the team meets the ideal described above. Over time, though, the client may come to feel more rapport with one member of the team than with another. That is often the person who is most securely inside the wall, the one who has intravened most successfully.

TECHNIQUES FOR MOVING INSIDE THE WALL

There are three general methods of working with a client in denial. The first two (bursting the bubble and peeling the onion) approach the denial from the outside. As such, they can be quite confrontational at times. But as we have seen, they work best when done in an intravention spirit, with an eye to the person behind that wall. The third method (see Chapter 6 on the practice of ENUF) deals directly with relating to the person behind the wall. Taken together, these three methods are the core of intravention.

Bursting the Bubble

When a therapist determines that an individual has a primary investment in one layer of denial (usually denial of facts), he or she may choose to intravene by penetrating this denial directly. The idea is to enter the bubble the client lives in and burst it to reveal the truth. This first method corresponds to what some people think of as a simple confrontation—you just gather the evidence that folks are addicted and then you "let them have it." However, there is an important difference: Therapeutic intravention is not so much a frustrated attempt to convince clients that they are "sick," as it is an attempt to get them to see that there is hope for them in treatment. "You don't have to use that crutch to walk. There is an operation available here and now that can help."

When a denial system is intact, confrontation is rejected or met with more denial. When it has been penetrated, the client responds with anxiety. Two roles played by anxiety come into play here. The first is an internal warning, like a smoke detector. It goes off when one's defense system is threatened (particularly the basic layer defending against floods of feelings). The second is a state of agitation, a diffuse but powerful pressure to "Do something . . . quick!"

An intravener can respond to this anxiety in two ways. One way is to talk about that feeling while demonstrating acceptance and support; this will also increase the sense of rapport between the client and the therapist. The other way is to focus on that anxiety by helping the client find the "right" thing to do about it, that is, go into treatment.

Bursting the bubble is a way of generating anxiety and focusing it on getting a client into treatment. It works well when the anxiety cannot be relieved by escaping, but can be relieved by entering treatment. If the confrontation is not designed to mobilize and channel anxiety this way, it may misfire, leaving the client more defended than before.

Vernon Johnson (1980) has developed a method of intervening that bursts the bubble by surrounding and squeezing it. Someone close to the abuser is trained by the professional in creating a confrontation called a "family intervention." The help-seeker, usually a spouse, initially meets with the therapist alone. He or she becomes educated about the disease of addiction (and co-dependence) and learns how to confront the addict with the aid of family and friends (and, of course, the intervention therapist who orchestrates the encounter). This confrontation is carefully designed to motivate the addicted person to seek treatment. Usually, arrangements are made to hospitalize the client immediately after the confrontation; a bag is packed and ready in the hall. The client's family, friends, and sometimes employers or neighbors are all assembled at once to present their concern and the "hard facts," the evidence of the abuser's problem. Their concern and affection for the abuser must accompany statements made to the person in denial or the result is only anger and isolation. It is necessary for each contribution to the confrontation to meet three criteria:

1. Participants must be willing and able to state their affection for the abuser.
2. They must be willing and able to describe the abuser's value to them and cite a specific way the abuse interfered with relating.
3. They must also express their eager anticipation of a return to a positive way of relating.

If a participant cannot meet these criteria, he or she is not included in the session.

Father (Abuser)   What's all this?

Wife   Jake, this is Ms. Morrow from Central Hospital. She's here to help because the kids and I have something important to say to you. We want you to hear us out all the way before you answer. Will you hang on until we've all spoken?

Father   Yeah, I guess.

Son   You know Dad, I love you and I'm worried about your drinking. I remember last year, you promised me you would take me to the baseball game, but when the day came you were drinking and we never went. Dad I want to go to ball games again with you, soon.

Daughter   Dad, you know I love you. I really like it when we do things together, just the two of us. When I see you start drinking beer before lunch on Saturday, I know we won't go bike riding. I hope you stop soon so we can have fun again.

Father   I'm sorry I let you kids down. I had no idea that my drinking had affected you so much. If it takes quitting the sauce, I will. I've done it before and I can do it again. [Silence]

Therapist   It's an uncomfortable silence, Mr. Wilson. Your family has expressed a whole lot of love and concern. But when you mentioned your previous attempts at quitting, everyone got quiet. Shirley, what does this mean?

Wife   We've seen you do it by yourself, Jake. You're so miserable—just awful until you start again.

Son   We want you to get well this time dad.

Father   [To wife] That bad?

Wife   That bad and worse, Jake.

Father   What is it? What do you want? You want more? You want me to get help, go to a hospital, see a shrink, what? [Gets up and paces; notices for the first time that his boss is there] I can't just take off work. I don't know what to do . . . where to go . . . What should I do?

Wife   I've made arrangements with your boss. That's why he's here.

Boss   Jake you *were* one of my most valued employees. You really blew it on the ACME Wire job. I almost fired you when I found out you had been drinking at lunch that day. When Shirley called me about today I thought about what a fine future you could have with us. So I contacted personnel and they told me that we have hospitalization for this sort of thing, and its completely confidential. No one at work but you and me ever has to know.

Therapist   What do you think of his offer, Jake?

Father   You all sure about this?

All   Yes.

Wife   Ms. Morrow and I have arranged to take you into the treatment
      program at Central Hospital.

Father   Now?

All   Yes.

A second way to break the bubble is bursting it with a sharp point, the
sudden terrible piece of evidence that demands a response. Many recovering
addicts talk about feeling the penetration of this point as "hitting bottom," one
terrible episode or frightening consequence when suddenly all their rationalizations collapsed. It may be an arrest, an accident with injuries, or some
terrible loss. They may go through several hair-raising crises, exhausting the
forgiveness and patience of those around them before one event turns them
around. Then again, after a brief period "on the wagon," they may turn back.
The family is left wondering, "Is this the time? Will it last?" Unfortunately,
the family and loved ones cannot just wait for the one event out of many that
penetrates the abuser's defenses. They may feel the need to create the "bottom"
via intervention. They search for the chisel to crack at the wall of denial.
Dene Stamas (1981) has recommended a technique which he calls "magnifying
the pain" to simulate the effect of hitting bottom. This technique is used when
the therapist senses a client has suddenly become aware of some painful
consequences of his or her abuse. Before the client can escape this awareness,
the therapist responds by focusing on the client's discomfort, putting the
feeling under a magnifying glass as it were.

Therapist   How come you're here Joan?

Client   My husband thinks I have a problem.

T   He's told you of his concerns?

C   He begs me to stop using coke and sometimes he even cries. I hate
    seeing him like that.

T   The picture of his pain from your using really bothers you. What is
    your most painful memory of your family's reaction to your using?

C   The worst? You mean like the kids?

T   Sure, tell me how your using has harmed your whole family.

C   Once I was partying with some friends all weekend. It got a little
    raggedy at the end. I came home strung out. I got mad and hit Stevie
    for no good reason. Lately I just see hurt in his eyes whenever I look
    at him. I never want to see that look again. I'd say anything to get
    back their love and respect! But it's too late. Too many broken
    promises.

T   Treatment has helped thousands just like you.
C   I guess actually coming here was more than just talk, more than just
    another promise.
T   It's a start! What's next?

In this example, the therapist is attempting to make the pain Joan has about
her behavior and the events surrounding the cocaine binge very clearly present
in her awareness by focusing on the way coke has hurt her at home, with her
family. Another approach would be to focus on the client's personal pain
about the past or fears about the future. Past pain and future fears dog all
addicts. There is always the specter of loss, sickness, even the fear of going
insane. When there is a new and compelling health crisis, the Stamas approach
is very effective; until some crisis focuses anxiety, magnifying pain will not
work well. It tends not to work when there is no crisis. The dim memory of
last Monday's hangover is not a strong motivation at 5:00 on Friday.

Clients do not have to be aware of the same painful consequences that are
uppermost in their spouse's or children's awareness. They need only be aware
of some negative consequence. Employee Assistance Programs (EAPs) are
great at this. Having one's job on the line creates just the sort of crisis (real
present danger) that mobilizes an addict. It may be more effective than another tearful scene with a spouse because the boss is not caught in a co-
dependent relationship. But the threat only works once. If the boss can be
conned, or says, "This time I mean it!" the boss *is* in a co-dependent relationship. In these bubble-bursting forms of confrontation, the goal is to move
rapidly from the denial of facts to an inner emotion. In the family intervention
example, pursuing that goal accessed so much anxiety in Jake that he was
willing to do anything to relieve it, even go into treatment. Time will tell if
he is willing to stop drinking as well. The confrontation is structured so that
the best option for Jake to bind his current anxiety is to go into treatment. "I
had to do something and the only thing left to do was to go to the hospital."
Jake, who is still in denial, may be escaping to the hospital to ease his tension,
but it will be much harder for him to maintain his denial there than it was for
him to do it at home.

One last but vital point should be made about bursting the bubble. It does
not do away permanently with the denial. It is only useful to get past a
particular sticking point by creating a crisis that demands a new form of
response (in this case, entering treatment). Once in treatment two things must
happen: Someone must develop rapport with the client and enter within the

wall, and the walls around the problem must be dismantled so that acceptance of the disease can generate a new, more adaptive response. Even though the client has come into treatment, the denial must still be dealt with.

Peeling the Denial Onion

When the therapist feels that the user's denial system is strong at all levels, or is not sure at what level the sturdiest protection exists, denial can be peeled back one layer at a time. The advantage of this strategy is that it provides ample time to establish a relationship with the user behind the wall of denial. The relationship is a force for growth from within, rather than an attack from without. The analogy of the flowering of a rose, rather than the peeling of an onion, might be useful. The rose opens one petal at a time. The process is gentler, and comes from the inside out. Flowering smells better too. Then again, the flowering analogy misses the connotation of spilt tears in the onion analogy.

In treatment the denial onion is peeled one layer at a time to ensure that the therapist can be present and offer a relationship to the client in lieu of the protection he or she has been using. Then, if the client's denial system should break, the client already has an alternative of value—the therapeutic relationship—on which to rely. Also, by proceeding carefully and documenting each breakthrough, the therapist can take steps to guarantee that the material that had previously been denied does not slip back behind the wall and become lost to awareness.

When bubble-bursting strategies are used to get a client into treatment, the client-therapist relationship is somewhat different from the rapport-based relationship that is established in formal treatment. The therapist in the family intervention example above does not have a therapeutic relationship with Jake. This method does not allow enough time to build such a relationship. The therapist relies instead on the power of the relationship between Jake and his family and his boss. These relationships are accessed by having each participant in the intervention begin by making a strong assertion of his or her concern. The therapeutic relationship with Jake is just beginning. Jake has had an opportunity to observe the way the therapist relates to his family and boss. He has also had an opportunity to experience the way the therapist has been present, and responded in a nonjudgmental way to his distress. The therapist also relies on the immediate entrance of Jake into the program to protect against the reassertion of his denial. Rapport has already been established with

Jake's wife and will be utilized in further work on her co-dependency issues. The plan of action for dealing with each layer of denial is summarized in Table 5.1.

PEELING BACK THE DENIAL OF FACTS

The plan of action for responding to the denial of facts is to collect more data about the problem at one time and in one place than can be dismissed. This is done during the intake and history-taking process. The client meets with intake workers, social workers, counselors, and other clients. Depending on the kind of program, the client may also undergo a thorough physical, psychological testing, lab tests, etc. The family members are interviewed. Employers, coworkers, and friends may be contacted, The staff gathers many behavioral observations from a variety of sources (including family, friends, work rec-

Table 5.1
Methods for Intravening on Denial

Layer of Denial	Example	Plan of Action
Denial of Facts	"I have not been drinking." "You have no right to accuse me." "That's not true!"	First gather observations of behavior from many sources, then present to the client without drawing conclusions.
Denial of Implications	"I only smoke pot." "Sure I like to drink, but that doesn't make me an alcoholic."	Provide client with experts to inform and educate about the disease concept. Provide lectures of education groups run by professionals.
Denial of Change	"Hey, no problem. I can handle things like this." "I'll try to stop."	Require client to perform recovery tasks and process resistance by exploring alternatives and choices.
Denial of Feelings	"It doesn't bother me." "If you let yourself feel stuff like that, you could make yourself nuts."	Support the client by using empathic, accepting, "feeling"-oriented responses (see practice of ENUF p. 154)

ords, and medical/psychological evaluations). These are then presented objectively to the client, without criticism, blame, and without drawing any conclusions. The search is for data, and the data are presented to the client for verification. Initially, the therapist will stick to the data the client has validated. The client may still be covering up or minimizing other data, but the focus will stay on what he or she has verified. If the case for addiction can be made on accepted data, then the hidden data (which will be more conclusive) can be picked up later.

Therapist Jake, your boss says you missed three days this month, all of them Mondays.

Client No, it was just two [thinking to himself, "God I hope he didn't mention the ACME Wire deal, or that stink about the phony expense reports!"].

T Okay two.

C The other Monday was last month.

T Okay, three Mondays in two months. Anything else?

C Well, I do have to drink with customers, sometimes, you know.

T What problems has that caused? [Notice the assumption that of course there have been problems.]

C Well, I guess my boss already told you about the ACME thing.

T You tell me *how drinking* was involved.

Two points in fact gathering are imperative. First of all, the incidents to be investigated must be related directly to the abuse itself. The target is the abuse, not the abuser; the addiction, not the addict. This is not the time to confront the client on table manners or insensitivity to in-laws. The therapist may ask clients if certain behavior occurs even if they have not been abusing. This question can reassure the client that the focus is on the negative effects of the abuse, not a personal attack on the user.

Second, the questions must come from a genuine concern for the client. By the time the family seeks intervention, most users are hiding a substantial amount of embarrassment or even shame and guilt. It is important to avoid gathering the data to force these feelings into public scrutiny. This could just strengthen the defenses such strong feelings require. It is not necessary to uncover all the client's dark secrets at the beginning of treatment. Their revelation will be part of the healing, but later, when it is safe. For example, the therapist may find out while taking a client's history that the client had blackouts and use this to help establish the diagnosis. Later, the therapist (following Stamas) might give the client an assignment to talk about his *most painful* blackout in group therapy.

Data gathering (as in family intervention) is not a witch hunt, nor are the participants there to do harm or exert their power over the client capriciously. They can only be there if they care about the abuser and need to tell him or her about the consequences of the abuse. The main reason for doing the confrontation in a spirit of love is obvious: The addict needs to know the truth, not defend against it. Somewhat less obvious is the possibility that should the user claim to be attacked, treated unfairly, or even plotted against, therapists who have allowed punitive or judgmental attitudes to affect the confrontation may be sidetracked into defending their own behavior.

The data are gathered in an objective way without making any moral judgments or drawing any conclusions. When people are in denial of facts, they behave as if no data exist to support the existence of addiction. It is impossible to persuade addicts to accept their addiction when they have not accepted the data on which that conclusion is based. There is no such thing as facing the "fact" of being an addict, because it is not a fact, but a conclusion. You cannot deal with denial of implications while the client is still in denial of facts. The family may see the addiction as a truth, and in that sense it is a "fact," but that "fact" is not data. It is a conclusion or abstraction based on a set of observations. Those observations are the facts. Some of these facts must be agreed upon by the client before any conclusion can be reached. In a court of law, an elaborate procedure exists so that the opposing sides agree about the evidence before it is submitted to the jury. They do not agree on what the evidence proves, only that it exists. The first step in intervening on denial is to assemble the observations upon which to base a conclusion of addiction.

As we have seen, the data gathering part of treatment is aimed at more than simple history taking. It is designed to bridge the client's denial system. It is true of the whole assessment and diagnostic process. The evaluation of a client actually involves four overlapping steps. The first is the gathering of the data. This stage confronts the client's denial of facts. The second is the professional evaluation of that data and the formation of the initial treatment plan. The third is the presentation of the conclusion or diagnosis to the client. These middle two stages begin the confrontation of the client's denial of implications. The fourth is the presentation of the treatment plan to the client. The fourth stage confronts the client's denial of change.

PEELING BACK DENIAL OF IMPLICATIONS

When an irrefutable set of facts validating the diagnosis of addiction has been established, the client and the therapist are ready to deal with the next layer of the onion, denial of implications. Inexperienced therapists are often tempted to reach the conclusion for clients rather than along with them. "Don't you see what this means? You're an addict!" This conclusion is best reached, however, by the client. As the old English observation goes, "A man convinced against his will is of the same opinion still." The task is to find the arguments that are compelling to the user. What will convince this client?

This task is best accomplished by an "independent expert" rather than someone close to the client or someone doing the initial confrontation of denial of facts. This therapist engages clients in the discovery that they have a disease and in learning about their disease. It is a two-stage process: first, the joint discovery, then, the intense study. Compare, for the moment, what happens in the early stages of the treatment of heart disease or cancer. All the test results are assembled and the conclusion shared with the client. Often, the client becomes very curious about his condition and asks for reading material to learn more about it. Some become quite sophisticated. They want to be on the cutting edge (so to speak) of the latest theories and techniques. Others want to get as far away from thinking about it as possible; they go into denial.

Structured addiction treatment programs (such as intensive outpatient and traditional inpatient programs) typically have a schedule of the topics to be discussed and the goals to be accomplished in each individual or group counseling session. Many of these goals relate directly to denial. First the data-gathering session takes place, then the staffing of the treatment team occurs, and then a separate feedback session, in which the treatment plan is presented to the client and discussed, is scheduled. Again, it is not necessary to end the interview with a formal diagnosis. The anxiety of awaiting "the test results" may be useful. It is often very effective to let clients think about the first (history taking) conference for a while and then ask them what conclusion *they* drew from the discussion. This avoids the problem of having prematurely labeled them as "addicts" on the first meeting. A premature diagnostic label often backfires. If clients feel manipulated or pressured into an admission of dependence, they could later reject it and become more defended than before. While clients wait for the team to evaluate the information and tests, they may be asked to write out use/abuse histories in their own words. The therapist can go on to asking them to note any particularly painful conse-

quences of their use. Did they have any sense of warning about the approach
of these consequences? What did they do about the warning and the events?
The client's version is discussed first, followed by the team's.

Often the question "Do you think I have a problem?" comes up early in the
process. Sometimes it comes up at the first moment client and therapist meet.
Counselors must be very careful in answering this question, because the issue
is not what the therapist thinks, but what the client thinks, and, most of all,
what the implications of those thoughts are for the client. The issue is the
process of denial in the client, not the ideas in the therapist. So the questioning
and answering are part of the process of peeling back the second layer of
denial.

Questions such as "Do you think I'm an addict?" may be a kind of test.
Clients have their own criteria for defining dependence. Some are personal
and secret ("if I ever go to a loan shark"); some are stereotypes held by the
general public (alcoholics are winos). Some of the criteria were changed as
their abuse grew and changed. A client's public criteria are usually symptoms
of severe addiction, certainly more severe than his or her current condition.
Persons who argue that alcoholics are skid row bums have defined alcoholism
in such a way as to allow themselves to continue to drink. The same is true of
clients who "only smoke pot" or "never used a needle in my life," etc. These
criteria tend to change as the disease progresses, so the user can still claim to
be on the safe side of the line—which means that there were several private
criteria, such as losing time from work or inability to abstain at will, which
were passed over long ago.

The best treatment approach to the denial of implications is education
about the disease. Patients can learn about their condition by reading pamphlets or books and discussing their conclusions with a therapist. They can
also learn a great deal by attending lectures on the medical aspects of their
disease and discussions of the progression of symptoms in addiction. Presenta-
tions about the family aspects of dependency (remember about half of all
alcoholic males come from chemically dependent families) or by viewing
dramatic movies about typical life experiences of dependent persons can have
great impact. Eventually, some of the material will correspond to the data
established during the peeling away of the denial of facts. Jake has blackouts
and liver disease. Joan has missed days from her job while on a coke run.
When the medical director lectures about liver damage, Jake may ask questions; when the therapist talks about the progression from use to abuse and
addiction, Joan may raise objections. Later, they both watch a movie in which

the hero of the movie experiences shame as his family physician diagnoses chemical dependency. The hero in the film rejects the diagnosis using the same arguments that Jake and Joan have used. They both can identify with the protagonist's feelings and rationalizations. When they say the hero should have done this, or was feeling that, they will be talking about themselves and to themselves. If they identify with the problem, they may also identify with the solutions the protagonist finds when he seeks help and accepts the diagnosis. After the film and during the lectures they ask questions, argue, object, identify. The internal argument now takes place in public. But this public (staff and other clients) is a much safer public than the one back home or in their family physician's office. It is just a discussion, a debate with an expert. Bit by bit their objections are spoken to. The clients begin to hear their own lives being described as they hear about the disease. Soon it becomes their disease, too.

Patients often report that the education was the best-liked part of a treatment program. It is not as threatening as other parts of the program. The lecture is relatively anonymous. No one sees Jake wince during the movie when the little boy says the same thing his son said last week. No one sees Joan blush as her favorite rationalization is shown to have fooled no one. The doctor is very matter-of-fact in explaining how alcoholic liver damage cannot be achieved by "a few beers after work and a couple of highballs on a weekend." The nurse-therapist is quite nonjudgmental as she explains how the cost of maintaining a drug habit leads even "nice" women into conning family and friends and even stealing from those who trust them. As Jake and Joan learn the definition and diagnosis of chemical dependency, the conclusion becomes inescapable.

Keep in mind that this education comes after the client has agreed to a set of facts. Yes, she missed mortgage payments to buy drugs and had to borrow from her father-in-law. Yes, Jake does drink in the morning. Joan hears about tolerance and learns that she is not alone in her sense that the "kick" doesn't seem to be there as it once was. So, when Jake and Joan are given the disease model interpretation of these symptoms (the symptoms they have *already* agreed do exist), they can convince themselves that they "have a problem."

Acceptance of the disease does not come when the client says, "Okay, I guess you are right." That is what Tiebout (1953) called "compliance rather than surrender." Acceptance comes when clients can put into their own words which symptoms convinced them and why those symptoms were convincing. If clients can only say, "You're right," and are unable to use their own words, they may be "complying" — telling the therapist what they think the therapist wants to hear. No one but the client can answer the question, "Am I convinced?" Many programs use a simple paradoxical restraint on clients in this level of denial by discouraging them from deciding "too quickly." Joan's therapist may tell her, "Don't decide today. Think about it. Talk to other clients, staff, whoever. In fact, I want you to promise you won't reach a final decision until the end of the week. Try out several ideas, but don't make up your mind until then." Of course, education about the disease concept will continue while Joan is "making up her own mind."

There is a very clear sign that the therapist is inside the denial of implications: When the therapy team hears Joan congruently (with integrated thought, feeling, and action) describe her addiction, they will know they are successfully inside this layer with her. This can take a lot of patience. If they think that they are not on solid ground with her, or that she is saying what she thinks the therapists wants to hear, they may give her an assignment to explain how she reached this conclusion to the other clients in group therapy. The other group members will pick up on any denial or incongruence. They are experts at evasion and cover-up. If her body posture is negating what her mouth is saying (e.g., by shrugging her shoulders or shaking her head when she says, "I guess it's true" or "Maybe I have a problem"), they will confront her. Counselors and significant others may be so eager to involve a client in active treatment that the minute they hear something like, "I guess I could be hooked," they are tempted to lay out an elaborate treatment plan. It is better to wait a bit and see what sense the client has made of this new idea. A client who has learned a lot about alcoholism and feels "sorry for the poor devils that have it," might respond to a premature assignment to attend an AA meeting with, "That's really a good idea. Right, and if my drinking gets any worse I should do that. AA is just the thing for alcoholics. If I were one I'd go." Many clients who are confronted about their poor attendance at meetings will eventually argue, "Well I don't really think I'm an alcoholic anyway!" These are clients who were moved from denial of facts into treatment without having had enough attention paid to the their denial of implications.

The second part of the intravention on denial of implications is a dialogue. Patients must integrate the conclusions from their own data with the educational material. They do this by dialoguing with many different people. Some of this dialogue is with the "experts." Some of it is held with clients and others in recovery. The most important work is done with the therapists, sponsors, and others who are inside the wall, the person with whom the client has established rapport. Clients hear themselves talking about the conclusions they have reached and how they reached them. They hear this reasoning out loud, with someone else whose opinions matter to them. Taking a position publicly is more integrating than keeping it secret. Clients can later say that they changed their mind, but they cannot claim they never said it. Even the most resistant clients find that it makes a difference to outline their logic publicly. It is hard to change a publicly held position. To profess a belief one day and change it the next seems erratic, even to themselves.

Many treatment programs place new clients in a special group to work on this level of denial before participating in regular group therapy. Patients stay in this "pre-counseling" group until they are able to identify the symptoms of their disease without denial or minimization. Some clients can do this rapidly and, after three or four meetings, move on. Those left behind may experience informal group pressure from the other clients on the ward, "You've been here much longer than Charley. Why aren't you in group yet?" For clients who are toxic, suffer from organic brain disease, or are limited in some other way, such a concrete approach can be more useful than traditional group methods. Groups can be run so that clients learn to confront each other; clients who cling to their denial can be confronted by their peers.

In the face of the reluctance and resistance at the denial of implications layer, the therapist has two basic options. The first is to persevere, to continue, or repeat the educational process. The second is to identify the barriers to forming that implication/conclusion. The therapist can review previously presented material and ask, "From what you have learned so far, is that true about addiction? Is that true about you?" Such a dialogue is quite confronting and must be done in a genuine spirit of inquiry. "You came to that conclusion the day before yesterday—now you're not so sure. Let's find out why that reasoning is no longer persuasive to you." The therapist knows that the client wants to present the "why-not" argument, so starts with the "why-so" argument. "Tell me what it was that first convinced you." Then, if the discussion reveals that the client is disputing the original evidence that symptoms of abuse even existed, or is reluctant to continue working, the therapist will go back and ascertain that the preceding level of denial has indeed been crossed. If there is reluctance to act on the diagnosis, the thing to do is to double back and determine if there is indeed an agreement about the facts which established that diagnosis. It may be adequate to review the abuse history with the client, or it may be necessary to gather more data and have a conference with others who know the using pattern of the client. Yet, the client may still want to minimize.

The same tactic is used if the client has accepted the symptoms and knows the disease concept, but is resisting the implications of the symptoms. This often happens when accepting the conclusion holds a particular dread for the client.

Client   Look, I don't think I belong here. These others are a lot sicker than I am.

Therapist   You've been comparing yourself to others and see them as different.

C   Yeah, they've all lost jobs, families. There's a lady in here who has been arrested for shoplifting four times. And those awful stories . . . Nothing like that ever happened to me.

T   When you contrast what has happened to them with what has happened to you, it raises questions.

C   Yeah. I'm not like that.

T   Uh huh, thinking about them, thinking about you . . . I'm curious about what part of your gambling experience you're thinking of.

C   I never embezzled from my employer, like what's his name.

T   That's right, you did not [referring to material which had been covered in the history-taking session and are used as facts to establish the diagnosis of a gambling addiction]. As I remember, you had other kinds of money problems. Tell me about how money was handled at your house.

C   Well, I handled the checkbook so it was easy. I would charge something and then take it back for a refund so I had the cash and it looked like a Sears bill. And, um, I would cheat on the grocery budget.

T   How?

C   Just keep part of it back. We ate a lot of macaroni and cheese. But you're right, I was always robbing Peter to pay Paul. There was never enough.

T   Is Peter your husband and Paul your bookie?

C   You know what I mean.

T   Yeah, and you know what *I* mean.

C   Well, I guess robbing is robbing.

T   Okay, that's one symptom of gambling getting out of control. What else have you experienced?

C   You mean the trouble with my husband?

T   Yeah, it says here, he left you last year because you were buying upward of $400 a month worth of Lotto tickets.

C   [Lowering her eyes] Oh, that. That was rough. We had a big fight in front of the whole family. I can't face that again. The humiliation, the "I told you so . . . should have dumped the lying bitch years ago." The whole family thinks that.

T   Did you stop?

C   Yes for a while, but I started in again.

T   Okay that's two more.

C   Right, just like on that chart they used in last night's lecture. "Failed attempts to cut down" and "Gambling a focus of family fights and stress."

T   What else have you got from that chart?

C   Well speaking of my life being unmanageable . . .

This counseling session has uncovered a specific barrier at this level: The client has trouble with her family. She does not have horror stories with loan sharks and the law. By keeping her focus on such differences between herself and the others, she is using the issue as a barrier to accepting her diagnosis. Things are not that bad, the kind of bad that would make her a gambling addict. But her denial is more than "hair splitting." For her, the issue is in the family and the terrible implication of accepting the diagnosis is that "they were right all along." For her, accepting the diagnosis seems like loosing the last shred of dignity in front of her husband and family. So the therapist presses on.

Therapist   Big fights about your money and gambling. Tell me about it.

Client   I think my husband thinks I'm just no good, like his parents have always said.

T   And that's what makes it hard to say "Yes that's true" to what you have learned about yourself and addiction?

C   I don't know how I could face them and say its true. I'm a hopeless bum, just like they said.

T   What would happen if you said, instead, "Yes, it's true; I have a disease, and I want to get well"?

C   Can I say that?

T   Try it out on me. See how it sounds to you.

C   I have a disease, and I want to get well . . . It sounds okay. Like there's hope.

PEELING BACK DENIAL OF RESPONSIBILITY

The focus of the next stage of treatment is denial of change, particularly denial of responsibility for change. As addiction progresses, promises to "reform" melt into the air. Someone or something else is always at fault when things go wrong. There is always an excuse for why things have not changed. Responsibility is simply refused and whatever sort of excuse or cover story that will work is substituted. This level of denial protects the client from the expectations of others. When stress is high, it may even be necessary to be protected from the expectations of oneself. The future is seen as totally unpredictable; anything could happen because there is no blame or responsibility, no success or failure. At this point in the treatment the stakes (and the expectations) are high—getting and staying sober.

Denial of responsibility for change is the primary mechanism for avoiding feelings of inadequacy and inferiority, which may be exposed when trying to meet the expectations of others and self. Excuses for failures and suppression of conscious choosing are at the core of this defense. It is as if these clients have to fail to meet any and all expectations in order to remain safely in denial. They cannot let themselves or others know this is happening. The excuses maintain the fiction that there has been no choice or actual failure. They seem to be proving that they are undependable, that others cannot count on them, and that they are just victims of fate. Patients who are stuck in denial of change can hold off responsibility for sobriety indefinitely, not because they are "willful" or "spoiled" or "self-centered," but because they are scared.

The outer two layers of denial are intravened on by focusing on the think component of the think/feel/act constellation (see figure 4.2, page 62). Intravening on this third layer of denial starts with the *act* component of responding. Clients are requested to act soberly. The treatment program will give assignments directly related to abuse education. The assignments will be an obvious extension of the addiction, which the client agrees to having. Clients are given tasks to carry out, such as writing their use/abuse history and sharing it at group sessions, listing the triggers for acting out, the early signs of addiction they did not heed, calling their employer and requesting a meeting, finding a sponsor, etc. Clients literally and explicitly contract to perform these actions when they accept the diagnosis and initial treatment plan. The assignments are so simple that only the client's denial system could prevent the completion of the task. Thus, if they complete their contract, they will have gained significant material to aid in their recovery. If they fail to complete the assignment they will, quite literally, display their denial in front of the therapist or the group. The therapist can then intravene by responding logically (but not punitively) to the thinking that created the excuse. The confrontation brings this avoidance/reluctance into awareness. It focuses on the think-act connection, choice.

> Therapist   So Ted, How goes it?
> Client   Okay.
> T   How was that meeting we talked about your going to?
> C   What meeting? Oh, you mean the new NA [Narcotics Anonymous] meeting on Sunday. I was going to go to with my sponsor.
> T   Uh huh.
> C   I didn't make it.
> T   Uh huh.
> C   I was gonna go. Honest. Ask my sponsor.
> T   You had the intention but . . .
> C   No *really*. It's not my fault. I had car trouble.
> T   Okay, car trouble. Anything else? [Notice that the therapist will not rescue Ted by offering alternatives, nor will she patronize him by lecturing him on what he should have thought, done, or felt.]
> C   Well, my mother-in-law is visiting, and the wife had the flu. But I'll make it this week for sure.
> T   Let's see, car trouble, visitor, and flu. Anything else?
> C   Not really.
> T   How did you handle the way the car trouble interfered with the plan?
> C   Well it was not starting right. I had trouble with it all week.
> T   So what did you do about that?
> C   Well, I've been using this new gas. I think it may not be good or something.
> T   No, I mean how did you handle the way having the car trouble conflicted with keeping to your plan?
> C   Like I said, I missed the meeting. I could have borrowed my mother-in law's car, but she isn't really hip to this meeting stuff.
> T   Okay, faced with the conflict, you could miss the meeting or borrow your mother-in-law's car. Anything else?
> C   What do you mean? I don't know. I could've called my sponsor, but I hate to bug him. He's a nice guy.
> T   Okay, that's three options: miss meeting, borrow car, call sponsor. Anything else?
> C   What? Take a bus, call a cab, that sort of thing?
> T   Okay, four options including public transportation. That it?

C   Yeah, I guess.

T   So with these four options, three get you to the meeting and one
    doesn't. How did you pick the one that left you at home?

C   You make it sound like I missed the meeting on purpose.

T   Going over it now, with me, it's beginning to sound to you like you
    somehow *picked* that option and got that result. But it didn't feel that
    way at the time?

C   Yeah, it just happened that way.

T   Four options and one of them just happened. No choice involved.

C   Of course, I guess I decided to take a pass on the meeting.

T   Okay, how? Decided how?

C   I didn't want any hassle. I could have done something else, one of the
    things we just talked about, but they all would have been hassles.
    Know what I mean?

T   I'm not sure. You were faced with a problem and what came up for
    you was avoiding hassle. Right?

C   Look, you don't understand. My mother-in-law was watching me like
    a hawk, my wife was looking at me like, "So what good are you now
    that you're sober?" [Silence] I felt crappy. I wanted it all to go away.
    But I guess I did, sort of, but not really.

T   [Looks puzzled]

C   Went away, that's it. I just sat there and watched TV. Solved the
    problem by ignoring it. Took the car in the next day. It was just a
    dirty filter in the fuel line. I'll make the meeting this week.

T   The car problem looks to be handled. What about the other "hassles"?

C   I guess I should have a talk with my wife . . . and my sponsor . . . I
    don't want to talk to my mother-in-law. She'll be gone in a few days.
    Can't I just let her go away?

T   Okay, that's one option. Anything else?

By focusing in a *non-blaming* way on the excuse system of the client, the
therapist helps the client take personal responsibility for sobriety. The denial
is confronted without attacking the client using it. The assignments and the
intraventions continue until the responsibility for sobriety is accepted and/or
the anxiety associated with accepting the enormous impact of dependency
begins to come into awareness. This change from blaming others to expressing
an internal state often starts with the emergence of anxiety (that is, the
warning that the primary denial may not be adequate). When this happens,
the therapist then shifts from a focus on the think-act axis to a focus on

the think-feel axis. The expectation to act soberly and fulfill assignments is maintained. The responses of the client are closely monitored to ensure that a return to denial of responsibility does not reemerge, particularly in the form of, "What do you want from me? I'm so anxious. What could I do?"

PEELING BACK DENIAL OF FEELINGS

Primary denial is the barrier to awareness of feelings. People who are utilizing the protection it affords will not attach feelings to their thoughts or perceptions. They will, however, substitute thoughts, judgments, and perceptions for feelings, or simply report having no reaction at all.

Anxiety is often the first feeling that clients experience as denial's protection diminishes. Their feelings are usually not differentiated—they are often described as global reactions of distress. "How did it make me feel? I'll tell you . . . It didn't feel good; I can tell you that!" The client will not yet be able to say, "Oh, I'm anxious because I'm threatened." They will say they are "nervous," or they are worried about some past or future circumstance. They may report no feelings at all, only thoughts. "I'm curious about how the kids are going to react when I get home. I thought about it all night long. Say, could I get some sleeping meds? For *some* reason I'm having a little problem with insomnia."

Sometimes the anxiety may become focused. When this happens, clients are most likely to concentrate on the obsessive thought or the compulsive behavior. For example, a client may receive an invitation to an important family wedding and talk about nothing else for days. This future event becomes the focal point of her anxiety about recovery.

Client   You don't understand how much this worries me. I have to go to this wedding. I can't get it out of my mind. This business of no more drinking changes everything.

Therapist   There's a lot of tension about this for you.

C   How am I feeling about going to a wedding now that I am sober? I feel that it is the right thing to do. All those people looking at me, waiting to see if I'm going to drink . . . they don't bother me. Why should I be bothered? . . . I feel the changes that will come with sobriety will be interesting, I will be curious to see if my husband will be supportive of this . . . yes, this will be a grand psychological experiment and I intend to remain an objective observer.

T   Standing apart from it seems like a good plan to you right now.

C   Right. Participate, but don't get emotionally involved. That's my
    motto!
T   Sounds like going into the fray under that banner really appeals to
    you.

At this point, the therapist senses the scramble to bind up all the anxiety
and decides not to press for more details about emotional responses. Rather
than interpret the feelings the client is defending against, the preferred response to primary denial is to respond with supportive counseling techniques.
Active listening and person-centered support are recommended. The therapist
and the client are approaching the wall of primary denial for the first time
together. Now, more than ever, rapport and trust are needed. It is better to
respond to such client statements as those given above by acknowledging the
tensions the client is aware of, than it is to demand that she uncover material
of which she is unwilling or unable to be aware. The therapist will first
respond to the anxiety and later respond to the conflict from which the
anxiety is derived. The therapist responded, "There is a lot of tension . . ."
rather than, "You have a lot of angry feelings about being in the spotlight at
this wedding. Perhaps because you are guilty about the way you have behaved
in the past." If the therapist had said the latter, the client might have responded, "Angry? Guilty? No, not really. I'm very objective . . . and I'm going
to stay that way . . . No matter what *anyone* [particularly you] says." The
client is "pleased," however. She is glad to have a plan, because it is a way to
bind her anxiety. At this point, the therapist will stay with this level of feeling
and say, "I have a sense of how important this plan is to you. Tell me more
about it."

The reason supportive responses are preferred at this level lies in the
relationship being built between therapist and client. When therapists are
accepting and nonjudgmental of the client's anxiety, they are more readily
trusted with deeper, more troubling feelings, such as guilt or anger. When the
denial of feelings is encountered, the therapist must focus on building the
relationship. After trust is established, uncovering will be useful rather than
scary. The need for denial is altered in the context of an accepting relationship
with the therapist. This relationship is offered in lieu of the defense. If the
therapist confronts before rapport is established, there is little for the client to
gain by surrendering denial. If the therapist accepts the feelings the client is
ready to communicate, a basis of trust and credibility is established which will
be important when there is difficult material to be faced. The therapist waits

for the client to be ready, rather than force the feelings. After all, recovery is a long process; it is done "one day at a time."

Confrontational techniques work at all the preceding levels of denial, but confrontation is not recommended at the level of denial of feelings for two reasons. The information being blocked at previous levels could be independently verified and validated. There can be no real argument about the liver test or the attendance record from work. The signs and symptoms of addiction are also objective. But there is no way to verify what the client is unaware of feeling. If the therapist asks, "Are you angry?" and the client replies, "No," there is no independent source of data to verify the blocked feelings. One can try saying, "Having all the relatives in the family staring at you must make you mad," or "Changing a whole life without your husband's support can be scary; I'll bet you've got some feelings about that." These responses start with acceptance and move on to ask for an elaboration of those feelings. An argument ("Yes, you're scared,"/"No, I'm not!") will not help. A therapist cannot argue with clients about feelings they claim not to be having; the therapist can only acknowledge that he or she is attending to what they are feeling, which in turn helps develop trust and rapport. The second reason that confrontational techniques are not recommended for working with denial of feelings is that building trust and rapport is the focus of work with primary denial, and arguing tends to polarize the therapist-client relationship, rather than enhance its development.

PRIMARY DENIAL AND SECRETS

Sometimes the wall of denial comes crashing down and all sorts of secrets, fears, and conflicts come gushing out. This leaves clients vulnerable and quite literally defenseless. Their only connection to hope and security seems to be this new relationship. What happens now? Does the therapist accept the responsibility for healing the deepest wounds of the heart and soul, or bail out? "You have to talk to a psychiatrist about that. I only deal with chemical dependency problems." Does the therapist try to cram years of psychotherapy into a few sessions, or advocate stuffing all those feelings back inside again?

None of the above. No rescuing, no abandoning, no stuffing. Instead, the client is redirected to the new knowledge he or she has acquired in all those lectures, discussions, and movies, through a process called *reframing*. Reframing is essentially the offer of a new or different perspective which opens new options in the think/feel/act system. Reframing is used when a client has become stuck in a particular way of looking at a problem. Being stuck is like having a kind of groove worn in the think/feel/act triangle. Certain ideas, memories, associations always result in the same feeling response, and those feelings always result in the same actions. Reframing provides an alternative perspective on the issue which opens up new information or new response possibilities.

The disease concept is the basic reframe used in treatment. When dependency is viewed as a disease (rather than as weakness, immorality, selfishness, or insanity), changes can be made in all three corners of the think/feel/act triangle. Within the think area, experiences and behavior the client once thought of as signs of weakness become identified as symptoms of the disease (e.g., a forgotten fight becomes a blackout; "pigging out" becomes a symptom of a binge/purge cycle). In addition, options open at the act corner. One can do different things about an illness than one can do about having rotten moral fiber. For a moral problem, one goes to confession; for a disease one gets treatment. So too, the feel component of responding is changed. Labeling oneself as "in recovery" generates a whole different set of feelings from such tags as "out or control" or "crazy." Most of all, this reframe opens up the think/feel axis of choice. It is not just that the old framework was "bad," but that the client was stuck in it. The disease model restores choice and with it opens the experience of mastery. From there congruence itself can be generated and with it experiences of the self as vital, insightful, etc.

The disease concept is used so that the therapist does not break the bond that he or she is forming with the client. For this bond to have its healing power, the therapist must not retreat into his or her own denial or encourage such retreat by the client. Ignoring painful issues would be such a retreat. A sudden referral to another therapist (particularly a "shrink") would be abandoning the relationship. It would send a potentially harmful message to the client. Reframing into the disease model maintains the relationship and puts "psychological" problems, such as depression, low self-esteem, anxiety, etc., into a perspective they can both use. The reframing works both ways. The problem is redefined in terms of the disease, and the disease is redefined in terms of the problem. The focus stays on recovery. The partnership is preserved. Aside from preserving the relationship, there are two good reasons for using this type of reframing at this point in treatment. The first is that progress on the "problem" will require a stable sobriety. It is usually recommended that a client have at least a year of sobriety before entering into intensive psychotherapy. The second reason is that success with recovery provides tangible proof to the client that he or she can find solutions to life's problems and even create a whole new life, regardless of the past.

The therapist can help the client reconceptualize even apparently unrelated problems by reframing the disease concept. The therapist opens up the think/feel/act system by linking the old feelings or the old behavior to the new thought—disease. This reframing extends the implications of the disease without diminishing or minimizing the "problem." At the same time, the problem is related to the disease/recovery process, which in turn preserves hope for the problem and the disease.

One way to help the client link the problem to the disease is by identifying it as a disease symptom. Typically, the problem is actually another manifestation of being "out of control." The therapist asks, "Would you have done this thing (struck your child, attempted suicide, stolen from your employer) if you were sober?" Usually the answer is, "No. Of course not!" Being out of control does not mean just the things that happen while one is intoxicated; it also means the desperate and reckless behaviors which have come to characterize one's whole life style. Here is an example: A client told off her boss—not at the office party, but the next day when she was hung over, guilty, and not entirely sure what had happened at the party. *Maybe* the event means that she has deep-seated hostility toward authority. *Maybe* it goes all the way back to her relationship with her abusive father. Maybe not. *Surely*, it means that her judgment had become significantly impaired amid the recurring crises of her chemical dependency. And the fact that she went on using, despite such disasters, is *definitely* a sign of addiction.

For problems of unacceptable impulses or intolerable behavior that is reoccurring, there is a similar reframe. It focuses on the thought-act connection of choice. Two things are true about an active addiction: (a) The "high"—intoxication—clouds judgment so that impulses seem irresistible, and (b) denial obscures alternatives. The lost experience of choice reduces life to the horror of compulsion and regret. The therapist says, "When you are sober, you can really choose what to do, when to do it, and with whom."

The following dialogue is an example of reframing and illustrates how the disease concept can help people who have deep-seated conflicts, shame, and guilt. People who feel they have been dogged throughout their lives by a secret inner life often conclude that their terrible pain is an unalterable part of them, a part that can only be managed by drugging it to sleep with food, sex, etc. The drug eventually becomes the only medicine available. Alone in their shame and guilt, they stop seeking alternatives and cannot bring themselves to ask for any kind of help for fear of having their secret exposed. Soon the shame/guilt of the disease is added to their pain. They have become addicted. As their addiction is broken, they are free at last to examine their pain and to explore alternative methods of pain management. The secret and the abuse have become all tangled up in each other. "Do I use because I am guilty, or am I guilty because I use?" While a secret was hidden, the client felt alienated, isolated, and kept from help and hope. Recovery programs offer help and hope, and clients become eligible for those benefits by accepting their disease. They are no longer helpless and hopeless.

> Client   I never told anyone this, but I had an abortion when I was seven-
> teen. It was one of those awful things in a shabby clinic in Mexico. I
> have never felt okay about myself since then. It was an accident. I
> was young. I was high. I have felt somehow dirty ever since then.
> Therapist   Since you have always felt guilty about that abortion, no won-
> der you couldn't see your drug use as a disease. Tell me about it.
> C   It always seemed like something I did because I was so guilty, not
> because I was addicted. Hell, I was probably addicted even then and
> didn't know it. Like you guys always say, "Would I have been in that
> jackpot if I wasn't using?" No. If I wasn't using, I wouldn't have been
> screwing around; and if I wasn't dependent I wouldn't have sneaked
> off in secret like that. You know, all I thought about on the plane
> coming home was getting high.

A secret often seems to be the single most important part of the client's identity. It seems to be the core of self and the final determinant of the think/feel/act systembelieve. A secret is a prison, just like addiction. Rather than argue with the client's belief the therapist may focus on welding the idea of recovery to this old belief. By inviting the client to accept the new aspect of identity and letting it interact with the old one, the therapist loosens the hold the secret had on the client's triangle.

> Client   I don't want any one to know this, but I'm bisexual.
> Therapist   Is that the issue, keeping it secret? The staff respects your need
> for privacy. Who you tell is up to you alone.
> C   No, I mean the other clients, and I guess my family. I'm not proud of
> - it, you know. But I guess it is the way I am.
> T   You've been troubled by this for a long time?
> C   Since my first experience. It made me feel not normal.
> T   Like you didn't belong?

C Yeah, and it got worse when I started hanging out in bars. I didn't fit in there either.

T Okay. So you are "bi" and you have been a "drunk," what now?

C What do you mean?

T You have been in conflict for a long time about your homosexual feelings and behavior. How will sobriety affect that?

C Well, for one thing I'm gonna stay out of those bars. For another, I heard there are even special AA groups.

T How about the other way? How will your sexual feelings affect your sobriety?

C Well, I'm just getting used to this idea of one day at a time.

T How does that apply here?

C I don't have to, as you guys say, "drink about it" today.

6

Rapport and the Helping Relationship: Intravention Behind the Wall of Denial

In previous chapters we have examined the dynamics of the person behind the wall of denial, what the wall is like, and how the addicted person and the co-dependent person need to change in order to recover. Now the question is how to get within the wall and beyond the incongruence that ensnares them. The key element in effecting change is the *relationship* between the helping other and the recovering person. The key to that relationship is *rapport*: a sense of trust based on a feeling of being understood and cared about. As discussed earlier, the protection of denial is only surrendered for something of greater value, that thing of value being a relationship that fosters human contact and growth. Of course, it is not necessary for the person meeting the addict or co-dependent to be a professional therapist. Twelve-step programs have been built on the relationship of the individual to the group (called fellowship) and in individual relationship between a successful old-timer and a newcomer (called sponsorship). Although the sort of relationship offered by either the seasoned amateur or the trained professional have a lot in common, this chapter will address professional counseling only. Since we will be discussing the therapeutic relationship, the recovering person will be referred to as the client, rather than the patient, addict, or co-dependent; and the person helping as the therapist, rather than the counselor, addiction worker, or psychotherapist. Although this chapter will focus on the relationship between clients in treatment for addiction and their therapists, everything in this chapter applies equally to the recovering co-dependent.

AN ALTERNATIVE OF VALUE

For a therapeutic relationship to be healing, it must, first of all, be different from what the client has been experiencing. It has to be different from the reactions of friends, family, or coworkers. Dene Stamas (1981) captured this point when he paraphrased Socrates as saying:

> Do what you've always done, and you'll get what you always got. Get what you've always got, and you'll think what you've always thought. Think what you've always thought, and you'll feel what you've always felt. Feel what you've always felt, and you'll do what you've always done. (p. 38)

When counseling begins, the feelings and the person who has them are hidden behind the wall of denial. Because of the distorted perceptions created by denial, clients often have little understanding of their feelings and few acceptable ways of expressing them. If the client had access to his or her inner self and the ability to express feelings, the client would have been congruent, out of denial, and into the healing process long ago. The ultimate goal of addiction counseling is congruence. To achieve that goal the therapist must first make contact with the person within the wall and use that connection to offer a way out of denial into congruence.

As noted in Chapter 4, congruence comes from performing the existential tasks of connecting the elements of think/feel/act/believe. Getting the client in touch with feelings (ownership) and learning to act on them (expression) in effective and ethical ways (choice) is the goal in primary treatment. Struggling with these tasks yields the experiences of insight, vitality, and mastery, respectively. As these new experiences are integrated into awareness, the distinctions between the natural self, the hurt self, and the adapted self emerge. The basic assumptions about who one is, and one's place in the world (i.e., the core of the belief system) then shift. New connections are forged between believe and think/feel/act. The tasks of dreaming, searching, and committing are approached in new ways. From the new ways come new experiences of the self: attaching to dreams that are better tied to the natural self, trusting one's inner gyroscope for guidance, and finding understanding emerge and are integrated into the experience of self (see Figure 4.5, page 96).

When the self starts to emerge, the client needs the relationship with the therapist, a relationship that bridges the wall of denial to achieve that new congruence. That relationship is the "alternative of value" (discussed in Chapters 1 and 5) to maintaining the protection afforded by the wall. Focus on the relationship as the alternative to denial is the core of intravention therapy. This relationship is not based on therapeutic techniques; rather, it is based on a set of attitudes about relating in general and counseling in particular that are part of the belief system of the therapist. Those attitudes and beliefs must be fully integrated into the think/feel/act/believe structure of the therapist's self for the encounter between the therapist and the client to be maximally effective. That is to say, if the therapist is to offer a healing/human relationship, then the therapist himself or herself must be congruent and present with the client behind that wall.

Vin Rosenthal (1982) used Antoine de Saint-Exupéry's fable, *The Little Prince* (1943) to describe the process of forging a relationship with someone behind a protective wall. At one point in his journey, the little prince asks a fox he has met how he might tame him. "What does it mean to tame?" asked the little prince. "It is an act too often neglected," said the fox. "It means to create a bond." It is the bonding dimension of "taming," not the behavioral control dimension that forms the basis of an intravention approach in addiction counseling.

> "Please—tame me!" he said.
> "What must I do to tame you?" asked the little prince.
> "You must be very patient," replied the fox.
> "First you will sit down a little distance from me—like that—in the grass. I shall look at you out of the corner of my eye, and you will say nothing. Words are the source of misunderstandings. But you will sit a little closer to me, every day . . . "
> The next day the little prince came back.
> "It would have been better to have come back at the same hour," said the fox. "If, for example, you come at four o'clock in the afternoon, then at three o'clock I shall begin to be happy. I shall feel happier and happier as the hour advances. At four o'clock, I shall already be worrying and jumping about. I shall show you how happy I am! But if you come at just any time, I shall never know at what hour my heart is ready to greet you . . . One must observe the proper rites . . . " (p. 37)

This chapter is about those rites and how the fox teaches the therapist.

UNDERSTANDING, EMPATHY, SYMPATHY, AND RAPPORT

Understanding: True Connection or More Denial

The first step in addiction counseling is to establish rapport with the client, and the primary basis of rapport is *the experience of being understood*. As a professional communicator, the therapist must know the dynamics of this experience. Help begins with the understanding of what clients are communicating about their experience; not just what they say, but, more importantly, what they mean. That requires a lot of patient sitting and letting the fox teach the therapist. It also means coming closer with each meeting and pushing the limits of their shared understanding of the client's world. At times, the therapist will question the degree of congruence between what the client says and what the client means. The intention is to *improve* the shared understanding of the client's experience, not to *correct* the client's experience, grammar, or presentation of self.

By the time a client has reached treatment, it has become hard enough for him or her to communicate effectively with the close friends with whom rapport has already been established, let alone with some stranger the client has just met. Fortunately, the therapist has learned how to move from stranger to intimate quickly and effectively. However, as we shall see, more than skill and training are involved. If therapists are to have consistent success in supporting recovery, they must have a particular attitude toward communicating with people, and substantial experience with their own congruence.

Most people trapped behind the wall of denial feel they are not accepted or understood. Even when they are withdrawing within the walls, they ache for a safe connection to the outside. They feel that no one is accepting their experience; rather, everyone is attacking, discounting, manipulating, punishing, or ignoring them. They expect misunderstanding, and they get it.

Aside from expecting misunderstanding, clients may also have unrealistic expectations of what understanding would be like should they achieve it. Indeed, most of us use the word "understood" to mean "agreed with," or "sympathized with." People in denial are often misunderstood. So, naturally, clients have come to expect to be misunderstood. The people around addicts may have become unwilling to accept "agreement" as a precondition of relating to them. "Look, I just don't want any more crap about the pills. I need them to relax. That's it! You just don't understand. I . . . Oh forget it!" The expectation of misunderstanding and the conditions imposed for understanding can combine to make rapport difficult to establish. Those that do accept the rules find that the price they pay is enabling, co-dependency, resentment, and, of course, denial. It becomes a vicious cycle, leading to further retreat behind the wall.

Therapy depends upon rapport between clients and therapists. Clients will not listen to someone who seems not to have listened to them. But the therapist offers a new kind of rapport. It is not the understanding of old friends who have a lot of shared history. Therapists cannot depend on having "been there" to form the bridge with all or even most of their clients. They meet all kinds of clients whose experience differs from their own. It is the therapist's responsibility to achieve an accurate understanding of their clients and to have mastered the ways and possessed the attitudes that demonstrate to clients that they do indeed know what they mean. Whether the differences are large or small, partial or total, the client's need to feel understood and to understand remains.

The addict craves relief and understanding. At best, relief is recovery: release from the prison of addiction; getting better, not feeling better. "My worst day sober is far better than my best day drunk." At worst, relief is just more escape: flight further inside the wall, retreat further inside the prison. At best, the understanding is successful communication: empathic, respectful, valuing, appreciative of the person of the addict. At worst, it is sympathy, collusion, or pity. "Buy that poor bastard a drink on me." Treatment is designed to lead to release rather than relief. It is based on the kind of understanding that is more like empathy than sympathy.

People feel understood when their communication is successful. So the accuracy of the perception of the listener is a key element in this success. Speakers feel that a listener is empathic when they feel assured that the listener has recognized the experience they are relating. Speakers may be hoping for more than an accurate perception of the experience being related. They may want sympathy or pity. They may want the listener to "see it my way . . . tell me I'm right" or even to "help me out . . . tell me what to do here." But those additional wishes also depend on the listener's having accurate perceptions of the speaker's experience.

Empathy

Empathy has been found to be the most important trait in a therapist. Truax and Carkhuff (1967), who did extensive research on the theories of Carl

Rogers, found this to be true of therapists working with a general population of clients. Sidney Wolf (1974) found that the ability to empathize was also the most important trait of an effective alcoholism therapist. His finding brings to mind the old saying attributed to Mark Keller, who, after many years of editing *Quarterly Journal of Studies on Alcohol* concluded that "Alcoholics are just like other people, only more so." Wolf used a very specific definition of this all important trait. He defined being empathic as having an "accurate perception of the experience of the other" (p. 27). An effective addictions therapist helps clients feel understood because the therapist is accurate in his or her perception of the client's inner world of experience.

SHORTCUTS TO EMPATHY

It is easy to confuse accurate perception with actually sharing the experience. Some people feel that the perception can only be accurate if the listener "feels the same way" or has had the same experience. We feel closest with those with whom we have shared common experiences; we can use communication shortcuts with them ("Remember the time when we . . .") to *recreate* an experience. Someone who was not there may find it difficult to understand what happened (let alone why it was important). Think about a wedding reception. Each family gets introduced to the other. Old stories and reminiscences are told. Do they really understand what each other's family is like?

It is hard enough to describe a wedding, a picnic, or a ball game to a willing audience. How will the client share the private shame of the end of a binge to a therapist he or she has just met? How does one get understanding for that? To be sure, many therapists are themselves recovering addicts. Believing that the therapist also has "been there" may help. That way the therapist and the client could use shorthand. "Well you know what I mean . . . you've done coke. You've been there . . . I don't have to spell it all out to you." Yet, that kind of understanding, based on shared experience, has its limits in counseling. First, therapists cannot expect to have had identical experiences with all the clients they meet. Second, the shorthand may allow (or even encourage) the client to leave out important parts of the story. If the shortcuts mean editing, then using them would enable the client to continue being in denial. The left-out details of what happened may include important *facts*. The omitted thoughts about the event may include important *implications*. The things not "spelled out" will probably include blocked *feelings*. Since the goal of counseling is to move the client's experiences out from behind the wall of denial, the shorthand may actually work against achieving that goal.

Moving feelings into awareness is one of the most difficult parts of addictions counseling. Empathic listening helps because the client's own perception of those feelings tends to become clearer as the accuracy of the therapist's perception of them increases. As the therapist becomes more accurate, the client becomes more congruent; and increased congruence is the goal of therapy. That goal can be short-circuited as well by prematurely saying, "I know what you mean . . . the same thing happened to me."

THERAPEUTIC EFFECTS OF EMPATHY AND RAPPORT

Acknowledgement of the addict's experience conveys understanding, valuing, and respect. Its effect is to encourage the client to disclose more of his or her inner world. It can facilitate the counseling process. If the connection within the wall is forced, superficial, or premature, it can have the effect of discouraging the client from further articulating his or her experience. The counseling process is thus defeated.

If rapport is based on matching some experience in the client with some experience in the therapist, searching for that match takes the focus away from what the client is experiencing and puts it on the experience of the therapist. They might end up talking about the therapist's home life instead of the client's. When the therapist is being empathic, he or she stays focused on the client, not on him- or herself. That is where Wolf's (1974) definition of empathy comes in. Empathy does not refer to the personal experience, feelings, or values of the therapist. Its total referent is in the experience of the client. This distinction helps differentiate empathy from sympathy.

Sympathy is a feeling response to another person. In contrast to empathy, sympathy involves an inner response of the therapist. The Greek roots of the word "sympathy" mean to *feel with*. It is coexperiencing with another. It is finding a component of one's own personal experience which matches that being experienced by the other. It is identifying *with* the client as opposed to identifying *what* the client is saying. That makes being "sympathetic" quite different than being "empathic."

When one is being empathic, one has one's attention focused outside one's self on incoming sensory data. Richard Bandler and John Grinder (1975, 1979) call this being in "up time." They use this term to refer to processing external data or current sensory experience. This state of awareness is in contrast with being in "down time"; that is, processing internal personal experience (e.g., memories or feelings). When the therapist shifts from empathic listening to sympathetic listening, he or she leaves up time and goes into down time. This means that he or she must stop being empathic to be sympathetic.

Sympathy: A Mixture of Pros and Cons

Some psychologists define sympathy and empathy in nearly the opposite way than is suggested here. They do this, in part, because most people take the word sympathy to mean "feeling for." That common sense of the word has some important connotations for the counseling process. When a friend is in pain, we offer sympathy. We intend the expression of this sympathy to be supportive. At a funeral one might say, "I am so sorry to hear of your loss. I know what you must be going through. I lost my father two years ago." When this sympathy is communicated, the focus shifts momentarily from what the mourner is feeling to what the supporter is experiencing. "I am moved by what you are experiencing."

As a communication, sympathy is more than a verbal or nonverbal acceptance of what the mourner is relating. Sympathizing involves a personal response from the sympathizer. Communicating it may require self-disclosure. The client may want this support and may even find the disclosure comforting. As such, sympathy may help the client put more of his or her inner experience into words. That might or might not help the counseling process. The therapist is concerned with both the positive and negative ways sympathy affects communication. Sympathy can distract the client from the task of self-exploration. It may permit the client to stop articulating his or her experience further, thus leaving important material unspoken. Sympathy's value lies in centering the therapist on the humanity he or she shares with the client; its danger lies in the potential for enabling denial and in the change of focus from the client's experience to the therapist's experience.

Expressions of sympathy can also create a problem in later communicating and relating. The word sympathy connotes an understanding that protects one from harsh judgments and criticism. One is sympathetic at a funeral precisely because one condones and shares in the mourning. A counseling session is not, however, a wake. When we offer sympathy at a wake, we hope the mourners will be comforted and *not feel* as much, or as badly, as they have been feeling. In counseling, the intention is increased awareness. Furthermore, the therapist wishes to avoid condoning the client's thoughts, feelings, actions, or beliefs. If the therapist condones some feelings, behaviors, or thoughts, might he or she later disapprove of others? "I guess it's all right to talk about my eating problems with Father Paulson. He's so patient and understanding. But he could never understand my affair with the bartender."

Here is another problem. If the client's feeling of rapport is gained through hearing sympathetic expressions of approval from the outside, from others, the client might develop (or extend) his or her dependency on others for self-esteem. In therapy, the client learns to evaluate his or her experience independent of others. The goal is exploration and integration of, by, and for the client alone. The therapist's goal is for the client to know and accept him- or herself, not to explore and accept only those parts that match the therapist's self and reject the rest.

There is no confrontation in sympathy. Sympathy connotes approval or confirmation that the feelings being expressed are right, just, and proper responses to the circumstances (see Chapter 4, Striving for Ownership; Achieving Insight, page 62). When the client feels sympathized with, feelings are not just accepted, they are taken to be condoned or approved of. For some people sympathy also connotes pity—a sense of being perceived as weak, helpless, a victim, or even inferior. All of these connotations are excellent examples of attributions, that is, characteristics arising from the internal process of the perceiver but treated as real traits of the perceived. Both the therapist and the client make personal attributions about sympathizing. Their attributions may conflict about whether sympathy is good or bad.

SYMPATHY AND MERGER

There is another problem with sympathy; it invites a form of relating called *enmeshment* or *merger*. Merger was discussed in Chapter 4 in the context of congruence and boundaries. This way of relating frequently occurs in dysfunctional families. Merger is said to occur when two persons share the same world view with a loss of psychological boundaries between them. Their two think/feel/act systems fuse into one. This co-experiencing can be so intimate and compelling that both parties seem to share a single reality. "He is my son. He wants the same things I want." But with only one system, somebody loses ownership, expression, choice, or all three. The perceptions of only one of these two people are given any credence. Merger creates problems for the subordinated one, who becomes absorbed into the dominant other. Only the dominant person's perceptions are validated; the subordinate loses his or her capacity to establish what is real for him- or herself. For example, a woman worries about her husband's gambling, but she finds herself saying that it is her duty to be sympathetic about his problems. Since being sympathetic in a merged sense means that she should have his attitude about the gambling and not her own, she loses a piece of herself when she is merged with him. She will not be sure of her feelings. They may not feel "real" or "justified." Without her own think/feel/act system she is not sure she is right to have such concerns, let alone her resentment and anger; she cannot own them. She may question if she should say them out loud—express them. She ends up feeling guilty for having hassled him. "After all, he only gambles to relieve the pressure from work." When she merged into his world view, she went into denial about her own. Her set of perceptions is invalidated. Her experience does not matter, is not real. She becomes an extension of him. After a while, she may tell friends she feels trapped, that there are no alternatives (choices) open to her.

In this merged, two-persons-as-one system, each person is *expected* to have the same feelings, values, and emotions as the other. "If you loved me you'd understand" (translated: agree, approve, etc.). For many clients, this obliteration of any difference between "you" and "me" is the only standard for "true understanding." The identification of this total absorption with caring accounts for some of the power of sympathetic responses. Caring and sympathetic understanding (in the sense of equated experiences) have become equivalent for many people. Many people feel safe only in merged relationships. As clients, they will expect the therapist to be merged with them; they expect the therapist to act congruently with what the client is feeling, to merge with the client, to not act congruently with his or her own feelings. Reproducing such a system in a counseling setting would perpetuate this fertile ground for addiction.

THE RELATIONSHIP BETWEEN A "PRO" AND A "CON"

The therapist is the professional in this relationship. He or she accepts the responsibility for walking the tightrope between the positive and negative aspects of sympathy. The therapist is aware of the pitfalls of forming a sympathetic relationship with a client and being "conned" out of confronting the client's denial. By the same token, the therapist brings to bear his or her own genuine presence into the relationship. He or she can, and does, "relate" to what the client says out of his or her own experiential base. He or she shares his or her own responses at times, as part of being a real person for the client to relate to behind the wall. To cut off access to their shared humanity would mean that the therapist was trying to be a therapeutic machine rather than a person.

THE BASIS OF A HEALING RELATIONSHIP: ENUF

After a lifetime of work in teaching and counseling, Carl Rogers (1961) concluded that the therapist is like a gardener rather than a mechanic. The therapist does not actually *fix* anything, but rather prepares a place where change and growth is natural. The gardener does not create the seed, but merely provides the cultivated soil, water, and nourishment the seed needs. The seed dose its own growing. He was describing counseling at its simplest and its best. Carl Rogers was the founding father of what grew into the person-centered approach to therapy. This analogy is at the core of what grew into the human potential movement. Rogers' theories included the idea that one could measure therapeutic success by simply asking clients to describe their real and ideal self and measuring the degree of correspondence and discrepancy. The outcome of therapy could be measured by how much the client brought the real and the ideal into congruence. Research on these theories, some of which was cited above, showed that Rogers' methods were quite successful and that the accuracy of empathy was the most effective aspect of the therapist. Rogers, in the meantime, came to feel that the *attitudes* of the therapist, particularly *genuineness* and *caring* were most important.

The minimum of good counseling is the therapist's willingness to take responsibility for creating a garden, an environment that encourages recovery and growth. The task is to do this without co-opting the client's responsibility. Ideally, there is no other purpose for that environment. It is just a garden. The seed does not have to promise to be a good carrot in order to be planted, nor does the tomato have to vow to be the fulfillment of a long-cherished dream or secret desire of the gardener in order to be watered. The opportunity is presented without making a priori demands such as those made by society, parents, spouses, or theoretical preconceptions about the role of client and therapist. A relationship is offered to the client inside the wall of denial and without the usual strings or preconditions. Neither merger with the therapist nor even agreement about values, such as sobriety, is the price for access to that environment. The commitment of the therapist, in the moment, to the relationship, is sometimes referred to as "presence," which Vin Rosenthal (1995) describes this way, "To be present, to be able to say, or not say, and mean: There is no place in the world I would rather be, no one with whom I would rather be, nothing I would rather be doing than being me sitting here with you, now."

This is not to say that the therapy has no demands at all, or that the therapist just sits there and listens actively to whatever the client says. This method was tried with alcoholics in the early fifties and was not successful. There are very real limits on time, place, and decorum. As the fox says, the rites must be observed. To suspend them would be to create a very artificial place—a hothouse, not a garden. More than that, unbridled permission is an inauthentic gift. It can come only at the cost of the therapist's integrity. Above all there must be a real person there for the client to meet. The therapist and the client are not meeting at a cocktail party; they are meeting at a treatment center. They are meeting there because the client's way of living his or her life is just not working. The therapist offers to accompany the client on the search for a better way (not to *direct* the client, which is why the method was once called "nondirective"). Most of all, the therapist wants that "better way" to fit the natural self of the client. This means that they *both* have to discover that self. By staying within the framework of the client's experience of him- or herself, the therapist encourages the client to explore and expand that experience. The therapist seeks to understand the experience of the self, how thinking/feeling/acting and believing relate *right here, right now, in this relationship*. Again, that is a matter of attitude rather than technique. Rogers called this attitude "unconditional positive regard." It is the key to being what he called "client-centered." The elements of this philosophy can be summarized in the acronym ENUF. The letters stand for the key terms in the phrase: The heart of good addiction counseling is Empathizing Non-judgmentally and Unconditionally, and Focusing on feelings. The unusual spelling is designed to emphasize that the attitudes of which Rogers spoke are basic to the work of counseling. Quite literally, ENUF is enough. New therapists often ask the question, "How do I know I have done the right thing?" It can be answered, "You have done the right thing when you have done ENUF." "How do I know that my responses are not going to harm the client?" "You know you have done no harm if you stop when you have done ENUF."

Empathizing

When the idea of being empathic is expressed as a verb, "empathizing" is used. If empathy is knowing the world of the other, then empathizing is communicating those accurate perceptions about the other's experience *effectively and in one's own language, style, and manner*. Empathy is not a technique. It is one of the four attitudes in ENUF that underlie the counseling relationship. It should not be confused with a therapeutic tactic of simply feeding back important components of client verbalizations.

Empathizing is often done using techniques similar to those that Rogers called "reflection," by which he meant mirroring, or echoing back to clients what they are saying about themselves. They can see themselves in those reflections, focus and adjust the image (without the interference of another set of perceptions telling them what they *should* see in that image). Over the years, Rogers and his followers came to see that this method left the person of the therapist out of the process. A mirror is not much better than the "blank screen" of classical psychoanalysis when it comes to authentic contact. In the attempt to appreciate what the client means, the therapist will take the risk of stretching *both* their perceptions. The therapist might say, "I hear this part, but it sounds like there is some of this over here mixed in too. Am I right?" The key is in the last phrase, checking back with the client for validation of the description of what the client is experiencing. In reserving the right to push the limits, the therapist also models the *client's* right to push the limits of his or her old perceptions, to try new ones, and to find the "aha" of congruence.

For many people, reflecting is a technique associated with "active listening." It denotes being involved, actively processing what the other person is saying, and repeating key phrases to demonstrate attention and involvement. The key to effective emphasizing is the *attitude* of the therapist, not what the therapist says or does. The therapist might summarize five minutes of conversation, just nod, or say "uh-huh." The nonverbal cues communicate, "I'm following what you are saying." The therapist might say, "I'm trying to understand . . . this is clearly important to you. Let me see if I get it . . . " Whether it is said directly or indirectly, the important point is the attitude, the commitment to understanding the thoughts, feelings, actions, and beliefs forming the experimental framework of the client. Therapy is no longer limited to pure reflection. It is a process, a dialogue in which the therapist utilizes his or her own language and experience.

Empathizing is, thus, a very active process that requires the therapist to be fully engaged and present. It is the concerted effort to both gain an accurate perception of the client's experience, and to check out the accuracy of that perception. By using their own words, style, and manner, therapists are required to bring all of themselves into each response. Because therapists continually verify their perceptions, they are interacting with their clients rather than reacting to them. The effort and the risk taking of the therapist matches the risks taken by the client. This mutual risk taking makes the relationship authentic and, thereby, a thing of value.

Without the attitude of ENUF, reflecting is at best a technique, and at worst a cheap conversational gambit. Without this attitude, reflecting is a "cookbook" response, not a relationship-building tool. The technique of reflecting (or for that matter *any* counseling technique) can come across to the client as a kind of wooden or mechanical response, parroting (or worse, mocking) what the client says. All technique and no concern. To avoid this pitfall, the therapist repeats what the client says, but uses his or her *own words*, always striving for accuracy. By using his or her own words, the therapist shows the active involvement that is critical to understanding. It also makes the conversation a dialogue rather than a monologue punctuated with a few nods and grunts. More than that it expresses the person of the therapist and invites the person of the client out from behind the wall. That in turn makes the goal of clarity and accuracy a joint process. In the following example, both the client and the therapist (for clarity referred to as Therapist or T) discover together the nature of the experience that the client was calling "irritating."

Client   My brother-in-law came along with my wife for a visit last night. Boy he really irritates me.
Therapist   So I see. You still seem bothered.
C   Not really bothered . . . come to think about it, I'm really ticked off. You see, I really hate it when people ignore me . . . "
T   Uh-huh, not so mild as irritated or bothered. Something is *really* under your skin in that relationship.
C   Right. I never thought about it before, but I just feel judged all the time around him. Like he's already decided I'm no good and he can't be bothered with me.
T   So for you the silence is rejection?
C   Maybe I make too much of it. I'm looking for it, so I find it. I don't want to come right out and ask. He might say, "Yeah, you are a jerk."
T   That's a rough combination. You're angry about what you *think* is going on, and afraid to check it out. Have I got that right?
C   Yeah, I don't know which way to go. What do you think?

In the above dialogue *both* the therapist and the client have come to a better understanding of what the client is experiencing. The offering of an empathic response tends to make the client feel valued. In this relationship the client is not being "ignored"; he is not too much "bother." The condition of worth is a building block of trust upon which therapeutic growth can proceed. In addition to experiencing being valued and listened to, the client whose communications are being responded to empathically tends to participate more actively in the relationship. Bandler and Grinder (1979) say that such effective empathizing (which they call "pacing") leads to four outcomes that facilitate therapy:

1. The client spends less time in his or her head relating abstract intellec-tualizations or stories about experiences.
2. The client spends more time reporting from internal experiences, or "coming from the gut."
3. The successful practice of ENUF leads to increased rapport (i.e., trust, the feeling of being understood and cared about).
4. There is increased willingness by the client to cooperate, listen to suggestions, explore alternative perspectives, etc.

The commitment to be empathic is an important decision. The therapist who undertakes this commitment is responsible for achieving accuracy in his or her perception of the client's communication. The therapist does not deny or set his or her own reactions aside, but *integrates* them into the response. That is why the response is not a simple parroting, but made in the therapist's own words about his or her own experience of the moment. The therapist in the above dialogue started with "So I see." The therapist kept an eye on achieving accuracy—trying to know what the language/experience meant to the client—and found that "irritated" meant "not knowing which way to go," rather than meaning "bothered." The therapist then integrated that accuracy into a genuine response, and acknowledged his sense of the client as torn between fear and anger. For the moment, the client is the absolute center of the therapist's attention. For that moment, in Rosenthal's (1995) words, "There is no place in the world I would rather be, no one with whom I would rather be with, nothing I would rather be doing, than being me sitting here with you now."

We all appreciate getting attention, certainly clients do. It is quite powerful to be the absolute center of someone's attention. If the therapist stays empathic in attitude, no matter where the client wanders, then the client keeps finding that the therapist is still there, paying attention. The client is not being "ignored." This can be hard work; it takes a lot of training, and, more importantly, a lot of experience in *being congruent* to do it effectively. There is a natural tendency to listen for a while and then react, to give advice, offer criticism, ask questions. But all of these reactions detract from empathizing. The job of the therapist is to remain present with the client.

Many potential problems are eliminated with this attitude. When centered in the client's experience, the therapist does not give advice, so he or she cannot misdirect the client. Further, the therapist stays centered on the material which is currently present in the client's awareness/experience so there is no danger of misinterpreting the client, conjuring up ghosts from the unconscious, or generating false self images. This is not to say that everything outside the moment is off limits. The therapist might observe later in the session that some of the client's reactions sound familiar. They have talked before about this experience of being "ignored" involving other people. The therapist may observe that the similarity might illuminate things. The issue, however, is not to uncover a deep-seated hatred of a long-dead grandfather, thereby explaining the anger at the brother-in-law, but to share that the therapist experiences the client as someone who feels the sting of criticism in many ways and that living under its lash is a major component of his experience of himself.

What if the client in the example had wanted more than understanding? What if he had wanted sympathy, rescue, or affirmation that someone else is to blame? These dimensions of the client's communication would have been acknowledged and responded to in the same way as the original feeling. If this client had gone on to decry the lack of understanding he felt in his family and asked the therapist to agree with him; the therapist might have responded by saying, "Let me see if I have this part straight, you're angry at your brother-in-law, and right now you'd really like to have me on your side, somebody to say you're right for a change."

The empathic therapist is a witness, not a cheering section or a critic. To remain so, the therapist must maintain boundaries between his or her ego and that of the client. A sign that they have merged would be the therapist's assuming the responsibility for finding *the* solution or the *right way* to act on the basis of the client's communication. The therapist can respond to the client's desire for sympathy (i.e., support) without becoming merged. The therapist might even say, "I can relate to that awful feeling of being alone with no one to protect me." But appreciation of the client's experience is not the same as losing oneself in it. The therapist might say, "I have a different frame of reference. Yours doesn't work, that's why you are here. You can find a new way, one that fits you like a glove. Let's try."

While practicing ENUF, the therapist will make few interpretations, no criticism, and no suggestions. The therapist listens very carefully and when he or she has comprehended the essence of the client's communication, offers a restatement of it as a demonstration of the accuracy of that understanding. The goal is not to avoid being wrong. Rather, the relationship is offered with an invitation for the client to tell the therapist where he or she misunderstood. "Here's my response. I'd rather take the chance of being wrong, than be dishonest with you. I can't work if the rule is I must never be wrong." Referring back to the client in the above dialogue, he was not "bothered" as the therapist initially said; he was angry, scared, and conflicted. Again the behavior and the belief are attached to the attitude that healing can come from within the client through the processes of clarification and congruence. This view is in contrast to the attitude of sympathy, which assumes that help will come from affirming the client from the outside.

Non-Judgmentally

The sense of self (particularly the hurt and adapted self-images discussed in Chapter 4) is initially learned in the context of a child's interactions with others. Too often those interactions are tinged with shame, blame, criticism, and judgment. Being judged is more like a trip to the principal's office than a chance on *Amateur Hour* or *Star Search*, so we all learned as children to fear being judged. Many people carry the pain of childhood criticisms all their lives. The criticisms and judgments of parents are rarely felt to be constructive. For most of us, judgment by others meant we were going to feel bad and we were expected to feel guilty. Judgment seemed to be a kangaroo court. The purpose of the trial was to prove our guilt rather than to establish our innocence. The goal was to prove us wrong/bad/to blame. Often judgment was meant to prove that we had to obey our judge, and/or that the judge had the power to make us feel bad. We had to feel bad and punished as long as the judge wished us to. We were to see our vulnerability and powerlessness and be ashamed of ourselves. Punishment was part of being controlled by others, and their power over us included their right to sit in judgment of us.

Control and discipline are part of parenting. Parents have an agenda for how children should think, feel, and act, and are always evaluating the child's performance accordingly. In trying to control the unacceptable expression of certain feelings and inappropriate behavioral choices, parents end up punishing both the act and the feeling it expresses. Usually they communicate that some emotions are good to have and others are not good. "Little ladies don't get angry," "Big boys don't cry." These injunctions are originally meant to inhibit the behavior congruent with these feelings, but end up inhibiting the feelings, thus affecting ownership as well. Now an adult (and in treatment), a woman who was taught in childhood, "Little ladies don't get angry," tells her therapist about her reaction in a group therapy session. "I got so mad! I know it's dumb and wrong. I shouldn't ever get mad . . . what's wrong with me?" She is describing her struggle to block the enactment of her feelings. She believes she should be incongruent, but her attempts as maintaining denial are not working. The willingness of the therapist to suspend judgment can be a condition for reducing that denial/incongruence and promoting growth.

Addicted people seem to have a great difficulty with criticism—as Keller said, "Just like other people, only more so." They seem either so resistant to external criticism that they obey only their own rules, or so vulnerable to it that they are constantly guilty and blame-ridden. Many addicts resist treatment because they dread the exposure to judgment (their own or others'). The idea that they are "failures" and that others will see that their lives have "become unmanageable" is intolerable. Some clients simply anticipate that counseling will be a continuation of the criticism that has dogged them throughout life.

The anticipation of external judgment is a great impediment to change, but the presence of strident internal judgment is an even greater barrier. Carl Rogers believed that our own internal judging of ourselves precludes change because these judgments distort our perceptions of our true (natural) self. An unrealistic ideal self is generated. Like the carrot on the end of the stick, it is always out of reach. We get so caught up in self-criticism (or avoiding it at all costs) that we cannot see ourselves clearly. As a result, our self-image becomes unclear or rigid. Saying, "I'm really no good . . . if others knew the real me, they'd reject me" implies that the person actually *does know* his or her true self and that the negative traits assigned to it by others (or self-assigned by the injured child) are accurate and permanent. So all judgments go back to the same place and reinforce the same damaged self-image. The adapted self then becomes rigid, insistent, and demanding in its mission to respond to this judgment. If clients could be in a place where the feedback they heard was not judgmental, they could accept and evaluate on their own what was true for them. The therapist's reflection of feeling without judgment could be the beginning of self-knowledge and self-acceptance by the client.

The therapist is responsible for temporarily setting aside all values and judgments about right/wrong, good/bad. The values are not lost, denied, or forgotten; they are just set aside. When listening to a client, it is only the client's values and feelings that matter. They are not being agreed with, they are being *noticed*. Now two people are focused on those values and feelings. As the client notices the feeling, it can be validated as real, owned by the client, and integrated into a congruent think/feel/act/believe system. Critical responses to the anxiety, and other feelings the client has heretofore screened via primary denial, result in the client shutting down or losing access to those feelings. Again, integration is forestalled. For example, the client who said he was angry about his brother-in-law's behavior might have been told by others in the family, "You shouldn't feel that way, he's family." While that matches what he *thinks* he should feel, it does not match what he *does* feel. Another might say, "You give too much importance to his actions" or "Don't hold resentments." If the therapist said such things, it is likely that the client would respond, "Oh, I know that." Practicing ENUF, a therapist might respond, "It sounds like you really did feel angry at him and, since you think you shouldn't, you ended up feeling angry at yourself" or "That resentment is really hard to shake." With any of these responses, the therapist can go on to say, '"Tell me more about that." If the therapist had said, "You shouldn't talk like that," it simply would not make sense to then say, "Tell me more about how you feel."

The willingness to suspend notions of "should" or "should not" also comes directly from the attitude of being non-judgmental. Feelings need no justification because they are not right or wrong. When the therapist can accept this principle, anything the client says is accepted as an expression of the client's reality. This is true even when the client wants to do something that the therapist cannot accept as ethical or safe.

Client   You know what I'm going to do? I'm going to go out and get good and drunk. What do you think of that!
Therapist   It sounds like you not only want to go out and drink, but that it's real important for you to tell me that, and to hear what I think about it. Is that right?
C   Damn right!

T   Yes, and the way you said "Damn right" I can really feel you coming right at me.

C   I ain't comin'; I'm goin'. I just feel trapped. Like *everyone* is expecting me to fail again, like all the other times. They don't know what it's like to try and fail, try and fail, and then have to try again. No one cares what I feel.

T   At first it sounded like you think I'll disapprove if you sound defiant, not care what you feel. I get the sense that you think I care more about your drinking than about what you are feeling.

C   Sure, why not? Everyone does. My husband said, "If you want to drink, bitch, drink." I felt so humiliated and belittled.

T   Feeling that way here with me now?

C   Yes. [Searching for handkerchief] Hurt and angry. When people doubt me like that, I always feel weak

T   Sounds like the focus in on *them* not *you*.

C   Sure it is. I feel like a freak in a circus. "Just wait for her to screw up; be the disappointment she really is. The other stuff is just an act."

T   I'm not seeing you as a freak. I see a lot of pain, but not a freak.

C   Okay, I see myself that way. My only hope of not screwing up was to remind myself of how big a disappointment I was to everyone. Then I'd get mad and "show them" how they hurt me. Sounds silly when you say it out loud like that doesn't it?

T   The logic might be flawed, but I still hear a lot of self-condemnation. Is silly the right word for you?

C   It's sure silly right enough. I've been doing this crap for years. I mean, it sounds like a ping-pong ball. Hurt to guilty. Guilty to angry. Angry to drunk. Drunk to hurt again. It is a *silly* way to live.

T   Each bounce leaves you bruised. Years of those back-and-forth feelings, no choice, just slam and carom off.

C   Well, I'm sick of it. I can't keep up this way, I mean, I'm really sick and tired of all this crap I'm stuck in.

T   Sounds like you're struggling to find a way out of this painful vicious cycle.

C   You bet I am. Can you help me?

T   [Nods silently, leans forward attentively, and waits]

C   Shit, I *could* go to a meeting instead of a bar, but God I want a drink.

T   It's hard to choose between the pain of giving up that drink and the pain of the vicious cycle . . .

C   I feel mixed up and scared. I don't know what to do. I mean, I know what I need to do. I need to talk about this in a meeting. I just don't know if I can do it. I want to, but I'm scared. I need to go to a meeting.

T   This time the cycle ended in a different place. A scared place, not a hurt place. And you are thinking of taking *this* feeling to a meeting, not to a bar.

C   Hey, how about that? The old bitch got a new trick!

In this example the therapist does not react to the stated plan in any judgmental way. The therapist merely recognizes that the idea has a great deal of appeal. The client's hurt feelings might not have been recognized and owned had the therapist reacted to her "planned drunk" by advising her how not to drink. They might still have made a plan to go to a meeting, but the plan would have started with the therapist, not the client. As such, it would have been communicated to the client as an expectation of the therapist. It might have felt like another expectation for the client to fail. Without finding and exploring the client's feelings, the therapist would not have discovered who the client was "showing" or why. The therapist could have asked what she was feeling, but the mere act of asking might have felt discounting to the client. She might have responded, "You don't think I'm going to drink? Watch me!"

The purpose of combining empathy with being nonjudgmental is to create a place in clients' lives where they have the freedom to feel without the injunctions that have come to surround the expression of their feelings. They need the freedom to explore (own) the feelings and to express them in ways other than acting them out (choice). When they know it is okay to know they want a drink, they will learn ways of responding to that feeling that are safe (e.g., sharing it with their sponsor or other members on their phone list). Being safe with the feelings meant that this client did not have to invoke guilt to control herself. She could *do* something else as a self-enhancing choice: She could go to a meeting. She can get beyond craving. She did, in part, because her threat to act in an unacceptable way was not met with the sort of judgmental reaction she anticipates from her husband. Her focus stayed on her own experience rather than being distracted into the reaction of another. Without a distraction distorting her think-feel connection, she could reconnect feel and act.

It is important that clients be aware of their feelings without the distortion their usual judgment process provides. The therapist does not correct them by making new judgments that the feelings are "normal" or "okay." In the example above, it would not have helped the client to hear that it was "normal" for her to want to drink or to feel hurt and angry. If the therapist says some feelings are normal, clients are left with the implication that other feelings are not; if the therapist is supportive in saying that they have a right to feel proud, and happy, clients are left with the implication that some feelings, such as anger or despair, are not right to have.

Positive judgments are a part of support and sympathy "That's right, chin up. You made a wise decision there. Atta girl. Poor dear." It might seem strange to avoid these in responding to someone's pain. The power of empathic non-judgmental responses is tied to the fact that all judgments, even positive judgments, are an invitation to the adapted self. Praise, as well as disapproval, evokes the pleaser/complier, the trickster, or even the reactor/rebel. "Oh, you like that stuff about my father? Well that's the last time you'll hear that, buddy!"

The therapist does not judge the actions of the client either. The competency of the client in the example above to enact her feelings either by drinking or going to a meeting is not evaluated for the client by the therapist. Think of how dismissing it would sound if the therapist said, "Oh, you're not going to drink so *forget* that!" The therapist might just as well say, "You better behave, if you know what's good for you! You'll just end up here again, or *worse*." Instead, the therapist's reaction is focused on the uncritical awareness of the client's feelings. Eventually, the client herself juxtaposed her feelings and her previous choice to express them. Now, new ways to enact them (going to a meeting) can be thought about. Her capacity for growth and change does not have to be pre-judged, as she felt at the beginning of the exchange.

The therapist might have responded to her assertion "I *could* go to a meeting instead of a bar" by saying, "That will be hard for you." But that response might have been heard as sympathetic. "Oh you poor thing." It might have been heard as a criticism. "How are *you* going to overcome a life of simpering ineptitude?" "How are *you* going to get off the pity pot and finally go out and do something right for a change?" Instead, the therapist just noted that this time the feelings ended in a different place. The way the client expressed this new thought and feeling (in contemplating an action of *her own* choice) was accepted and empathized with, just as previous ones had been. It became another part of the client's reality, which the therapist then affirmed. Whatever this client does now when she is hurt will become more data to the client about herself. She can look at this data directly, without having it filtered through the expected criticism of others. Again, the therapist did not act or recommend an action. We do not know what is best for the client (perhaps she might also profit from talking to her sponsor, or arranging to meet someone at the meeting, or both, or some other action). We can't be sure. No matter how good our guess might be, we do not *know* what would be best for *this* client at *this* time. To be sure, we also cannot trust that the client always knows what is best. After all, if her judgment was good, let alone infallible, she would not be in treatment. The client will ultimately be the evaluator of any experience she has. It is the *process* of these evaluations we hope to change. We want her choices to be self-enhancing. The experience of mastery comes from performing the task of choosing in the context of congruent awareness. The client learns best by performing the evaluation herself, trying out the "fit," so to speak, of a new option into an emerging (sober) self. Developing realistic mechanisms for self evaluation is an important goal in sobriety.

Is there any drawback to being non-judgmental? Can it be inappropriate? The answer to both questions is yes, if the therapist acts non-judgmentally but is not congruent when doing so. If it is just a technique, an act, or a role, it can backfire (like reflection without the attitude of empathy). Non-judgment is not a technique; it is an attitude (or belief) about relating to clients. If the therapist really believes his or her values are *necessary* for the client's well-being and recovery, the congruent expression of that belief is to give advice, instruction, or critical feedback. But if the therapist acts in opposition to those beliefs and just nods, the therapist shifts into incongruence. Remember when you wanted to spend your whole allowance on something foolish and your mother said, "Well it's your money, dear" with *that look* on her face? It was time to change the subject and the plans real quick. The client may notice incongruity in the therapist and react, possibly by shutting down. The problem is worse if the therapist is unaware of the mismatch. It is hard to make progress when both parties are in denial. The task of counseling involves facing feelings, not avoiding them. This is true for both client and therapist.

The suspension of judgment is not the suspension of involvement. We all have run into people who can shrug and say, "It's not my problem, I don't care." They use a withheld opinion as an excuse to act out passively, without regard for the impact of their own non-caring behavior. It is a kind of denial. Some people present the belief that "we should all do our own thing." They appear to be non-judgmental and may have integrated feeling and action but are still in denial. They have not accepted the need to choose actions on the basis of the consequences or impacts of their behavior. Therapists avoid turning the attitude of non-judgment into a breezy *laissez-faire* demeanor. "Do your own thing. It doesn't matter" implies "It doesn't matter to me . . . you don't matter to me." This is clearly not being person-centered; it is being indifferent.

There is also a danger in overuse of this non-judgmental attitude. Any part of the think/feel/act/believe construction can become inflexible, even the practice of ENUF. When one of those elements gets locked in concrete, there will be problems in the other. A belief in being non-judgmental can become an injunction rather than a guide. It can be incorporated as a rigid rule and make the therapist rigid, and thus a poor model of congruence for the client. Inflexible rules on how to behave can serve to cut off the therapist's own feelings. In this way one gets back to judging feelings all over again. This paradox is captured in such prescriptions as, "It is wrong to say someone is wrong" or "You shouldn't say shouldn't." Some therapists become so involved with the N in ENUF that they confuse any decision or evaluative act on their part with the kind of judging Rogers talked about, or that one dreaded as a child. It is not. When a conclusion is reached without denial by the therapist, as the result of his or her own internal process, and is given ethical and effective expression, it is not judgmental. Furthermore, the presentation of a congruent self, someone not in denial, is fundamental to intravention counseling. The therapist cannot afford to be dishonest in that presentation.

There are two inauthentic and detrimental aspects of being judgmental. The first is captured in the distinction between the words *judicial* and *prejudicial*. The former implies an attitude of fairness and a complete hearing of all the facts. One can be discriminating without discriminating against. The latter implies a foregone conclusion and the kind of deafness empathy mitigates. Prejudice is a kind of stereotyped thinking and as such echoes the issues of the hurt child. "This is happening because of how I am, not what I do."

The second component of a judgmental attitude is a false sense of superiority, which comes from the *judge's* adapted self. Judging has, at its heart, a promoting of oneself to a superior position over the judged one. It is a one-up position. If one reaches a conclusion from this superior attitude, it probably will be judgmental, not a judgment. The perspective the therapist takes when evaluating rightness or wrongness of a client's behavior makes the difference. The therapist in the above dialogue can conclude that the client will be at risk of relapse when hurt and angry. That is not a judgment of the client, of her worth and value as a human being; that is a prediction. However, if on the basis of that prediction, the therapist prescribes some behavior ("You better get to a meeting . . . *I* know what is best for you"), the attitude of ENUF will be lost. The danger of judgmentalism has emerged. Shoulds and shouldn'ts (with all their guilt, their power struggles over the right and wrong, their punishment and obedience) are triggers for the hurt and adapted self. It is the inference about self inherent in these demands that is so dangerous. One can say to a client who relapsed, "You didn't make it" and not be judgmental. On the other hand, saying, "You should have gone to more meetings" is more than advisory; it is judgmental.

An additional point can be made here about being advisory. One of the many hats worn by addiction therapists is that of the educator. In many programs, staff lecture clients on various aspects of recovery. In those settings, clients are often told what they "should do." Keep in mind, however, that those settings are designed to deal with problems of denial of implications, (see Chapter 5). One does not deal with denial of feelings in those settings. A medical lecture is not group therapy. ENUF is a therapeutic attitude, not an educational or behavior modification concept.

Unconditionally

Conditionality is contingent acceptance. All of us have experienced love with strings attached. If we want to be liked (or safe), we must please people, be good. Praise weaves very subtle strings. Warmth, love, and praise can hang on pleasing (or not displeasing). It is not difficult to imagine the client who had the negative encounter in group therapy as a little girl. She babysat her little brother after school. Mother came home and said, "What a good girl! You minded the baby. Mother is so proud of you!" For the moment there are smiles all around. Yet, if that is the only positive attention she received from her mother the message is "You are good (loved, safe) *because* you did a good thing," which in turn implies that her *goodness* depends on doing good deeds. Can she ever just *be* good (with all the love that brings)? Will goodness ever be hers without such deeds? Hopefully the baby has it without such strings. Baby just lies there and coos. When baby cries, baby gets held and shown lots of love. When the older sister cries, she is told, "Grow up!" Parents say that they wish little brother could "stay a baby forever." What's the matter with the little girl? Why is she so punished, *sentenced* to growing up, banished from the lap of Eden? When she is upset, mother sends her to her room, to be alone and "think about acting more civilized." For her, love has strings. She has learned that she is not quite okay the way she is. She gets the message that she is not quite acceptable until she does something good. She can earn love by performing for others. An adapted self based on "people pleasing" emerges. The role as family hero is born. An adapted self will protect her from hurt with compliance and emotion stuffing. That self will have a credo based on what transactional analysts, call "drivers," for example, "Try Hard, Please Me, Be Perfect, Hurry Up, Be Strong" (Kahler, 1977).

Some people introject parental demands and become people pleasers. Others become rebellious, but they are no freer of the mandate. Their behavior is as automatic; it just goes in the opposite direction. As adults, clients who learned the lessons of contingent acceptance are very sensitive to strings attached to the counseling relationship. Rogers felt that it was the therapist's responsibility to communicate to the client that the client's right to be loved, to be cared for, and above all to be respected is inherent in his or her humanity. The relationship is offered to the client just because he or she is there. The client does not have to earn the relationship by saying, doing, or feeling what the therapist wants. Furthermore, the client's right to caring respectful relationships cannot be lost. It is not earned through good deeds, or forfeited through misdeeds. To be sure, a relationship can be damaged or lost. Treatment can end if rules are not obeyed. But the *right* to have a relationship, and beyond that to have recovery itself, is never lost. That unconditionality precludes the proposition that this client *should* stay abstinent or sober to please her family or the therapist.

Clients develop fantasies and expectations about the way significant others will respond to their sobriety. These expectations express the client's beliefs about the way strings will *always* work in his or her world. If the motivation for treatment or recovery is to please a spouse or parent, it usually falters. Conditionality means strings and secret bargains. Often the conditions of the agreement are never spelled out. One client may not be aware of her expectations of her husband. She may not be able to put into words what he is supposed to do for her (if she gives up using); how he is supposed to make sobriety worth it. He, too, may be unaware of the arrangement. When he fails to keep up his end of the bargain, the risk of her relapse is great.

By offering a relationship of unconditional positive regard, the therapist has the opportunity to discover these strings, and clients have the opportunity to question the place of these strings in their lives. Clients must internalize their own value for sobriety—to stay sober because they are worth it to themselves, not because others want, expect, or even need it.

Unconditionality is particularly important in working with issues of depression, acting out, merger, or low self-esteem. Such clients are often profoundly influenced by the expectations of others. Some are so sensitive to what others want of them that they seem to incorporate the value system of the other and lose their own boundaries. Others compulsively rebel without thought to consequences. Either overcompliance or unthinking defiance shows a similar surrender of power to others to define one's world. When unconditionality is present, clients can effect change on their own and test it themselves for congruence. In an atmosphere of unconditionality, clients are not dependent on the therapist in any way for their self-esteem nor for their right to treatment. They do not have to surrender denial, stay sober, talk about feelings, love AA, or meet any other condition in order to have a human relationship.

Unconditionality, empathy, and non-judgmentalism are all aspects of a basic commitment to honor the client. This client-centeredness does not mean the loss of the therapist's person or values. Meador and Rogers referred to empathy as follows:

> The term *empathy* refers to the accurate perception of the internal frame of reference of another with the emotional components and meanings that pertain thereto, as if one were the other person, but without ever losing the "as if" condition. (1984, p. 162)

In the context of this discussion, "without ever losing the 'as if' condition" can mean the therapist's not going into denial. One can have many feelings about one's clients and find effective ethical expression of those feelings without resorting to the denial of them. Unconditional positive regard does not mean the falsification of one's true feelings. Nor is it a universal mandate. In the previous distinction between sympathy and empathy, the value of sympathetic responses was identified as being a way for therapists to connect with their clients, to find the parts of themselves that match the clients. Unconditional positive regard is the belief that this connection is a basic human right and possible for all people. Meador and Rogers were clear—those parts of another person that match every other person are worthy of positive regard. This is the bond of mutual humanity. Nonetheless, no one feels it all the time or for all people at any one time. We do not always have "positive regard," even for the people we love. Like love, unconditional positive regard serves as a beacon that orients us, rather than an anchor that ties us down. Like all of the principles of ENUF, unconditional positive regard is not so much an ideal as a frame of reference for the therapist's mission. In fact, the principles of

ENUF are often most instructive to new therapists when they step outside its parameters. They can use its guidelines to identify the feelings clients raise into their awareness and work to understand the source of these reactions. A therapist who becomes advisory or critical with certain clients may be reacting from his or her adapted self, losing genuineness, and thus not offering an authentic presence.

Some clients will be irritating when they do not meet the therapist's timetable for improvement. The frustrated therapist might say, "He's not ready to stop using." Other clients might generate frustration when they cling to their denial. This frustration may be denied, only to emerge disowned and projected onto the client as an attribution: He is "resistant." Faced with uncomfortable feelings about a client, the therapist may be tempted to shut down emotionally and try to find a "good" response for a "bad" client. Now there are two people in denial. Who is to lead whom out from within the double walls?

Again, we can go back to the definition of denial. Denial buys time until safety can be found. Clients have a right to that safety (and yes, even to the resistance they use to protect that need). Denial is basic to the human condition. It is our shared humanity that makes unconditionality possible and realistic. As one old trooper put it, "You gotta love 'em to work with 'em . . . or you'll kill 'em," to which we might add, "and love them without strings, or you'll kill the humanity in both of you."

This is not to say that love and unconditionality are the same thing. One should not confuse that attitude of unconditionality with the hurt child's yearning for *unconditional love*. All our hurt children dream of Eden. They want a magic space and time when there is absolute safety and bliss. Most of all they want the special love that relieves them of all fears, pains, and burdens forever. For the hurt child, adulthood's freedom is just the burden of responsibility, banishment from the garden where "loved" meant "cared for" and "cared for" meant "taken care of." This is the magic love of which the hurt child dreams. The unconditional positive regard of the therapist does not carry with it the magic release for which the hurt child yearns. "If *everyone*, not just me, is okay (i.e., has a right to unconditional positive regard), then I'm not *special* to you. I will only be really okay when I am *special* to you." The hurt child believes that happiness, love, and unconditionality should all cause each other. He or she does not want to "dwell in the land east of Eden." It is not just the problem of earning one's daily bread by the sweat of one's brow, but also the burden of all the difficult tasks in the think/feel/act/believe configuration, the aloneness, the frailty, the uncertainty. Most of all, a part of us protests the aloneness, and decries the fact that bliss is not guaranteed, even by love. The loss of symbiotic bliss and the fearfulness of being on one's own is repeated in all of the subsequent Eriksonian developmental crises. That is why the hurt child is with us always. Some might argue that birth and death are not metaphors of separation; they, like ambiguity and suffering, are inseparable from existence itself. The child is always with us because we, like the child, must struggle with these issues over and over again. ENUF is a breathing space in this struggle.

The U in ENUF is a linchpin. This open-ended positive regard binds together the other attitudes of ENUF. A dispassionate ruling from a black-robed judge is not healing—even if it is fair. Empathy alone, without positive regard, is not sufficient—neither is a response that is unconditional but without the positive regard.

Focusing on Feelings

The heart of intravention therapy is offering a relationship within which emotionally charged topics that have previously been buried and distorted can be examined and responded to without denial on the part of either the client or the therapist. Working *together* with the therapist on primary denial establishes the ownership of feelings in the client. Working with primary denial brings the task of expression of feelings to conscious awareness. Alternative expressions of those feelings can then be chosen. The new choices allow new integration. Thinking, feeling, and acting become congruent, without denial. Awarenesses such as insight, vitality, and mastery lead to new experiences of the self, a new self, a congruent self, a natural self. Therapy closes the gap between the real and ideal self in an unexpected way. One does not, as many people expect, get rid of one's disease and become transformed into one's ideal self. That "ideal" turns out to be composed mainly of missions dictated by the adapted self. Its agenda is be a perfect fixer/pleaser/complier, rebel/reactor/malcontent, or trickster/performer/manipulator. Furthermore, the initial "real self" turns out to be contaminated by false self-images from the injured child. As its claims about one's true nature and place in the universe are revealed to be false, an undistorted view of one's natural self emerges. There is no gap to be closed, only a path to be followed. As one recovering adolescent put it, "I used to be different, now I'm more the same."

To accomplish this goal, the therapist practicing ENUF keeps the dialogue focused on the client's feelings. This focus is maintained by selecting the feeling/valuing/wishing component of the client's communication and responding to it. Talking about feelings, not events, contrasts with working with denial of facts. When the purpose of the interview is to deal with denial of facts, the therapist avoids the discussion of feelings so that the feelings do not distract from the compilation of evidence. When dealing with anxiety and denial of feelings, the focus must be on how clients *feel* about events, not what they and others saw, heard, or did. The reactions of the clients move to center stage, and the therapists' job is solely to identify and mirror, that is, to be empathic with those feelings.

The therapist will, however, stay within the limits of the client's awareness and usually will not ask questions about those feelings. It is hard to understand without asking questions, but getting the details of the story straight in the therapist's mind is not the point. The point is for the client to sort things out. In ordinary conversation, questions can imply interest in the topic being discussed, but they are avoided when working with primary denial and the anxiety-laced feelings which surround it. Keep in mind that the client is struggling to admit into awareness feelings which previously have been shut out. Many beginning therapists are surprised to learn that clients feel as if they are being interrogated even when the therapist asks questions with the sole intention of better understanding. From the client's point of view, a question often implies that the client's communication has not been adequate, that important details were left out, or that the account is illogical and flawed in some way. Specifically, for many clients, questions imply that the therapist thinks the client is lying. Also, there is an implication that more details would help the therapist make a fair and objective decision regarding the matter. That implication is the anticipation of a judgment and does not fit with ENUF. Finding out all the facts makes sense if you are going to make a judgment about the facts or the client, which is not what the therapist wants to do. Questions often warn of an impending judgment, and the client may respond accordingly with more denial. Having "the facts" also would help if the therapist was going to have to take some action and want to take the *right* action. But, the therapist is not going to do that. Again, when practicing ENUF the therapist is not making judgments and not problem solving.

There are two good reasons why the therapist will not get involved in problem solving with clients. The first reason relates to therapeutic philosophy. Most therapists believe that sobriety is the responsibility of the client. Many therapists feel it is bad clinical practice to take over responsibilities that belong to the clients, and so in order to avoid taking too much responsibility, they take none. They leave *all* decision making to the client. They never tell a client what to do. Some therapists help the client clarify the alternatives, but even then they shy away from making suggestions. They go as far as saying, "You *could* . . . "; they never say, "You *should* . . . " Even those clinicians who feel *joint* problem solving is sometimes warranted in treatment are extremely careful about giving advice. A sponsor, on the other hand, is like a coach or tutor to the newly recovering addict. They are instructors showing the newcomer the ropes. They are very advisory, but their focus is "working the program."

The second reason for therapists' reluctance to become involved in problem solving relates to the anxiety that accompanies the rise of feelings in the client. Anxiety is experienced as the need to do something and, thus, can divert the discussion of feelings into problem solving. Problem-solving activity is intellectual and objective—"up in the head." It signals the increased use of denial, which is at cross-purposes to the therapist's goal, that is, to facilitate the experience of feelings. Helping the client find the right thing to *do* will keep the feelings buried beneath the wall of primary denial. Problem solving does have a place in addiction treatment; the choice "to do" is reflected as just that, a choice. As clients become aware of the task of choosing, they tend to become clearer about the other tasks as well. Doing sober activities is established as a treatment modality alongside of working with feelings, and vice versa.

THE PRACTITIONER OF ENUF

The experience of the field indicates that the core of good addiction counseling is a combination of skills and attitudes. Eric Berne (1961) spoke of potency, permission, and protection. Father Joseph Martin (1976), in his film *Guidelines for Helping the Alcoholic*, summed it up using three Cs: competence (training and skills), caring (an attitude of genuine concern, such as ENUF), and charisma (personal strength and congruence). It takes training, a genuine concern for clients, and a sense of one's own personal power to work effectively with dependent clients. In terms of our discussion, good therapists possess the skills and attitudes to work with all levels of denial. This means not only having the ability to work with the outer layers, but also having the ability to relate to the client in a healing way when the denial system finally collapses. In the previous chapter, we discussed the skills and techniques used for working from the outside of the wall of denial to the inside. At each point, however, there was a look forward to the time when the therapist had established a relationship inside the wall. Since that was the ultimate goal, the basic skill of good counseling must be the ability to work effectively with the feelings behind the layer of primary denial. As the denial system crumbles, feelings of anxiety and intense affect may emerge. This is the time clients need someone to be with them behind the wall.

Rapport is the beginning of the client's relationship with the therapist. Rapport is a sense of trust based on the feeling of being understood and cared about. Thus, the ability to establish rapport (for working with feelings), not skill in confronting (for working with denial), is the starting point of counseling.

Skills, theories, and techniques are not enough. That is why Father Martin added his other two Cs, caring and charisma. Therapists are a dedicated group. As a whole, they love their work (despite its frustrations), and they love the clients with whom they work. They owe a lot to Carl Rogers, and those who followed him, for showing them how to express that caring in effective ways. The techniques do not substitute for the caring, but facilitate the expression of it. The same is true for charisma. If therapists do not feel competent and on top of their own lives, good training and masterful techniques will not bail them out of tough situations. In fact, the techniques will interfere with being genuine, open, and available to the client. They may become a wall of professional behavior behind which the therapist is only an obscure presence, yet another person hidden from the client. When any behavior, even the best trained set of counseling techniques, is not congruently integrated into thought, feeling, and belief, the result is a wall between two people; the result is denial.

For these reasons, the ideas presented in this chapter were discussed as components of a belief system, a set of tenets about working with people in pain. In terms of the think/feel/act/believe figure presented on page 96, the techniques of counseling are a set of behaviors which come under the heading of act. Ideally, each element of the configuration is connected to all the others. When those connections are solid, counseling behavior is a congruent expression of the whole self of the therapist. The acts of counseling become an integrated expression of the beliefs of the therapist, because the therapist has successfully performed the tasks of linking act to thought (through choosing), to feeling (through expressing), and to belief (through valuing). Thus, the therapist's beliefs about ENUF guide the behavior of counseling. Integrating this belief system allows the therapist to present a congruent, genuine self to the client and to respond authentically in a relationship behind the wall of denial. That relationship is the alternative of value to the protection afforded by the wall.

Below is an example of a counseling session in which the therapist practices ENUF. It is intended to illustrate how this practice allows the client to experience feelings in the special atmosphere of acceptance without denial. You will notice how the client, Jerry (who is in treatment for compulsive masturbation and high-risk behavior with prostitutes), goes from criticism of these feelings and reluctance to accept them toward better integration and congruence.

Therapist   Hi Jerry.
Client   Aren't you going to ask me, "How's your sobriety this week, Jerry?" I don't see why you guys always question me about SA [Sexaholics Anonymous] meetings. You make me feel like some kind of prisoner on parole or something.
T   You're feeling kind of "quizzed" by my hello . . . is that it?
C   Every time you guys ask that, I feel as though I have to report to you like some father confessor or something, and I hate it.
T   You don't like the feeling of *having* to tell me things.
C   Yes. [Silence]
T   I have the sense of your feeling caught between what you think you're *supposed* to say and what you *actually feel*. Not just with all us guys, but right here, now, with me.
C   I'm not upset. You just make me feel, I don't know, guilty sort of. Like I should be telling you it's going to be fine. Well, it's not! I feel like I've failed you unless I tell you I'm doing fine and SA is wonderful.
T   Feeling like a liar or a puppet if you say the *right* things and a failure in my eyes if you speak your truth . . .
C   God, I'm so tired of trying to please everyone. Even you. Hell I just met you a few weeks ago and there you are jerking my strings.
T   You felt all of that: guilty, cantankerous, conflicted, checked up on, pushed, judged . . . all that from my "Hi Jerry." With all of that going on inside you, it seems like there are different parts of you having different reactions to me.
C   I guess that's what I mean; the one who is jerked is the jerk. I keep trying and just never make it. Like a part of me wants to say, "Why don't you just leave me alone? If I'm a pervert, sex-drunk, then just let me be one, instead of push, push, push all the time."

T   You *are* feeling pressure from me, or a part of you is.

C   Seems like I have failed all my life . . . and now I'm failing at recovery. Why don't you leave me alone? What do you want from me? Can't you see I'm no good? That I'll never make it? You're a professional. You could put me out of my misery like a horse with a broken leg. Why don't you do it? Tell me why I'm no damn good.

T   Somehow, getting condemned by me could really do it for the part of you that carries all those hurt angry feelings.

C   I *am* no good . . . I mean, that's what explains things doesn't it? All those years of family and friends saying things like "Gee, maybe you found yourself this time Jerry." "Maybe this time you got it together, Jerry." "Gee, we're sorry, about the divorce . . . getting fired." All that stuff they said. [Lowers his head and then sits in silence for a moment]

T   Somehow, attempts at comfort do not help that angry part. He wonders when the axe is going to drop, when I am going to come out and say it and end the farce. It's all too damn painful.

C   Just once, I'd like the inside and the outside to match. You know, that's part of what I always liked about the pros. Not you guys, I mean the girls. She's a filthy slut and I'm a dirty old man. Nothing phony, no pretense. We are what we are.

T   Okay. One way to get the match is for *them* to play a role that matches your sexual addict/bad boy. Is another way for *me* to play the role of parole agent to your hurt child? Then the way you feel and the way I behave would match? Is that it?

C   I guess, sort of.

T   Well, that way I am in charge of who and what you are.

C   Yeah, well screw you.

T   Does that make me a "pro"? [Both laugh] Seriously Jerry, can I only be with you if I play a role? Can you be with me if you don't play a role?

C   Who would I be, if I were not a pervert or a puppet? NO! Damn it! To hell with them and all their strings and rules! I don't need that failure bullshit coming from outside me or inside me either. Why should I submit myself to your judgment? Who the hell are you? Who the hell are they? Who the hell am I anyway? I'm not a bad boy, I'm a man . . . *screwed up*, but a man. I can't say I know how to cut the strings. I *do* know I'm sick and tired of wearing a "kick me" sign, being the poor slob everyone else is superior to!

T   Your whole feeling about yourself and me and judgment seems to have changed in the last few moments.

C   Hell, if you can stand me, maybe I can stand myself! [Pause] If I stay
     in that judgment place, *I* treat *myself* like a failure. Like that's actually
     an identity or something. "Hello, my name's Jake-too-screwed-up-to-
     get-straight." Like in the meeting last night I was feeling real dumb
     about the fourth step, so I wouldn't make any comments. But I had
     this question I needed to ask. But I didn't because I thought they
     would reject me or something. I don't know . . . too dumb to take
     the fourth step . . . so naturally I'd relapse. I actually sat there and
     thought about getting laid. In a meeting for Christ's sake.

T   [Nods. A long silence ensues]

C   God, sitting in that meeting, I was doing what I've always done. It felt
     just like the way it was at home as a kid all the time. [Long pause]
     But, you know, I don't feel that way now talking to you. I did, but I
     don't. Does that make sense?

T   What are you feeling now?

C   I don't know. Weird. Like what I'm saying to you is true not held
     back, really me. I can make it here. I'm not too stupid here. I feel
     like I'm into the fifth step right now, here with you. You know,
     "admitted to ourselves . . . and another human being . . ." I never
     admitted shit to myself. Accused, yes. Argued, yes. But admitted . . .
     how I felt. No way. I'm not stupid, just scared. Say, do you put
     about being scared in the fourth step?

7

Addiction and Loss: Grieving and Recovery

Sooner or later, the addict will confront loss and grief. It is an unavoidable crisis. The dynamics of grieving (including denial and acting out) can be seen at several stages of the addiction and recovery processes. Grieving often leads to acting out, which sets up a use-abuse-addiction progression. Trauma, grief, and loss during recovery can derail treatment and program efforts; they often precipitate relapse. The pain of loss calls forth denial, and any increase in denial increases the risk of relapse. Painful losses lead to anxiety and depression, which can activate postwithdrawal syndrome (see Chapter 3, page 30). The losses need not be new. Recalling past, addiction-related losses without the protection of denial can threaten sobriety during the first-step catalogue of the ways the addict's life has become unmanageable, during the fourth-step inventory, the fifth-step admission, or while making a ninth-step amend. Last, full recovery requires a shift to the *pou sto* of the natural self. It is an enormous change in self-image and self-awareness. To make this change, the recovering addict must face his or her inner children and *their* lost dreams.

The disease of addiction shatters the innermost hopes and dreams of those addicts and co-dependents caught in its web. Dreams they had for themselves as individuals are lost. "I'm gonna make it on this job. This time it will all work out." Dreams they had for themselves as family members are lost. "I know I haven't been the best wife, but I could be." Some addicts find, while taking the first step, that they are not going back to "normal" as soon as this "crisis" is over. Whatever they thought "normal" was is now gone. They have to build a life with the reality of their addiction and the havoc it has caused. For some abusers, the admission of the first step, that their lives have become "unmanageable," leads them right to a series of lost dreams. Facing the truth that "all the king's horses and all the king's men" cannot fix it this time, means surrendering cherished dreams.

Thanks to early intervention, it is no longer necessary for an addict to lose family, job, health, and self-respect before gaining sobriety. Still, hitting bottom is just that. You cannot hit bottom without breaking a few Humpty Dumpty dreams. Just having to give up the ego behind the words "I can manage it" is a loss. For some addicts, sobering up means losing the wish to "use safely," the wish to have only the "good times." Some former users speak of the addiction itself as a "lost friend." Most addicts will have to sever relationships that centered around using. Others see that they have lost the illusion that tomorrow will magically be okay. They find themselves facing more and more losses, a life-long series of ungrieved losses. Undoubtedly some of their despair and "self-medication" involves attempts to flee from this awful reality.

The true nature of some of these losses can be difficult to characterize. The fellowship of the program is richer than barroom camaraderie. Jobs can be replaced; second families can be started. We are reminded by Ken Moses (1995), whose work was cited in Chapter 1, that we do not lose things or people; we lose the *dreams* (fantasies, illusions, projections into the future) they represent. For newly recovering addicts, these dreams include illusions about indulging their addiction without consequences, being normal, etc.

The people, the events, even the objects that are most special to us represent those values, issues, and beliefs that are closest to our core. Underneath the deepest protection of our defense system, our inner core attaches to the world outside by dreaming, imagining, yearning, and projecting a future in which those core values, hopes, and aspirations are validated. Ironically, the more they elude our grasp the more cherished they seem to become. The farther away we are from a "happily ever after" ending, the more tenaciously we cling to our dream of getting there.

Loss assaults us, and like the flimsy shelters of the hapless little pigs the comforting, albeit fragile, structure of our lives comes tumbling down. People who are grieving traumatic losses are said to be bereft.* A disaster rips apart

---

*This word comes to us from the Old English word "reave" which means to rob, seize, or carry away by force. Although the use of the word "bereft" in that violent sense is now archaic, I think it accurately reflects the experience of the bereaved, who rarely feel they have lost someone or something in the sense of having mislaid it, but rather that he, she, or it was taken from them.

all of the connections between think/feel/act/believe. This is the "tearing away" in the meaning of the word "bereft." People who have received tragic news are shocked, stunned, in a daze. They say things like, "I feel empty, lost; nothing matters anymore." Their feelings are numbed. The hoped-for future is gone. All future, all hope, is gone. Gone is any sense of vitality, mastery, or insight. Gone too is any sense of guidance, understanding, or attachment. It will take time to recover an integrated sense of self, time to hope for a future, and to attach to it. In the context of grieving, denial is positive and necessary. Denial buys the time needed to identify the external supports (information and people) and the inner strength necessary to reintegrate and reattach. It buys this time, not just by stonewalling, but by gradually easing one into a painful reality. One has a little more time at each of the four levels of denial.

A terrible truth cannot be absorbed all at once. The emotional impact will be hardest of all; unless it is tempered by denial of feelings, it will come in waves and floods. Never is the blessing and the curse of denial so clear. It is vital to the task of surviving loss, but it creates a great vulnerability. It makes it possible to both perform mundane tasks and meet the highest ethical commitments of living. But at the same time, it creates blind spots and a false safety.

As the bereaved struggle to reconnect think/feel/act, they find that the truth of the loss has also disconnected believe. They need to reconnect to some basic assumptions on which they can build their lives. Bereft of the old ones, and without adequate replacements, they wander in a frightening void. The terrible truth of the loss exposes one's belief system. The reality of the loss continually asserts itself. It is always there, always pressing at old beliefs, raising questions. "How can *that* exist, if *this* is so?" Thus, a shattering loss temporarily opens up the system of the self to the harsh light of examination and demands incorporation of today's reality. It can illuminate the schemes of the adapted self and the world view of the injured self. Denial filters that light, so one does not become disoriented and unable to function. If denial does not shut off the light completely, a "re-vision" of self can take place. The *pou sto* of the hitherto eclipsed natural self can be located, and a new congruent think/feel/act/believe system erected. The belief systems of the adapted self and the hurt self do not change. They remain. What changes is the clarity about who one *really* is and what the path of the natural self really is. The opening may not last long; denial can close the door.

This chapter is about the journey from loss to transformation of the awareness of self. It brings together the core concepts of this book: denial, think/feel/act/believe, the inner self, and ENUF. It examines addiction as a kind of grief, discusses how denial perpetuates that grief, and describes how people emerge from it into the light.

BELIEFS AND LOSS

In Chapter 4 a fourth element was added, called believe, to the think/feel/act triangle. Believe was described as the sense we have made of our experience, of ourselves, others, and the meaning of our lives. Our deepest convictions about living derive from this sense of what *has been*, of what *should be*, and of what *we must do* if we are ever to be complete, safe, and happy. Our beliefs set the parameters for relating to others and write the scripts we use to cast our relationships. The credos of the hurt and adapted selves influence and control thoughts, feelings, and actions. The hurt self is forever caught up in its struggle against ambiguity, blame, betrayal, and abandonment. The adapted self has developed well-crafted personae to protect us and pursues its mission with deadly earnestness. Denial protects this mission from criticism and control by others. The natural self on the other hand seeks integration of think/feel/act/believe through the existential tasks that lead to true congruence. It pursues the types of awareness these tasks bring as its birthright. The tasks and the awareness of self are as much a part of its unfolding—becoming— as are the other developmental forces. Believe, in the configuration of the natural self, is connected to thinking through the existential task of searching for meaning. "Here is what matters to me about what is going on and why it matters to me personally." The connection to acting is through performing the task of valuing. "I commit to this because it fits my sense of self." And the connection to feeling comes through daring to dream. "I give my heart to this."

True congruence comes only when think/feel/act/believe is integrated into the emerging awareness of the natural self. The awareness of the natural self is based on the experiences of insight, vitality, mastery, understanding, guidance, and attachment, which derive from pursuing the aforementioned existential tasks. In that process the natural self unfolds. It is fluid, changing, ongoing, becoming, emerging. Most of all, it is not distorted by denial. Congruence cannot come from enacting the mission of the adapted self, nor out of the negative self-image of the hurt self. The adapted self is surrounded by the shield of denial, which precludes integration. As it pursues its mission to protect the hurt self from further injury, it sabotages successful completion of existential tasks. There is no simple word for the false congruence of the adapted self; it is a world of illusion and denial. As Table 4.2 on page 92 indicates, the sense that one is doing the *only right thing*, despite the protests and advice of others, is a clear indication that one is inside the system of the adapted self.

Denial protects the injured self and stabilizes the world view of the injured child, frozen in time at its center. The adapted self is rigid and maladaptive. Successes have special meaning for the adapted self. Its cadre of protectors (the fixer/pleaser/complier, the rebel/malcontent/reactor, the trickster/performer/manipulator) seizes on the slightest victory. Successes (i.e., dreams that come true) prove their worth and validate their *raison d'être*. They justify whatever version of "*how I have to be*" is emblazoned on their battle shield. Failures (i.e., losses) strengthen their grip as well. They are taken as proof that real success requires more diligent effort. The injured self discounts the validity of success and takes failure/loss as irrefutable proof of the truths discovered by the injured child. Denial, designed to protect and stabilize these core beliefs, is reinforced. When it breaks down as the result of a terrible loss, changes in beliefs occur. The soul-wrenching pain that accompanies those imposed changes is called grieving.

Daring to dream plays a special role in the expression of the self/selves. It provides the sense of attachment and hope which is vital to living. Grieving is the natural response to lost attachment. That is one of the reasons that the natural self is never lost, no matter how many times it is eclipsed by pain, denial, and adaptation. When we dream we are vulnerable to loss, but the capacity to dream, indeed the *need* to dream, is central to the human experience and a trait of the natural self. So to is the capacity and the need to grieve, and the capacity and the need to attach anew.

Daring to dream is the existential task that connects our beliefs to our emotional responses. Our fondest hopes for relationships with others grow from the belief system. In fact, dreaming those dreams is the *way* we attach to others. It is *how* we rehearse and ultimately commit to loving others, loving ideals, missions, God, life itself. Grieving is the process of separating from a lost dream. The more this dream expresses a profound belief about self (natural, hurt, or adapted), the greater the pain of loss and the more difficult the grieving.

Because grieving has its roots in the natural self, there is a natural process involved. Three things happen. First there is shock and denial. As the denial reduces, because inner strength and external resources have been identified, the way in which the dream expressed the mission of the adapted self becomes clear. Second, as the protection of denial is shed, the way the loss reflects the world view of the hurt self emerges. This in turn takes one back to the world of the injured child and the primary definition of existential values it found in its struggle with its primal pain. Third, the pain of loss drives the bereaved so deeply into the world of the injured child, that one cannot help but become painfully aware of its values. The bereaved one comes to know the meaning his or her hurt child's dreamed life could have, but this knowledge comes while he or she is painfully aware that life no longer has that possibility. "If only . . . " starts the dream of the hurt child. If only the values of the hurt child could still be true, then life could still have meaning and hope. Without those values in life, life is meaningless and hopeless, and the bereaved is lost. But he or she is "lost" in a familiar place: in the hurt child's world. The bereaved is right back in original anguish; but he or she is there with certain adult awareness. There is an *unresolvable* conflict between the hurt child's value/meaning system on the one hand, and the adult's terrible truth on the other. This conflict polarizes the self. It drives a reexamination of the bereaved's previously unquestioned childhood-based assumptions about life. From this reexamination, a shift in the concept of self can emerge. It emerges because there is an awareness of an adult *I* who sees this hurt self. Thus, a boundary line is drawn between the world of the inner child and the sadder-but-wiser adult. This adult can uncover and reintegrate the natural self, long obscured by the hurt and adapted selves. This process has many pitfalls and dangers and if the fear and pain are too intense, or the pursuit too lonely, he or she will retreat again into the protection of the adapted self and its denial skills.

THE MOSES MODEL OF GRIEVING

Ken Moses (1995) has developed a conceptualization of grieving that greatly illuminates this process. Key concepts of his theory are summarized in Table 7.1. Briefly, grieving takes place when we are forced to separate from a lost dream, wish, or projection into the future. The more cherished the dream, the more shattering the loss. In the end, it is not people (or even things) we lose; it is the dreams they represent. Some dreams are not fulfilled, others are achieved and lost. Some, particularly dreams of the adapted self, are achieved, and found to be hollow. Others, particularly dreams of the hurt child, are achieved and found not to be magical. When a cherished dream is shattered,

Table 7.1
Key Concepts in Grieving

Grieving is the spontaneous, natural, necessary feeling-based process that moves one to separate from a lost dream, fantasy, illusion, or projection into the future, impels a search for meaning in the light of loss, and then guides one to more authentic being, expressed through new attachments that are more congruent with one's evolved, natural self. The process of grieving is driven by the interplay of denial, anxiety, depression, guilt, anger, and fear, each of which serves a specific function. Denial and anxiety are the forces that govern the process of separation from the lost dream, and impel one to undertake the search for new meaning. Depression, guilt, anger, and fear are the affective states that impel the examination and redefinition of core existential values, and prepare one to recommit to the existential tasks of authentic being.

Denial helps one buy time to find the inner strength and external resources that are needed to cope with traumatic loss. Through the gating process of the layers of denial, one is eased into an unacceptable, incomprehensible reality in manageable steps.

Anxiety first mobilizes energy, and then impels the search for viable ways to make the internal and external changes that a core level loss demands.

Depression impels one to examine personal definitions of competency, capability, value, and potency, and how such assumptions shape one's beliefs about the nature of the universe and one's place in it. Ultimately, depression prepares one to establish new criteria for personal worth and self esteem.

Guilt impels one to examine core assumptions about causality and responsibility, and how such assumptions shape one's beliefs about the nature of the universe and one's place in it. Ultimately, guilt prepares one to make new commitments, and to assume authentic accountability for them.

Anger impels one to examine core assumptions about the nature of fairness and justice, and how such assumptions shape one's beliefs about the nature of the universe and one's place in it. Ultimately, anger prepares one to maintain authentic boundaries that are consistent with the natural forces of being.

Fear impels one to examine the basis of one's personal courage, and how such assumptions shape one's beliefs about the nature of the universe and one's place in it. Fear prepares one to face the existential dilemma inherent in risking attachment. Ultimately, fear impels one to search for the courage to be

Transition is the phase of the grieving process shaped by the dynamics of denial and anxiety, and focused on the discovery and separation from the adapted self.

(continued)

Table 7.1
Continued

Active grieving is the phase of the grieving process shaped by the dynamics of depression, guilt, anger, and fear, and focused on the discovery and separation from the injured self.

Transformation is the phase of the grieving process shaped by the dynamics of congruence and the authentic performance of existential tasks, and focused on the uncovery and empowerment of the natural self.

Adapted from Moses & Kearney, 1995.

we experience great pain because a precious part of ourselves has been torn away from its hoped-for realization. Dreams express our beliefs; loss forces us to change how we can enact those beliefs. Deep losses can change the belief system itself. That is how the hurt and adapted child were first born, and it is the path back to the natural self. However, in order not to reinforce the preexisting belief systems, the response to loss must have one element that was tragically absent at the time of the griever's primal pain. There must be a safe place to do the work. The work of grieving takes place *only* in a relationship with a significant other. In this context, "significant other" has two meanings: (a) someone whose opinions, reactions, and responses matter; (b) someone who can share the grief work without retreating into his or her own denial, or enabling us to hide behind our own. The terms presence and authenticity should be added to the description. Although these terms were discussed in the last chapter as they applied to professional counselors, they have added meaning in the context of grieving. The "somebody" one turns to must be "real." Of course, this does not mean that the significant other must be a professional helper. It means that the raw emotions and unbearable vulnerability one experiences in grieving require that one share them with someone who is important and willing and able to share the work. The natural forces of grieving are impelling the bereaved to seek out and make contact with those around them with whom they can do their work. At the same time, family and friends may be repelled by what they see as too much feeling. Often the bereaved are treated with kid gloves by those around them, who consciously, or unconsciously, communicate their own discomfort at the emotional storm raging within the bereaved. The bereaved may be isolated, placated, infantilized, or medicated—as much for the relief of others as for the comfort of the bereaved.

Doing the work of grieving means going back to the roots of the loss, which are in the hows and whys of attaching or committing to a relationship, object, or plan. One attaches by daring to dream. Dreaming is a way of planning to express feelings, so there are many kinds of dreams. A mother singing lullabies to a sleeping infant, or a father buying him a football are imagining a future of feelings. There are also dreams for expressing anger. An abused child may dream of revenge. The frightened and the guilty dream. There are dreams of serenity held by recovering addicts. Dreaming, imagining how it might be, could be, *should be* are part of attaching. Whether one is talking about Cinderella fantasies from childhood, or plans to climb the corporate pyramid, dreams express something deep inside us. Unfulfilled dreams connect us to our future. Lost dreams haunt us from the past.

To let go of a dream means to rework some of our deepest beliefs. It requires—indeed is *impelled* by deep painful feelings. Moses finds that the feeling states of grieving (depression, guilt, anger, and fear) are not only *natural* reactions to loss, they are also *necessary* to the process of separating from a lost dream. Without letting go of the old dream, we cannot attach to new ones, and part of ourselves stays wrapped in denial. He defines grieving as a process of transformation. This transformation occurs because the feeling states of grieving impel us through an examination of our deepest existential values. Following a great loss, our whole belief system is under siege. In transforming it, we transform ourselves.

Once denial has been breached by the painful truth, the work of grieving is driven by powerful emotions. These feelings come tumbling out, and with them, profound questions. The pain of the current loss opens us to the world of the injured self, which is the part in each of us that understands our pain, that finds ways to make it meaningful. Neither the griever nor those around are likely to be comfortable with the intensity or duration of these feeling states, let alone with the awful questions that come with them. Everyone wants things back to normal, even if there is no normal to go back to. If we claim the *feelings* are "the problem," we may even come to pathologize the process, to call it "morbid grief" or "nothing but self pity." If life drops a big rock on your foot, however, the problem is the injury, not that you cried out in pain. If we see feelings as the problem, we may try to medicate, to "stuff," or to deny the feelings, and in so doing, cut off the work of grieving.

A dream creates an anticipated state of real or false congruence for thought, feeling, action, and belief. When the object of the dream is lost, the anticipated ways of expressing the feelings bound up in that dream are also lost. The loss means that the person's inner life has become disconnected. The rehearsed way of expressing feeling has become blocked while, ironically, the bereaved is flooded with feelings. "He is dead. What can I do with all the anger I feel?"

To understand the consequences of this blocking, we must again contrast the effect of having congruence with the consequences of losing it. Until the depth of those feelings is reached, congruence cannot be restored or achieved. When people can find congruent expression for their feelings (in the form of talking with someone they trust inside the wall of their denial), they tend to experience a sense of inner openness to those feelings. There are no denial barriers to those feelings nor to the ownership of self. A world-shattering event can be followed through all of its implications, all its associated feelings, and all the changes in responsibility for action attending the event. The inner constellation of think/feel/act can shift, and the individual can experience changes in feeling tone, behavior, and self-concept. The altered self-concept is based on the new experiences of insight, mastery, and vitality. This new self-image is a glimpse at the natural self and is quite different from that of the adapted or hurt self. Along with these changes the individual becomes able to reattach to newer, more attainable, dreams. The new dreams will be more congruent with the natural self and not just substitutes in the ongoing schemes of the adapted self. Thus, the concept of denial yielding to the power of a relationship with someone inside the wall takes on special importance when working with grieving persons. And the value of the practice of ENUF is extended to its maximum.

We cannot let go of the dream until we can own our investment in it. That means feeling the loss to its fullest. Typically, those around the bereaved will offer comfort and make attempts to ease the pain. We try to cheer up someone who is depressed, calm someone who is anxious, reassure someone who is frightened or guilty, and cool off someone who is angry. The "comfort" is an invitation to denial. "The best thing for you is to get your mind off it for a while. Why don't you . . . " Denial buys time until safety can be found. Denial is a safe resting place, but it is not a safe dwelling place. The griever needs to do the work of grieving; being surrounded by denial delays getting on with it. Instead of buying time, such "comfort" stalls the process. We have seen that change takes place when someone special is with the person behind the wall, who neither uses nor invites denial. Healing the wounds of loss demands that the griever experience someone else's acceptance of his or her feelings of grief, in a non-judgmental way. Empathy around the lost investment ultimately leads the bereaved to the core beliefs the dream had expressed.

In the Moses model of grieving, the griever is not seen as working through the feelings in an orderly, progressive way. Instead, Moses talks about the feelings as "affective states" rather than stages. When grieving is active and intense, the griever may move rapidly from one feeing to another or stay stuck in one feeling for a long time.

Figure 7.1 shows these four grieving affect states arranged in a tetrahedron. The configuration is meant to depict the fact that one can go directly or indirectly from one feeling state to another. For example, a grieving person may be feeling depressed, empty, and worthless. The internal monologue about these feelings may focus on low self-esteem. Ruminating on this self-image can lead to remorse and intense feelings of guilt. The guilt can trigger anger at imagined judges. The sense of alienation from others who judge the bereaved can accentuate his or her sense of aloneness, and bring up fears associated with the vulnerability tied to risking attachment to someone on whose acceptance the bereaved might come to depend, only to lose it through some future loss. Awareness of the yearning for this acceptance could raise doubts about the bereaved's worthiness to attach and bring him or her back to depression. This cycling of emotions is very much like the affective potentiation seen in postwithdrawal syndrome.

On the other hand, one feeling can dominate awareness. To depict this

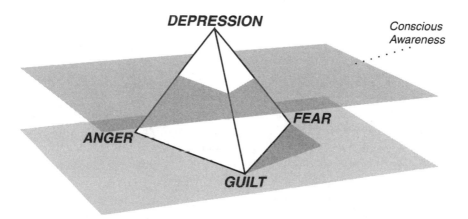

Figure 7.1. The feeling states of grieving.

circumstance, a plane labeled "conscious awareness" is drawn across the figure. Above the plane is what the griever is aware of in the moment. The other feelings are connected to it, and may come into awareness in the next moment, as in the example above. They may not, however, come into awareness, because primary denial blocks them from awareness. It is important to note that all four of these feelings (depression, guilt, anger, fear) are part of grieving. Separating from a dream means that somewhere along the way all of them must come into conscious awareness. All of them must be owned and fitted congruently into the self. Obviously, one feeling may dominate because there is a lot of work connected to it. Not so obviously, one feeling may dominate so as to keep one or more others outside awareness. For example, a rebel/ reactor/malcontent is quite comfortable with anger; focusing on it will keep him or her away from sadness or guilt. The fixer/pleaser/complier knows guilt inside and out, but often fears his or her own anger. The trickster/ performer/manipulator can deftly juggle all four feelings at the same time. No one, him- or herself particularly, knows what is really going on inside, but the show is terrific.

Some feelings are thought of as safer than others. For example, our culture links depression with suicide, and anger with violence. There are often powerful subcultural injunctions against feeling and expressing certain emotions. Sometimes it is a matter of the support network surrounding the bereaved. For example, a widow is "allowed" different feelings than a divorced woman. When the widow says, "He was so good to the children," she may be told by her friends, "There, there," and get a sympathetic hug. If she says, "The rat has gone and left us penniless!" they will hush her. "Try to think about the good parts," they will tell her. The divorcee may get lots of support for her anger; but if *she* says, "He was so good with the kids," her friends may say, "Never mind that, he was a rat!"

The personality style of the bereaved or constrictions in his or her defense system may block grieving. Some people have characterological resistance to experiencing one of these feeling states. Others may have a tendency to dwell on one affective state. People who are habitually angry, sad, guilty, or fearful *before* a loss will find that this feeling will dominate their awareness. As such, it can function as a shelter, or a distraction which protects their awareness from the flood of the other feeling states. For example, anger often masks fear or sadness. If the divorcee mentioned above was chronically bitter, her anger might keep her from experiencing her depression.

The tetrahedron in Figure 7.1 can be thought of as an iceberg. Only the tip is above the surface of awareness. Ice floats. If the part above the surface is reduced (burned off by the sun, broken off by the wind and the waves), the iceberg rises. It does not sink. More comes to the surface, dissipates, and gives way to more exposure. As the iceberg rises, its center of gravity can shift. Suddenly it rolls over and a face which had been deep below the surface is suddenly on top. This is often seen in grieving. When the significant other is empathic and non-judgmental, more feelings come to the surface. In the presence of such empathy, the iceberg effect can happen; suddenly the whole gestalt shifts and a new affective state emerges. Indeed, deepened experience is one of the four benefits of the practice of ENUF (discussed in Chapter 6).

THE PATHS OF GRIEVING

Even though grieving does not move through orderly stages, there is some order to the process. In this process there are three overlapping areas: transition, active grieving, and transformation. The bereaved enter transition when they are first confronted with the terrible truth. Transition is dominated by the dynamics of denial and anxiety. When denial finally collapses, the bereaved are actively grieving. Out of the struggle with the existential issues (impelled by the feeling states of grieving), the bereaved uncover a natural self. In pursuit of the existential tasks of integrating that self, they undergo a transformation.

Transition

When first confronted with a loss, there is shock and denial. Denial takes the same form as it does around addiction. "I can't believe it's really so; I keep expecting to see him walk through the door." "I don't like good-byes; let's just say see you later." "It won't be that much different; I still have the kids and my friends." "There's so much to do right now; getting back to work as soon as possible is the best medicine." Moses (1995) says denial buys time to find the safety, the external resources, and the internal strength to face the fact, the implication, the responsibility, and the feelings about the loss. Although the external resources are often concrete forms of help, such as medical specialists, rehabilitation centers, and the like, the critical resources are the significant others who make the work possible. The inner strength is not some miraculous power which rises to meet the occasion. It is the rediscovery (usually in the context of a relationship) that not only is one surviving, but also that the capacity to do the work of grieving is innate and is taking the addict through the journey despite profound doubts and misgivings about the final destination.

As recovery progresses, and the reality of the addict's many losses creeps through denial, anxiety mounts. The pressure to do something (*anything* . . . the *right* thing) becomes greater and greater. Relief from that anxiety is sought in familiar ways. It may even get medicated. Medicating the pain of grief with chemicals (licit or illicit) delays the work of grieving, but it is particularly dangerous for addicts. The risk of relapse is never greater than when a recovering person is grieving. AA calls this "drinking at a feeling." Acting out *any* addiction provides immediate relief from the tension and anxiety generated by resisting the compulsion. As the addiction progresses, acting it out becomes a panacea; the addict is "psychologically dependent" (see Chapter 3). The relief is, of course, replaced by more anxiety. Now there is the problem of what one has just done, and there is usually a flood of remorse and waves of self-recrimination, self-deception, and self-deprecation. These pains set up another round of compulsivity and impulsivity.

Even if the pain of anxiety is not medicated by relapse into a previous addiction, relief is sought in various ways. The alarm spoken of in Chapter 3 (p. 52) gets louder and louder. Anxiety is a response to the impending collapse of denial's protection. This is why Moses (1995) calls denial and anxiety "preparatory" forces in the grieving dynamic. They work together to accomplish a very important goal, namely, an understanding of the role played by the adapted self and an awareness that its mission, protection, and core-level dreams have been shattered. The louder the alarm of anxiety screams, the more frantically we try to fix, comply, or do "good." The more insistently it shouts, the more earnestly we trick, manipulate, and perform. The more it says disaster is coming, the more we rebel.

Anxiety first mobilizes energy to try harder to solve the unsolvable problem of loss. This makes us try the old ways. When they do not work, we try harder, and become an unvarnished version of our adapted selves. Still the anxiety mounts. "It's not working. It's not working! *It's not working!!*" At some point, the energy of the anxiety focuses down on, and impels one into, a terrible realization. The *it* that is not working is the whole structure of the adapted self.

While the twin forces of denial and anxiety are exposing our "act" to us and those around us, we experience a series of "threshold moments" (Moses & Kearney, 1995). These thresholds are accompanied by feelings of anxiety, panic, and dread, mixed with embarrassment, humiliation, and shame. They range from a momentary "Uh-oh" to the profound "Oh my God." These thresholds are the moments when one catches a glimpse of one's adapted self running the show, and one senses the burgeoning awareness that one can no longer sustain this way of life. The first uh-oh opens a crack in the carefully constructed universe of our everyday lives. It exposes the terrible truth that the fortress we built in childhood to protect us from blame, ambiguity, abandonment, and betrayal has become a prison. Ultimately, the natural forces of grieving will impel us through that crack into the profound, uncharted world of active grieving.

There are three paths associated with transition. Loss places the bereaved at a crossroads. Down one path lies the intense pain and inner turmoil of grieving. Down another lies dissociation.

> Splitting off of part(s) of self on a continuum from anesthesia through disconnection between feelings, thoughts, actions, and/or beliefs, to serious emotionally disturbed states including severe neurosis, psychosis, affective disorders, etc. (Moses & Kearney, 1995, pp. 178–179)

Down the third path lies acting out:

> Consciously choosing a solution to a problem that is known to be ineffective, and in addition is one or more of the following: immoral, unethical, illegal, unhealthy, or dangerous to self or others. Nonetheless it is still enacted because "bad" feelings and distressing issues are avoided. Examples include substance abuse, child abuse, overeating, sexual indiscretion, financial irresponsibility, desertion, criminal acts, workaholism. (Moses & Kearney, 1995, p. 179)

These three paths are never far away from each other. At any point along the path of grieving, one may escape to the hoped for comfort of dissociation or acting out. At any point along the path of dissociation, new traumas or losses may trigger grieving. At any point along the path of acting out, a crisis may trigger an intervention, or "bottom" may be hit, taking the abuser back to the crossroads. Everyone, abuser or nonabuser, samples all three paths. There may be a great deal of switching from one path to another. Finally, for many reasons, people commit to one path; such factors as genetic predisposition, personality structure, subcultural patterns, and support system ethos can all play a part. The process is as impossible to predict as charting the course of sobriety and as impossible to anticipate as guessing when an abuser will hit bottom. At any point along the way the process can get halted, shunted aside, or buried, only to spring up at another unexpected and inconvenient spot. A person can arrest, that is, stay stuck in an ungrieved loss for a long time. When later losses occur, they too are buried, because to mourn them would open the old wound. Like Marley's ghost in the *Christmas Carol*, one can walk around in chains of ungrieved losses.

Transition is the domain of the adapted self. The adapted self has an enormous capacity to dream. It resists any awareness that its plans have truly and irrevocably failed. The acknowledgment of loss can call the adapted self's entire mission into question. This accounts for some of the tenacity of denial around loss. If the most diligent effort to achieve the most prized goal has failed, the plan to achieve that goal itself can be invalidated and the "planner" called into account. What is the point of being a sensitive fixer/pleaser/complier, a skilled trickster/performer/manipulator, or a powerful rebel/reactor/malcontent if success in that role does not keep love from hurting? A major loss takes one back to the original, survival-based mission of the adapted child. "All of my life I have wanted . . . It's all I ever wanted. Ever since I was a little kid. Now it's gone." "It" can be anything or anyone. It can be what that thing or that person *represented* to the adapted self. The loss shattered the current updated version of the adapted child's dream. The dream was going to validate his or her most advanced repertoire of techniques for manipulating life. Loss of the dream spirals one back to the original bargain with life, the original "If only . . . I'll never . . . I got to." The failure of the protectors leaves the bereaved with no way to mediate pain, quite literally alone in the world of the injured self.

There is a lot of vacillation during transition. Glimpses of the adapted self and the mission of the adapted child are disconcerting. Their rationales are not easily abandoned. After all, survival itself once seemed to come from their development. The growing threat of impending collapse of the denial system demands some way to bind the growing anxiety. The impending flood of feelings creates pressure to find comfort and relief. For these reasons there are many forays and false starts into active grieving, and many retreats. So there is no clear boundary between transition and active grieving.

Strict adherence to a recovery program can be difficult during transition. The risk of relapse is great and the experience of starting and stopping can create a discouraging sense that one's recovery has stalled or is going around in circles. Furthermore, sponsors and other old-timers may be intolerant of the grieving process, and admonish the recovering person to "get off the pity pot."

Active Grieving

When the feelings finally come unfilterred by denial, they come in four affective states: depression, guilt, anger, and fear. Each of these feelings is directly connected to personal definitions of worth, responsibility, justice, and attachment. When the feelings are felt and shared, without distortion or minimization, with a significant other, the path of active grieving has been committed to. The work of redefining these issues (i.e., grieving) is going on.

Just having the feelings without experiencing the change in the belief system is pain without purpose. But it is still pain. For this reason, a distinction could be made between mourning and grieving. We mourn when we feel the pain of the loss; we are bereaved. Bereft means to be deprived or to have had a valued object taken away by force (as in losing a loved one through death). Mourning and bereavement are the expression of pain caused by loss. Grieving, on the other hand, is pain that changes us; it moves us from the transition imposed by the loss to the transformation of self. It is pain that has found its purpose. The mourners at a funeral express their sadness, fears, even anger, at their loss, but their pain is only the start of the process of separating from their lost dreams. It is a cry of anguish, of the terrible pain of having their sense of security cruelly stripped away. The rituals of funerals and mourning provide a framework for the shared expression of pain. Participation in these rituals serves to establish the loss by penetrating all four layers of denial. The wake makes the fact inescapable. The eulogy and the expression of the attachment of the other mourners illuminates the magnitude of the loss and some of its many implications. Solicitous friends and family ask, "What will you do now?" and press against the denial of responsibility for change. The tears of loved ones call forth waves of feelings. These rituals prepare the mourners for the task of grieving, but are not the work itself. Long after the tears are dried, and the comforting hugs have been exchanged, the changes in the mourners' belief systems will be working their way into awareness, or they will be blocked out in order to maintain unexpressed beliefs and unexamined self-concept tied to the lost dream.

Active grieving is the domain of the hurt self. The acute pain is directly associated with the current loss. However, without the protection of denial, this pain spirals downward into the world of the injured child—the core of the hurt self. "It" is happening all over again. This injury proves that life is really all about the hurt child's struggles. The pain can never be escaped; it always comes back. That is the child's fate and its nature. Precisely because fate is doing what it has always done to this child, the way the child has structured its universe becomes clear. Out of its pain it found meaning for sadness, guilt, anger, and fear.

The affective states will be discussed one at a time, but keep in mind that they do not neatly sort themselves out in actual experience. In fact, the labile affect of grievers adds to the confusion of both the grievers and anyone trying to comfort, support, counsel, or sponsor them. This joint confusion can have a negative impact on critical relationships of the recovering person, particularly significant others, such as family and sponsors.

DEPRESSION

A lot has been said about depression: that it is more than simple sadness; that it is characterized by a sense of being hopeless, helpless, and hapless; that it is anger turned inward; that it is biochemical; even that it is just self-pity. But in the context of loss and grieving, depression takes on a special meaning: *It is the feeling state that opens our beliefs about competency, capability, personal worth, or potency.* Like anxiety, it first mobilizes energy, and then impels the search into the deepest reaches of the psyche, into the very pain from which those concepts originally took meaning. It is first mobilized during mourning. At that time, however, the questions raised by the bereaved take the form of agonized protests about the loss, rather than the deep existential evaluation of these issues which takes place later, when depression impels them on their search.

In the light of a lost dream, that which makes us, as people, and life itself worthwhile, comes into sharp relief. Grieving people ask terrible questions. "What's the point?" "What good is it?" "What good am I?" Such questions come up precisely because the dream that was lost was an answer to those questions. If you lose a cherished friend, a part of your own self-image is lost. If the meaning of your life centered on having friends, then *being* a friend is very much a part of how you define who you are. When a friend is lost, the central way of being your best is lost. If you can't be a friend, what good are you? What are you supposed to do? Go out and get a puppy to feel better? Make a new friend to replace the lost friend? Diminish your friend's value by how quickly he or she can be replaced?

A women whose definition of the best in her was connected to the mothering of her children will be devastated by the discovery that her child has some dreadful impairment. She will cry for the child, for herself, and for the loss of mothering. The mother of a child born with severe cerebral palsy once expressed her lost dream by simply saying, "I'll never dance at her wedding." Clearly it will do this mother no good to hear how others find meaning in their life, or how others center their worth. She must again search for meaning in her life. Although the woman must find her *own* answer, she is not necessarily searching *alone* because grieving takes place in the context of a meaningful relationship, that is, while feeling the connection to whomever is with her behind the wall (e.g., a counselor, a friend, a clergy member).

Another woman, who has a child with a fetal alcohol syndrome, will probably have fewer people volunteering to be with her behind the wall. She will be more apprehensive about the messages those outside the wall may be carrying. Her journey may be longer and harder.

Because the resolution of the issue of worth (or any grieving issue) is unique, personal, and individual, it is not possible to say what answer this work will produce. It is possible, however, to say how that answer feels. When you come to a new definition of a core value in your belief system, its presence affords new opportunities to experience congruence because it brings new awareness of understanding, guidance, and attaching. The new belief feels integrated, whole, and very much yours. It expresses a new awareness of self. Perhaps that is why the values that are dearest to us are born out of the struggle with adversity. It is also why our deepest values will always have a connection to the struggles of, and with, the hurt child. Depression goes right to the heart of the hurt child, because it goes directly to its sense of worth. It goes directly to what is *wrong* with the hurt child, which accounts for its pain. The hurt child knows *why* it is unhappy, *why* it is in pain, *why* it is unloved. These answers are the core of its sense of self.

People who want to help with the depression of grief are frequently frightened by the depths of despair into which the bereaved plunge as they search for reasons to feel competency, capability, personal worth, and potency. Recovering addicts may be facing the depression of grieving, without an anesthetic, for the first time in their lives. Because our culture links depression to suicide, helpers may fear that if grieving addicts look "too hard" at the issue, they might harm themselves.

The frequency of suicide among alcoholics is a serious concern for professional and nonprofessional helpers. Ironically, the "chronic suicide," which Carl Menninger (1938) called alcoholism, may become "acute" when the addict struggles with grieving during recovery. It is well to keep in mind that depression does not cause suicide, anymore than it causes addiction (see discussion of anxiety as the cause of addiction on p. 31). The depression of grieving first energizes and then impels a profound existential search for new meaning in one's life. If that search is frustrated, particularly by the absence of an authentic, present other to accompany one on that search, the despair of the bereaved is magnified. Suicidal gestures—"cries for help"—are an expression of profound frustration, not an *effect* of depression. Suicide expresses despair, it is not caused by loss.

GUILT

Guilt is part of the experience of a loss. The griever knows what has happened and how "bad" it is. The pain is proof. But the pain drives the question, "*Why?*" What accounts for this bad thing happening to him or her? We all have explanations. "Good things happen to good people; bad things happen to bad people." "One gets punished for sins of thought, word, or deed." "It's my fault and I can prove it."

Friends and relatives may be inclined to try to relieve the guilt. "It's not your fault; these things just happen!" Somehow this does not seem to help. It does not redefine or ease the guilt, but rejects it. The guilt feelings are there because the griever is working on a new definition of causality and responsibility in the light of profound loss. This work is extremely difficult when there is confusion between responsibility and blame (see Chapter 2), or when there is confusion between causality and the need to have a sense of control.

The attitude of ENUF, with its feeling-focus and non-judgmental attention to guilt feelings, will make it possible for the griever to explore his or her old belief system which was rocked by the loss. The following dialogue illustrates this type of exploration. Elsa is in a group therapy session struggling with her guilt about her child's impairment; Gregory, another member of the group, and the therapist also participate.

Elsa   Sarah is almost six years old. Not a day goes by that I don't feel racked with guilt about her Down syndrome. Friends and family tried to comfort me in the first few months, but I have alienated all of them by my obsession with this guilt. My husband is a saint, but I am afraid that I will drive him away as well. He can't take much more of my behaving like this.

Gregory   [Very excited, blurts out] But it's not your fault. Down syndrome is genetic!

Elsa   [Looks at Gregory and sighs] Perhaps I left something out in my introduction of myself. I have a Ph.D. in biology. I work as a genetic counselor down at the medical center. I know quite a bit about trisomy 21.

Gregory   [Embarrassed, stares at the floor and then at his watch] Oh.

Elsa   [Addressing the group as a whole] Maybe this will show you how pervasive the guilt is. I told you my husband was a saint. He's perfect. That's the point. Don't you see? That proves it's my fault. It must have been my genes!

[The whole group is overwhelmed]

Therapist   Since it feels like your fault, no wonder you have felt so bad. And no wonder there has been no relief or comfort from others. It seems to me that when they try to prove that it is not your fault, they miss the point. Somehow, it is vitally important that you be the cause of this awful thing, that you be responsible for it. Can you tell us more about what being responsible means to you?

Elsa   [Looks directly at the therapist and begins slowly] I have to be responsible. That child is no one's responsibility but mine. *I'm her mother*. [Pauses, focuses on some point far away] Its funny, no, ironic, to hear myself say those words. My father was a drunk like I became after Sarah was born. Mom had to work so I was put in charge of my sibs. The younger ones were okay. But the older ones were hell. They always said, "You can't tell us what to do. You're not our mom!" I still remember the exhausted, overwhelmed, and betrayed look in Mom's eyes when she would come home and find bedlam. Her eyes silently said to me, "You failed. You didn't do your job." [Pause] I knew some day I would have a baby. It would be mine. Then I could do it right.

In the context of grieving, guilt is part of the way all of us evaluate our impact on our environment. "Oh my God, look what I did!" Knowing and, more importantly, experiencing accountability takes us directly to the issue of responsibility. Guilt is the feeling component of responsibility. In evaluating our impact we explore the personal standards for responsibility to which we can commit. We do this in the light of the feedback loss provides about reality and our own limitations. As such, feeling the guilt helps us come to a full and mature choice about our future actions and to congruence in a new responsible way.

It would seem as though a woman who has a child with fetal alcohol syndrome is really guilty of causing her child's impairment. It is not neurotic, or irrational guilt. It's "real guilt." However, it is as important for her to explore her guilt feelings as it is for the mother of the child with Down syndrome, and for the same reason. Both of them must redefine what being responsible means to them from this point forward, in the light of their losses.

Guilt is an answer to the question "*Why?*" "Why did this happen? Why did it happen to me?" The adapted self protects us by defending against confusion and ambiguity. It insists on black and white depictions of causality. A core loss is incomprehensible. The only way to explain it and still keep order in the universe is to assume blame oneself. It does not matter that there are logical inconsistencies in this theory of causality, or that the concepts of fault, blame, responsibility, control, and causality have all run together. What matters is that the terrible "WHY" is answered. For many people this question takes them directly to their belief about God. "Where was God? How did He allow this to happen?" There are many ways to answer this. We all learned one set of answers while we were children getting our first religious instruction. Most of our answer seeking and spiritual development stopped in childhood. Someone taught us that God was good and that God was running things, and we continue to believe that view—until grief forces us to redefine it and recommit to a new definition. In the light of a terrible loss, we are forced to examine what those ideas mean *now*. Again there is no fixed answer. No other person's answer will do; one has to find one's own.

Many people find comfort in religion at times of grief. Grieving and the comfort of faith are not incompatible, neither are they substitutable. When people with firm religious beliefs finish their grief work, they often report experiencing what they call a renewed faith. They report that their relationship with their higher power has changed. Some find it alive again, after years of sleeping in Sunday school. Some lose the faith of their childhood completely and find another. Others find faith for the first time. Bill Wilson (Kurtz, 1990) traced his recovery from alcoholism to what he called a "spiritual awakening."

For many people, the challenge to their beliefs about God is unbearably painful. They cannot accept that a good God would do this. So they are thrown back into accepting blame themselves. There *must* be a cause. If not in God, then in themselves. "I did it. It's my fault. I can prove it." It really makes no difference whether this proof is logical to others or not. It makes perfect sense to the injured child, whose belief about God it is, after all. The mother of a baby with fetal alcohol syndrome feels her guilt just as strongly as the widow of a man killed while driving drunk ("If only I had not fought with him . . . If only I had made him call his sponsor . . .). Each must find a new definition in the light of their own limitations and frailty.

Even when guilt does not take the form of remorse or assumed responsibility for cause, it often takes the form of regret over lost opportunities. "I should have visited Dad more often." "All those stupid arguments." "Could I? Should I? Would I?" Again it is a lonely quest, because the bereaved must find answers for themselves. In grieving they are found, as the saying goes, *for* themselves, not *by* themselves.

Guilt, anxiety, denial, and responsibility are all interrelated. There is no way to say how much cause we *should* assign ourselves. But it is important to say how much responsibility we *can* undertake, and then to act in accord with this belief. In the process of working a 12-step program, the recovering individual has an opportunity to explore guilt at many steps. The fifth step ("Admitted to God, to ourselves, and to another human being the exact nature of our wrongs") captures the essence of this part of grieving.

The guilt/responsibility connection also has special meanings for the hurt child. The hurt child made sense of its pain by taking responsibility for it. "It's my fault. I did it wrong, or I was not good enough. Either way I am the center of pain, all pain." Whether or not this is still as true as it once seemed to be in the experience of the wounded child is the core question during grieving. If the griever incorporates the current pain into the preexisting model, then the whole universe is still balanced. The way out of pain, found years ago, can still work. If this world view is questioned, or, worse yet, rejected, then the center of meaning is lost. One is abandoned in the same cruel universe that once threatened one's entire existence. The hurt child came into being to check the free-fall of incomprehensible pain. Its existence is the answer to the original "*WHY?*" One's hurt child found the *only* answer there was. If that is lost, there is no answer, nothing to stop the free-fall.

Again, the energy for this work is first mobilized and then impelled by the feeling state attached to it. Guilt gets us asking the question "Why?" If we stop at the old answers provided by the adapted self, we are still in transition. Guilt keeps us examining until we get to the hurt child's answer.

ANGER

Anger is another form of the question "Why?" In the context of grieving, it is a vigorous "Why *me*? Why not *him*? Why not *you*? . . . *It's not fair!*" The anger of grieving is not a schoolyard pout. Anyone who thinks so and responds,

"Life is not fair, you know," is likely to have his or her head taken off in a roar. "What the hell do *you* know about fairness?" Indeed, what do any of us know—for sure—that cannot be shaken when the dearest part of our world falls apart? In each dream there is a buried expression of our concept of justice—what is right, how things *should* be. "You work and slave to make a good life for your kids. What happens? You wind up identifying his overdosed body in the county morgue. Why? I was gonna do it right, you know. Damn it, I *did* it right!"

Being around someone who is actively grieving produces a profound visceral reaction. One feels either compelled or repelled, either drawn into the existential struggle, or driven to escape its force. In much the same way that we tend to fear depression will lead to suicide, we fear anger will lead to violence.

The anger of grieving can be frightening to family and friends. Not that anger is any more irrational than any of the other grieving states; it is just more frightening to most people. It can be particularly disconcerting for one who is meek and mild-tempered. It is often the most difficult of the feeling states for others around the griever to "bear with." One recurring problem is that anger is never handled well in a dysfunctional family. Violence, denial, blame, and shame are real and omnipresent dangers. Dysfunctional families script the response to anger. The rules identified by Claudia Black (1982)—don't feel; don't trust; don't talk—do not prepare one for congruent handling of anger or other feeling states of grieving. Nor do they prepare one for responding to them in a loved one.

The anger of grief drives a redefinition of one's core beliefs about fairness and justice in the universe. First it mobilizes the energy and phrases the questions, and then it holds our feet to the fire until our own unique and personal answer emerges. Anger challenges justice. There must be a place in justice for anger. Without it, right and wrong are just empty rules someone else dictated. The rules are intended to bind us, but not necessarily others or life itself. Rage against injustice is a fire that forges new rules. The fire makes it hot for all of us, because we are all rule-givers, rule-followers, *and* the rule-breakers. It forces us to "own" the real rules we live by.

The anger of grieving affects recovery in many positive ways. Many people get angry at the disease. Some make a personal enemy of John Barleycorn. Anger can make the second line of the Serenity Prayer ring with meaning and power; in the crucible of anger, the phrase "courage to change the things I can" is more than mere words.

The hurt child is a volcano of anger. He or she was born out of injury(s) which occurred because of repeated or traumatic assaults on the natural child's autonomy. The pain existed and persisted because caretakers willfully or negligently violated the just terms of their obligation through abuse, neglect, or exploitation. Anger is the other half of the fight or flight response (See Chapter 3). It is a capacity of the natural self to defend against harm, intrusion, and violation of one's boundaries. It is basic to the assertion of self. From its appearance in the small child's discovery of the word "NO" to the toddler's defense of his or her territory in the sandbox, it is the energy to create and defend boundaries. Socialization will civilize this energy in most; but hurt children exist because their defenses and boundaries were overwhelmed, and the anger stuffed back down their throats. Fairness and justice are powerful dreams of the hurt child.

FEAR

Fear is last on the list of the affective states of grieving. None of us is really safe, and loss makes this terrible fact terribly real. Security is an illusion. Why should we love, if we just get hurt? Why attach to anything, anyone? What worth can there be in all this pain? Fear makes it seem safer to live our lives half alive, not fully investing or feeling with any depth. Don't get too close. Don't let others get too close. We may make an exception for a friend, our spouse, or our child. Some people train their children from early on to "trust only family." If we draw a circle with most of humanity outside and only one or two people inside, we are no safer from the vulnerability of attachment. We may find that, like a foolish little pig, we are dwelling in a house of straw. Narrowing the heart does not solve the problem. We are no safer when we love only one person. We can live our whole lives focused on that one person, only to find that all our dreams can be lost at once. To be real, alive, present, and dreaming with only one person is the adapted child's solution to the existential task of daring to dream. It places a huge burden on the one selected to be our safe haven. That one person takes on the burden of making life itself worth living. He or she takes on the impossible task of keeping fear away from our door. We may not even know we have done this until loss strikes. The griever cries out, "I want my safety back! I want to be alive *and* protected from life at the same time. I want to be alive without living—safe and alone. Let life go on and leave me alone."

Fear in the context of grieving is the experience of the risk of living with attachment. Again, no one can establish for the griever what makes that risk worth taking again. Without love we are only partially alive. We are existing in a world without meaning or hope. We have safety, but it is the safety of the grave itself. We are already in it, while still walking and talking. With love, we risk life, we risk loss.

The hurt child knows the risk of life and the terrifying aloneness of losing love. Protection, safety, and love are all fused together in the natural child. Yes, there are bumps and scrapes which momentarily shatter its magic bubble; there are times when munificent mother says "No," when she drops our hand in a crowd, or does not come to rescue us quickly enough from a nightmare. But in a moment there is a kiss or a hug, and Eden is restored. All children must leave the garden eventually, and once it is left, the gate is locked behind. While no one willingly gives up the *right* to its joys and comforts, the natural force of maturation takes us all away from home. Ideally this loss is adventure, not trauma. It comes when the individual is able and eager to encounter the outer world. No child surrenders a beloved blanket because *someone else* thinks it's time. In time the nook will be discarded for the Nintendo, and waves of nostalgia can flood an adult who comes across a box of old treasures in an attic. All children must face the loss of their artificial Eden. All children must build a fort against the disconcerting forces of ambiguity, blame, betrayal, and abandonment. Everyone has a hurt self. Everyone is in danger of having their childhood fort become a prison. It is this fort that must be taken down and reassembled in grief work.

Some children are forced to leave Eden too soon. This is particularly true among addicts, the majority of whom describe their childhood homes as dysfunctional (see Goodwin, 1976 and Vaillant, 1983). They are forced to deal with levels of pain associated with ambiguity, blame, betrayal, and/or abandonment before their natural selves have developed the necessary skills or the requisite desire. Their pain is not comforted, the "good mother" does not return at all, let alone in time, and they are left to their own devices to plumb the depths of dark, cold pain, while an abusive father rages just outside their bedroom door. The hurt child accounts for the loss of protection and safety by accepting the loss of love as his or her personal fate, and then goes on to account for this "fact" by discovering his or her own flaws. No wonder the hurt child believes in magical love, and dreams of safety from vulnerability. No wonder the primary job of the adapted self is to protect against ever experiencing such pain again.

Perhaps the most compelling thing about the hurt child is that it is a child. It has kicked off its blankets in a bad dream and cries for comfort that does not come. It cannot climb out of the crib and retrieve the cover itself. It cannot rub the sleep from its eyes and go down to the kitchen and fix its own hot cocoa. Its helplessness and dependency are givens. Therefore, all adult capacity for self-care disappears when one tumbles into its world. It not only disappears, it is rejected. If a stranger were to enter the nursery and attempt to tuck the toddler in, he or she would howl in protest. "You're the wrong one. I want my mommy. You won't do. Go away!" Our hurt children feel that way about our "adult." It's the wrong one. In fact, for many hurt children, growing up was a curse. "No, I won't do that for you. Do it yourself. *Grow up!*" Actually growing up is a double-edged betrayal. It is following the hated injunction, and thus caving into the unjust demand to grow up. By ending childhood, it ends the need for parenting and thus lets the caretaker off the hook. Worst of all, becoming an on-your-own adult threatens to disqualify one from ever being eligible for care and nurturance, which are the birthright of childhood. No wonder the hurt child wants nothing to do with the adult it has become. "Go away. You are definitely the wrong one!"

Arrested Grieving

A person arrested in grieving cannot get on with life because he or she cannot close the chapter on a lost dream. Each time he or she thinks about the loss, he or she is overwhelmed with a feeling such as guilt, anger, etc. Completing the work of grieving requires enormous change. Changing the old ways of thinking about, experiencing, and acting while in grief involves one general and several specific changes in think/feel/act. The general change is realizing that grieving is necessary and important work. The specific changes are associated with identifying each feeling with the existential value, which is changing as the result of the loss. Yet some people seem to get stuck in the process. They seem to "die with the loss." For them, one of the feeling states of grieving becomes a life style—much in the way that acting out can become a life style and an addiction. They take on the *identity* of a depressed, angry, guilty, or fearful person. For them, the feeling is no longer part of a search; it is a cul-de-sac which has become their new home. The emotion serves as what some psychologists would call a "character armor." In terms of the discussion of character in Chapter 4, it has become a consistent way of perceiving and interacting with the world. For the most part, people who arrest in grieving are people who experience a life-shattering loss on top of a preexisting emotional problem. This raises the intriguing question of how much so-called mental illness is in fact arrested grieving. Often it turns out that persons who have been suffering from life-long difficulties uncover a childhood loss which they were unable to grieve at the time. In this context, posttraumatic stress disorder can be thought of as impacted grieving.

Transformation

Time loses meaning during active grieving. The grief promises to go on endlessly, like the pain that gave birth to the hurt child. Time will take some of the sharp edges off, but any chance reminder or subtle cue can take one back to pain years or even decades later. Again there is no clear boundary between the work of grieving and the work of transformation. Softly, slowly, time heals. But this healing is neither forgetting nor denial. Grieving does not end just because everyday life distracts one back to the world of the adult. Active grieving ends because there is in fact a transformation occurring. It occurs because grieving has its roots in the willingness, ability, and need of the natural self to find congruence. The natural self is latent in all of the capacity of the adult. In fact, as we said earlier, the anchoring of the adult in the here-and-now experience of life is what exposes the schemes of the adapted self in transition, and contrasts with the logic of the hurt self in active grieving. During the whole process there is a conflict. "I always thought (felt, acted, believed) that way, but now I don't know." The "I" that no longer "knows" is the natural self. As the once-too-terrible-to-think-and-feel experiences gain awareness and articulation, a powerful new truth, unknowable by the hurt child, emerges: *The loss has been survived.* The darkest fantasies of the hurt child have not, as it always dreaded, become reality. The "I" that is left standing is not crippled, helpless, and dependent on the source of its agony for meaning and survival. This "I" is not bound up in the old universe; it is free to find its own way, a path of its own. There is a burst of freedom. Like the toddler discovering walking, the first new steps are uncertain, determined, filled with awe, and very exciting. Things are new and familiar at the same time, but there is excitement, risk, and possibility—there is *hope*. Excitement is easy to confuse with anxiety; risk, with danger. Hope is risky; it is not dangerous. Attaching to new dreams is risky; it is not dangerous. The informed adult can tell the difference, the injured child cannot. Because there has been a separation between the adult and the inner children, the recovering griever can take those steps and journey down a new path. New, more authentic dreams tied to this path can be made, and pursued congruently. The hallmark of this path is congruence. Without the distortion of denial, the existential tasks required to pursue this path can be accomplished, and with them the experience of a congruent self can be achieved.

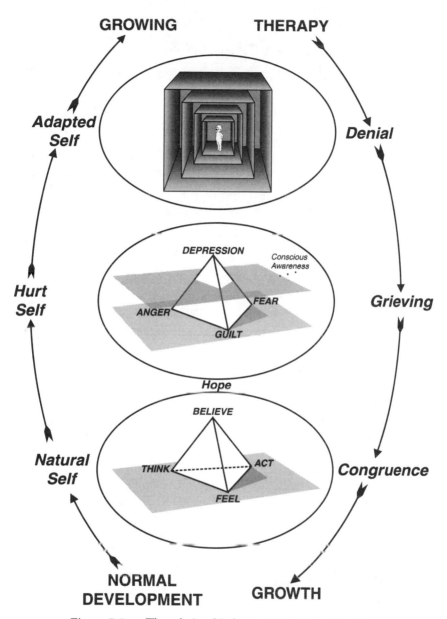

Figure 7.2.   The relationship between denial and grieving
in normal development and therapy.

RECOVERY AND GRIEVING

Ultimately the process of grieving takes one into the belief system of his or her inner children. These children's most cherished dreams still bind the adult to the love that once was, a love that once was almost grasped and then was lost, a love whose loss seemed unendurable and the end of being itself. And so they cling, regardless to the damage to themselves and the years of lost living. What does it matter? All can be fixed when the dream comes true. Then the dream is lost. The grieving of the recovering addict may begin with the crisis or trauma that brings him or her into treatment. It uncovers the lost dreams of the adapted child and exposes the pain of the hurt child. Ultimately, grieving takes the recovering addict to the final wall, the sanctuary/fortress of the hurt child which has become the prison of the natural self. Grieving ends when there is freedom for the natural self. When the natural self is the center of the existential tasks of owning, expressing, choosing, valuing, searching, and dreaming, true congruence emerges out of insight, vitality, mastery, guidance, attachment, and understanding of self.

Figure 7.2 depicts the relationship of denial and grieving to recovery from loss. On the right of Figure 7.2 is an arrow marked *therapy*. It points downward marking the path of the patient as he or she moves through sobriety and healing on the journey inward. On the left of the figure is an arrow marked *normal development*, which points upward. At any point in the struggle with the beliefs of the child within, a person may escape into denial and strive again to make the old dream come true—until the next loss, and the next opportunity for grieving and for growth. In the end, the small word *hope* seems lost in the swirl of ideas and arrows. Perhaps it should be written in bigger type, because it is the thing of value for which denial is surrendered. It is the light that takes us out of grieving. But in reality, moments of hope are easily lost. That makes them special in a book about denial, as well as in life.

References

American Psychiatric Association. (1980). *The diagnostic and statistical manual of mental disorders* (3rd ed.). Washington, D.C.: Author.

American Psychiatric Association. (1994). *The diagnostic and statistical manual of mental disorders* (4th ed.). Washington, D.C.: Author.

Bandler, R., & Grinder, J. (1975). *The structure of magic* (Vol. 1). Palo Alto: Science and Behavior Books.

Bandler, R., & Grinder, J. (1979). *Frogs into princes: Neurolinguistic programing and transformation of meaning.* Moab: Real People Press.

Berne, E. (1961). *Transactional analysis in psychotherapy.* New York: Grove Press.

Berne, E. (1964). *Games people play.* New York: Grove Press.

Black, C. (1982). *It will never happen to me.* Denver: M.A.C.

Bradshaw, J. (1988a). *Healing the shame that binds you.* Deerfield Beach: Health Communications.

Bradshaw, J. (1988b). *Bradshaw: On the family.* Deerfield Beach: Health Communications.

Bugental, J. (1987). *The art of the psychotherapist.* New York: Norton.

Dorpat, T. (1994). *Denial and defense in the therapeutic situation.* Northvale: Jason Aronson.

Erikson, E. (1964). *Childhood and society.* New York: Norton.

Frank, J. D. (1961). *Persuasion and healing: A comparative study of psychotherapy.* Baltimore: Johns Hopkins University Press.

Frankl, V. (1963). *Man's search for meaning: An introduction to logotherapy.* New York: Pocket Books.

Glasser, W. (1965). *Reality therapy.* New York: Harper & Row.

Goodwin, D. (1976). *Is alcoholism hereditary?* New York: Oxford University Press.

Hilgard, E., & Marquis, R. (1964). *Conditioning and learning* (Rev. ed.). (2nd ed.). New York: Appleton-Century-Crofts

Johnson, V. (1980). *I'll quit tomorrow* (Rev. ed.), New York: Harper & Row.

Jung, C. G. (1968). *Archetypes and the collective unconscious.* Princeton: Princeton University Press.

Kahler, T. (1977). The mini-scrip. In A. Barnes (Ed.), *Transactional analysis after Eric Berne: Techniques and practices of three schools* (pp. 223–256). New York: Harper's College Press.

Kohut, H. (1971). *The analysis of the self: A systematic approach to the psychoanalytic treatment of narcissistic personality disorders.* New York: Intrernational Universities Press.

Kübler-Ross, E. (1969). *On death and dying.* New York: Macmillan.

Kurtz, E. (1979). *Not-God: A history of Alcoholics Anonymous.* Center City: Hazelton Foundation.

Levin, J. (1991). *Treatment of alcohol and other addictions.* NorthVale: Jason Aronson.

Levine, J., & Zigler, E. (1973). The essential reactive distinction in alcoholism: A developmental approach. *Journal of Abnormal Psychology, 81,* 242–249.

Martin, J. (1972). *Chalk talk* [Film]. Aberdeen: Kelly Productions.

Martin, J. (1976). *Guidelines for helping the alcoholic* [Film]. Los Angeles: FMSP.

McCord, W., & McCord, J. (1960). *Origins of alcoholism.* Stanford: Stanford University Press.

Meador, B., & Rogers, C. (1984). Person-centered therapy. In R. Corsini (Ed.), *Current psychotherapies* (3rd ed., pp. 142–195). Itasca: F. E. Peacock.

Menninger, K. (1938). *Man against himself.* New York: Harcourt Brace.

Mosak, H. (1979). Adlerian psychotherapy. In R. Corsini (Ed.), *Current psychotherapies* (2nd ed., pp. 44–94). Itasca: F. E. Peacock.

Moses, K. (1995). Grief groups. *Voices: The Art and Science of Psychotherapy, 30*(2), 70–77.

Moses, K., & Kearney, R. (1995). *Transition therapy: An existential guide to grief counseling.* Unpublished manuscript.

Rogers, C. (1951). *Client-centered therapy.* Boston: Houghton Mifflin.

Rogers, C. (1961). *On becoming a person.* Boston: Houghton Mifflin.

Rosenthal, V. (1982). How to tame a fox. *Voices: The Art and Science of Psychotherapy, 18*(2), 83–87.

Rosenthal, V. (in press). Essentials of an experiential psychotherapy, Einzigerlebnistherapy. *Voices: The Art and Science of Psychotherapy.*

Rovee-Collier, C. K., & Hayne, H. (1987). Reactivation of infant memory: Implications for cognitive development. In H. Reese (Ed.), *Advances in child development and behavior* (Vol. 20, pp. 185–238). New York: Academic Press.

Shakespeare, W. (1959). *The tragedy of Macbeth.* New York: Washington Square Press.

Stamas, D. (1981). *The trap map.* Lombard: Adult Children Center.

Saint-Exupéry, A. (1943). *The little prince.* New York: Harcourt, Brace.

Tiebout, H. (1953). Surrender versus compliance in therapy, with special referrence to alcoholism. *Quarterly Journal of Studies on Alcoholism, 14,* 58–68.

Tillich, P. (1952). *The courage to be.* New Haven: Yale University Press.

Truax, C. B., & Carkhuff, R. (1967). *Toward effective counseling and psychotherapy training and practice.* Chicago: Aldine.

Vaillant, G. (1983). *The natural history of alcoholism.* Cambridge: Harvard University Press.

Winokur, G., Reich, T., Rimmer, J., & Pitts, R. (1970). Alcoholism III: Diagnosis and familial psychiatric illness in 259 alcoholic probands. *Archives of General Psychiatry, 23,* 104–111.

Winokur, G., Rimmer, J., & Reich, T. (1971). Alcoholism IV: Is there more than one type of alcoholism? *British Journal of Psychiatry, 18,* 525–531.

Wolf, S. (1974–75, Winter). Counseling for better or worse. *Alcohol Health and Research World,* 27–29.

Index

abstinence, 101
acceptance
  of addiction, 19, 129–30
  of diagnosis, 131–33
  role of client dialogue in, 130–31
  of self, 62, 152
  in therapeutic relationship, 168–72
acting out, 38–39
  denial and, 40–41
  grieving and, 179
  as learned habit, 39–41
  response to, 41
  as response to loss, 193
adaptation
  in chemically dependent families, 5
  vs. denial, 4–5, 28
adapted child
  adaptive role of, 85–87
  challenges for, 89–90
  denial system of, 91, 93, 182–83
  family role of, 88–89
  recovering client's perception of, 93–94
  response to loss, 194
  social relations of, 90–91
  survival strategies of, 88–89
  in transition stage of grieving, 194
  world view of, 87–88, 92–93

addiction
  acceptance of diagnosis, 19
  acting out behaviors in, 38–39
  alcoholism, 31, 32
  anxiety as cause of, 31–33
  assessing client's perception of, 127–28
  client's public discussion of, in therapy, 130–31
  denial of diagnosis, 17–19
  habitual behaviors and, 36–40
  hitting bottom, 28, 56, 101, 121
  incongruence of feeling and action in, 73
  irresponsibility in, 67
  loss and, 100–101
  other than chemical, denial in, x
  personality patterns, 76
  physiological vs. psychological, 39
  reframed as disease, 140–42
  resistance to change, 12–13
  resistance to change in, 5
  self-concept in, 97
  self-esteem issues, 77, 152
  sensitivity to criticism in, 161
  shame of, 48, 141–42
  in think/feel/act model, 101
  think/feel/act model of, 60–61
  tolerance effects, 57
  see also chemical dependency